A Study of
ST. JOHN'S REVELATION

by the late
James Turley van Burkalow, Ph.D.

Edited by
Anastasia van Burkalow

DORRANCE PUBLISHING CO., INC.
PITTSBURGH, PA 15222

CONTENTS

EDITOR'S INTRODUCTION   v

PROLOGUE: THE THEME, FORM, AND SYMBOLISMS OF
ST. JOHN'S REVELATION   1

A FOUR-FOLD INTERPRETATION:
  REVELATION AS A WORSHIP DRAMA   15
  I. The Letters to the Seven Churches   17
    Act 1. The Parashoth—Readings from the Law
  II. The Seven-Sealed Book   41
    Act 2. The Haphtaroth—Readings from the Prophets
  III. The Seven Trumpets   69
    Act 3. The Targumim—Translations of the Haphtaroth
  IV. The Seven Bowls of the Wrath of God   107
    Act 4. The Derashoth—Expositions of the Haphtaroth

A THREE-FOLD INTERPRETATION: REVELATION AS A
FORESHADOWING OF DEVELOPMENTS WITHIN AND BETWEEN
CHURCH AND STATE   141
  I. Surveys of Church and State Separately   146
    (Acts 1 and 2 of the Drama)
  II. Conflicts Involving Church and State   148
    (Act 3 of the Drama)
  III. Church and State United   150
    (Act 4 of the Drama)

THE MESSAGE FOR TODAY'S CHURCH   155

* * * * * * * * *

APPENDICES   171
  1. The Primordial Apocalypse of the Stars   173
  2. The Parables of the Seasons and the Allegory of
    Israel's National Epos   199
  3. Rituals of Ancient Synagogue and Early Christian
    Worship   221
  4. The Symbolism of Numbers   241
  5. The Apocalyptic Sevens and the Book's Recapitulations   253
INDEX   265

Editor's Introduction

For many years my father, the late Rev. Dr. James Turley van Burkalow, devoted much study to the writings of St. John. He often discussed his ideas with me, and shortly before his death in 1959 he and I began to assemble his manuscripts for publication. Because of my own professional obligations it was for many years impossible for me to continue this undertaking, but now at last I have been able to complete one aspect of it, the study of St. John's Revelation presented here. Because of my father's theological background, his thorough knowledge of Greek and Hebrew, and an understanding of ancient Middle Eastern culture and thought gained from a doctorate in Assyriology, he was able to offer new understanding of the symbolisms in the Revelation and new interpretations of its structure. Other aspects of his interpretations of the Johannine writings will follow in other publications.

Scripture quotations are from the King James Version unless the letters AST indicate that they are from the American Standard Translation (1901).

I acknowledge with deep appreciation the help my sister, Elizabeth van Burkalow Curral, has given me as I have prepared this material for publication. Because she, like me, had often talked with our father about his work, she has been able to give invaluable advice and support.

Anastasia van Burkalow

New York City, 1990

PROLOGUE:

THE THEME, FORM, AND SYMBOLISMS OF ST. JOHN'S REVELATION

PROLOGUE

The Theme of the Apocalypse

The Book's Form: (1) As a Four-fold Worship Drama

The Book's Form: (2) As a Three-fold Foreshadowing of
Developments within and between Church and State

The Book's Form: (3) The Apocalyptic Sevens

St. John's Symbolisms

PROLOGUE:

The Theme, Form, and Symbolisms

of St. John's Revelation

In his Revelation—or his Apocalypse, as it is often called—St. John is concerned with the fulfillment of God's great plan for the salvation of his earthly children. His purpose is therefore to foreshadow the developments in Christendom that will lead eventually to the Savior's return in his second advent and his final establishment of a new heaven and a new earth.

In order that we may better understand the book's message the present monograph offers new interpretations of its apocalyptic symbolisms and of its complex form. It is the latter that is the chief concern here and it is interpreted in two ways. The first of these, to which the greater part of this study is devoted, suggests that the obvious four-fold pattern of the book represents an apocalyptic worship drama based on the ancient Hebrew synagogue ritual as modified by the early Christian Church. Symbolisms of course play an essential role in this drama. The second interpretation, really an outgrowth of the first, points out a three-fold foreshadowing of developments within and between Church and State as they are revealed in the action of the drama.

THE THEME OF THE APOCALYPSE

First let us summarize the book's message as it will be interpreted in this study.

This last book of the Bible carries to completion the unfolding theme of divine revelation that is begun in the first book and is continued throughout the Bible as a whole—the theme of the promise of divine intervention for the salvation of a fallen world. We find its first and germinal announcement in the Protevangel, made after humanity's "fall" in the Garden of Eden. In that old parable we are told that "Jehovah God said unto the serpent...I will put enmity between thee and the woman, and between thy

5

seed and her seed; and he shall bruise thy head, and thou shalt bruise his heel" (Gen. 3:14–15 AST).

The historic fulfillment of the latter part of that promise is found in the Gospels, which tell of the Savior's coming as the Lamb of God. Fulfillment of the former part, the Savior's coming again as "the Lion of the tribe of Judah" (Rev. 5:5; cf. Heb. 7:14) to crush the serpent's head, is the theme of the Bible's last book, the Revelation of St. John. There, in a parable of apocalyptic symbolism, we are shown the anti-Christian perversities whose hate-urged culmination of abysmal and all-threatening evils will make necessary a hastening of that divine intervention; and we see the glorious consummation that will follow it when the whole earth, made new, is to become the kingdom of the Lord. Through the first advent the fruits of the Christ-like spirit—works of lovingkindness, faith, service, and steadfastness (Gal. 5:22; Eph. 5:9)—have been spread abroad in individual lives. The second advent will insure the dominance of that spirit in the life of the world. And just as the sacrifice of the Passover lamb, which foreshadowed the sacrificial first advent, was not an accomplishment complete in itself, but the first effective movement that made possible the pilgrim journey to the Promised Land, so also the first advent began the work of the great salvation, which will be completed by the second advent and the coming of the New Jerusalem.

Our usual English translations of the first verse of the Apocalypse make it appear to have been written to tell of things that were to come to their consummation in St. John's time or shortly thereafter. As the King James Version expresses it, the book was "to show unto his [the divine author's] servants things which must shortly come to pass." But *genesthai*, the significant Greek verb of this declaration of purpose, means specifically "to come into being" rather than "to come to consummation." It is the radical of *genesis*, "birth, beginning." The real purpose of the author was, therefore, to show to his servants things that were shortly to *begin* to come to pass. And the most cursory glance at the contents of the book discovers the fact, made clear even to the mind that is altogether ignorant of apocalyptic symbolisms, that the consummation of these "things" was not meant to be reached until after the end of the age, which was to be marked by the personal return of the Savior. And the rest of St. John's brief introduction and greeting to the seven churches (1:1-8) makes this clear, as he goes on to give praise and glory to Christ, recognizing him as the one "who is and who was and who is to come, ... the first born of the dead, and the ruler of the kings of the earth... who cometh with the clouds"—the sign of the Savior's second advent first used by Daniel (7:13) and cited by Jesus himself (Matt. 24:30)

The "things" foretold in this Apocalypse are, therefore, the great events and movements that will lead up to and culminate in the promised consummation in the age to come. Here we have a prophetic history of the development of Christendom and its two great social institutions, the Church and the State, during the centuries of the ebb and flow of its struggle upward from the heathendom out of which it came and to which it so easily reverts. We see the varying fortunes of our warfare against the evil forces of the present age, a warfare led by the Captain of our Salvation in preparation for the establishment of his kingdom on earth. And we see foreshadowings of that new age, which is shown as coming into being with relative suddenness through a cataclysm that will sweep away old wrongs.

The outstanding feature of this coming age will be the second-advent presence of the Savior, a spiritual presence manifested through the Church whose head he is. It is the Church, a kingdom of priests (5:10; cf. 1:6 AST), that is to constitute the larger incarnation through whose hands he is to wield the "rod of iron" (2:26–27) with which his rule must begin, and through whom he is to bring to realization the ideal of earthly conditions, the kingdom of heaven on earth. In the closing vision of the book we see that ideal pictured as the New Jerusalem, "coming down from God out of heaven"—the City of God that is both the goal of earth life and the vestibule of heaven,

THE BOOK'S FORM: (1) AS A FOUR-FOLD WORSHIP DRAMA

The first and more complex interpretation offered here regarding the form of the Apocalypse suggests that the book is a four-fold worship drama. Self-evidently, the message of the Apocalypse is "signified" or made known to St. John and to us by means of dramatic action; and that the resulting book can be characterized as a worship drama is evidenced both by its content and its form. As regards content, among the many activities dramatized in the Apocalypse worship is recurrent. It begins

7

with the silent spiritual devotion of the lone prisoner on Patmos, enlists the thousands of voices of the angelic choirs of heaven, and eventually includes the still mightier chorus of all created things. As regards form, the four major divisions of the book—the letters to the seven churches of Asia and the oracles of the seven-sealed book, of the seven trumpets, and of the seven bowls of the wrath of God—are here interpreted as symbolizing four of the major features of the ancient Hebrew synagogue ritual, as modified by the early Christian Church.

Thus the four divisions of the Apocalypse, which serve as the "acts" of the drama, are here interpreted respectively as representing: (1) the readings from the law (the parashoth); (2) the readings from the prophets (the haphtaroth); (3) the translations of these prophetic readings, from ancient Hebrew to the vernacular (the targumim); and (4) the expositions or sermons based on them (the derashoth). Here then are three parallel versions of the lessons from the prophets; and because these were always chosen to reinforce the readings from the law, a further parallelism results. This means that each one of the four acts tells, from a different point of view, the same story—the foreshadowing of the developments that will lead up to the end of the age and the Savior's second advent. Such parallel but differentiated versions, interrelated and cooperative, provide ample opportunity for and understanding of the recapitulations that are so characteristic of the book.

To make the worship ritual as complete as possible St. John includes, symbolically, the ceremonials of Yom Kippur, even the fearful one of the scapegoat, for it was only on that Great Day of Atonement that the Holy of Holies, pictured in the book's visions, was employed in any service or could be entered even by the high priest. Indeed, we find that the penitence and cleansings of atonement are doubly emphasized in the Apocalypse; for in addition to the ceremonials of the regular Day of Atonement, one of which is represented in each of the four acts, a special anticipatory day of atonement is found as an episode in the third act, introduced by the archangel who brings the "little book open" (Rev. 10:2). This serves as the megillah of the service, a short sacred writing sometimes added as a supplement to the haphtaroth.

In the early church, as in the synagogue, the services also included appropriate prayers and hymns, represented in the

Apocalypse by the prayers of the saints (5:8; 8:3–5) and the matchless music of the heavenly choirs. And at any time in the midst of the regular service there was complete liberty for spontaneous utterances by those who had received spiritual gifts, such as those of prophecy and unknown tongues. This enabled the revelator to introduce a number of significant proclamations.

In the worship of Israel the great seasonal festivals were of almost equal significance with the great fast of Yom Kippur. They were indeed of supreme significance in all the ethnic religions of the Middle East, but as they were developed by Israel—Passover, Pentecost, Rosh Hashana, and Tabernacles—they had a peculiarly prophetic symbolism, just such as to make them most serviceable to the apocalyptist. This was their association with the wilderness journey from the bondage of Egypt to the freedom of the Promised Land, which was accepted as a glorious parable of the final deliverance of the whole of earth life from its bondage to Satan and the final establishment of the kingdom of the Messiah, the Christ. Since this is the very theme of the Apocalypse, with its final vision of the New Jerusalem, its four acts must represent not only the major elements of the synagogue ritual but also the temporal suggestions of the four festivals, one of which is symbolized in each act, but without details of their ceremonies.

The Apocalypse is therefore a composite worship drama, and combining its various symbolisms we can summarize its four acts and their related festivals thus:

1. The parashoth, or seven-fold setting forth of the law of Christ (substituted for the Mosaic law), represented by the letters to the seven churches. These provide an outline of the inter-advent history of Christendom from the religious point of view and include symbolisms of the Feast of Passover and the first atonement ceremonial.
2. The haphtaroth, or seven-fold readings from the prophets, represented by the book sealed with seven seals. These lessons, chosen to reinforce those from the law, tell of Christendom's civil history and include symbolisms of the Feast of Pentecost and the second atonement ceremonial.
3. The targumim, or translations of the sealed book of prophecy, represented by the messages of the seven trumpets. Included are various interruptions, one of them being the introduction of the megillah (the "little book open"), its

9

translation by the seven thunders, and its exposition in the vision of the two witnesses. Here also are symbolisms of the Feast of Trumpets or Rosh Hashana and the third atonement ceremonial.

4. The derashoth, or expositions of the haphtaroth, represented by the oracles of the seven bowls of the wrath of God. The Feast of Tabernacles and the scapegoat ceremonial of the Day of Atonement are included symbolically.

In accordance with the fact that these visions are seen on the Christian Lord's Day, which takes the place of the Jewish Sabbath, St. John has followed the Jewish custom of reading seven passages from both the law and the prophets in the Sabbath service of the synagogue. What he actually pictures in the drama, however, is the Day of Atonement, for the Holy of Holies, seen in these visions, could be entered only on that day; and on that day only six portions of each scripture were read. Therefore in all four acts St. John contrives to separate the seventh reading, or at least to differentiate it in some way, from the first six; and in the vision of the seals, while seven are opened, only six are actually read, though we shall find that the seventh seal and its related trumpet and bowl of wrath are by no means supernumerary or perfunctory.

Regarding the targumim or translations of the scriptures, it should be noted that these became necessary after the Babylonian exile, for by that time the ancient Hebrew in which they were written was no longer understood by most people. In this Apocalypse, however, no translation is needed for the parashoth, since the letters to the churches of St. John's time would of course have been presented in the vernacular (nor are they expounded, as will be explained in Act 1). And though it was the custom of the synagogue to translate each of the several passages of a lesson from the law or the prophets immediately after it was read, in the case of the oracles of the seven-sealed book St. John waits until after the reading of all of them has been completed before presenting the seven trumpet oracles that translate them and those of the seven bowls of wrath that expound them.

In this dramatization of the service of the Christian synagogue we thus have set before us three prescribed scripture readings—the parashoth, the haphtaroth, and the megillah. The synagogue service provides for a three-fold presentation of each one—the reading of the original Hebrew text, its translation into the vernacular, and its exposition—and if St. John had seen fit to follow this pattern entirely he could have told his story nine times, each one, of course, being from a different point of view. This would be only one less than the ten versions in Robert Browning's masterpiece, *The Ring and the Book*. Nine versions, however, would have overcrowded the stage of this apocalyptic drama, and so four of them have been relegated to the background, leaving only five to be set forth in the drama's four acts and one special episode. These are: one for the parashoth (reading—or rather dictation—only), three for the haphtaroth (reading, translation, and exposition), and one for the megillah (exposition). Although the point of view is different for each one (see Appendix 5 for a discussion of their parallelisms), the theme is the same—the foreshadowing of developments that would lead to the Savior's promised return as the Lion of Judah, the King of kings and Lord of lords.

In the form of his apocalyptic worship drama, then, St. John has followed the principal features of the synagogue ritual, but in a number of ways he has varied it, availing himself of an entirely legitimate measure of dramatic license.

THE BOOK'S FORM: (2) AS A THREE-FOLD FORESHADOWING OF DEVELOPMENTS WITHIN AND BETWEEN CHURCH AND STATE

In the dramatic action of the Apocalypse major roles are played by Church and State, and if their varied relationships are followed through the four acts of the drama it becomes evident that they are shown from three different points of view. (1) Separate surveys of Church and State are found in acts 1 and 2 of the drama. (2) In act 3 there is a review of conflicts between Church and State and between their true and pervert forms. (3) Act 4 pictures the Church and State united.

Thus in terms of Church-State relationships a three-fold structure can be discovered in the midst of the four-fold worship drama.

THE BOOK'S FORM: (3) THE APOCALYPTIC SEVENS

The number seven, which plays a prominent role in the Apocalypse, has special symbolic significance, for it is the sum of three, which represents the triune God, and four, which to the ancients represented the four "elements"—earth, water, air, and fire—which they thought made up the world created by God. (See Appendix 4.) Thus this number could well be considered in the following section on symbolism. In his Apocalypse, however, St. John uses seven as an element of the drama's form as well, and so it must be given separate treatment here.

Seven is a difficult number to work with, for it cannot be divided into equal parts, a four–three or a three–four division being the nearest approach to such equality. Such groupings are readily resolved, however, into two equal parts of four each when the subject matter permits the middle unit to be counted in both halves. In all of the Apocalyptic sevens just such a commutation is indicated, with four–three or three–four becoming four–four.

The significance of this pattern is not far to seek. As has been noted, the purpose of this Apocalypse is to foretell things that were about to begin to come to pass in the history of Christendom, and it is evident that the emphasis of its foreshadowings centers, not on the beginnings of these "things," but on the consummation to which they are all to lead. We would expect, therefore, to find, in the symbolism that represents the action of the drama, some device that would focus attention upon the end of the age covered by the foreshadowings. Just such a device is clearly provided by a four–four division of the sevens that make up the scenes of the drama and set forth its action.

Applying this pattern we find that in the oracles of the seals, trumpets, and bowls of wrath the first four can readily be interpreted as foreshadowing the significant features of the history of Christendom, divided into four chronologically successive periods, just as the allegory of Israel's ancient pilgrimage is set forth by the four traditional Hebrew festivals. And just as that old journey led through the troubles of the wilderness to the freedom and rest of the Promised Land, so the history of Christendom is pictured as leading through successive struggles and, in the fourth scene, to the final cataclysm that ushers in the New Jerusalem. Further details of that final period are provided in the last three scenes. Although this pattern is not so immediately evident in the case of the letters to the churches, it can readily be applied there once it has been recognized in the other oracles. (See Appendix 5.)

Thus what appears at first glance to be a four–three or three–four division becomes, by counting the fourth oracle twice, two groups of four, and their relationship can be illustrated by the carpenter's square. Using it as a pattern, we can picture a vertical arm representing the four successive periods of time and a horizontal arm showing four scenes—the fourth or final one in the time sequence plus three more that concentrate on that last period, the end of the age. The fourth member, at the corner of the square, is therefore included in each arm.

The parallelisms between these Apocalyptic sevens will be noted from time to time throughout the first interpretation, and they are summarized in Appendix 5.

ST. JOHN'S SYMBOLISMS

Apocalyptic writing is largely symbolic, and the present study shows that in his Apocalypse St. John draws his symbolisms from a number of sources, a major one being the star lore and cosmography of the ancient world. Thus in this worship drama enacted in the inspired imagination of the seer the action takes place in the starry heavens, and the actors are represented by stars or star figures. This was easily accomplished, for the theme of the drama, the story of the salvation of the human world gone wrong, was foreshadowed in the primordial apocalypse of the stars. (See Appendix 1.) There the zodiac is represented as the two seven-branched candlesticks "standing before the Lord of the earth" (Rev. 11:4 AST) and symbolizing the Church and the State, the two institutions divinely ordained for the ordering and developing of human society. And there we see under what influences the mutual and interdependent activities of these two indispensable social institutions must be carried on during all the millennia of the moral and spiritual warfare involved in earth-life's salvation from its own perversities. On the one hand there are the celestial agencies represented by the supernal constellations or star pictures of the northern heavens, while on the other hand there are the satanic agencies represented by the dragons and wild beasts pictured in the southern or infernal heavens, an interpretation of the heavens held widely throughout the ancient Middle East. These star figures, the actors in the drama, are construed by St. John primarily in accordance with the cosmic myths associated with them from

13

time immemorial, but on occasion he does not hesitate to vary his interpretation within the limits allowed by the shapes and relationships of the figures.

Here we must mention also the ancient concept of the earth as a double pyramid, its northern part reaching up to the heavens, with the Garden of Eden at its top. (See Appendix 1.) Temples of the old Middle East were copies of this pyramidal earth mountain, and symbolic representations of the structure and furnishings of the temple in Jerusalem form the background of many of the Apocalyptic visions.

Use of symbolisms found in apocalyptic writings of the Old Testament will be noted from time to time in the presentation of the drama's four acts, and of course the worship rituals, the seasonal festivals, and Israel's wilderness journey all add their symbolisms, as has been noted earlier. The symbolic significance attached to certain numbers is evident also. (See Appendices 2, 3, and 4.)

In the Apocalypse, therefore, we find a multitude of symbolisms, all of which are fully discussed in the Appendices, and all of which are drawn from the age-old heritage of which the religion of the New Testament is the consummation. The complexity of the book, only glimpsed here, will become more evident as its four-fold pattern is interpreted as a worship drama and its four acts are examined in detail. Its many symbolisms give coherence and significance to its picture of worship and provide the organic divisions, stage properties, and dramatis personae required to set forth its revelation. For its full understanding all of the symbolisms must be interpreted, and for the most part this will be done as they appear in the action of the drama. However, in order to tell the Apocalyptic story with as little interruption as possible, consideration of the atonement and festival symbolisms will be presented separately at the end of each act.

The three-fold interpretation, based on the four-fold one, emphasizes those parts of the dramatic action that reveal Church-State interrelationships. Only the symbolisms associated with those interrelationships are pertinent to this discussion, and they will be mentioned only briefly, as they are treated fully in the four-fold interpretation.

A FOUR-FOLD INTERPRETATION:

REVELATION AS A WORSHIP DRAMA

I. THE LETTERS TO THE SEVEN CHURCHES
Act 1. The Parashoth—Readings from the Law

The Setting

The First Vision and Its Astral Figures
   The Seven Stars
   The Seven Golden Candlesticks
   The Theophany

The Seven Letters: The Worship Drama's Parashoth

The Seven Letters: Their Messages
   Ephesus
   Smyrna
   Pergamum
   Thyatira
   Sardis
   Philadelphia
   Laodicea

Atonement and Festival Symbolisms
   The First Atonement Ceremonial
   The Festival of the Passover (Now Easter)

I. THE LETTERS TO THE SEVEN CHURCHES

Act 1. The Parashoth—Readings from the Law (Rev. 1–3)

THE SETTING

The stage is set in the open country, and the drama begins with worship as we see St. John, a lone prisoner on Patmos, "in the spirit on the Lord's day." Here, however, as again in the final vision showing the New Jerusalem, we see no temple, no synagogue, no man-made sacred edifice of any sort. In that last vision "the Lord God Almighty and the Lamb" are the temple of the city; and so it is with St. John in this first act. He needs no temple, for his worship is in spirit and truth, like that described by the Savior in his words to the woman of Samaria (John 4:21–24), and that makes his retreat on Patmos a true sanctuary.

St. John's worship was interrupted, however, by a loud voice like a trumpet, a typical apocalyptic symbolism representing an archangel. This is evidently the angel by whom Jesus Christ "signified" his revelation to "his servant John," and we need not seek far to identify him. Immediately we think of Gabriel, the "man of God," who is represented in the scriptures as the chief of God's special agents to humanity. It was he who announced the first advent of the Savior (Luke 1:19,26), and so it is appropriate to find him setting forth the apocalyptic foreshadowings of his second advent. To John his words were: "What thou seest, write in a book, and send it unto the seven churches which are in Asia."

Thus through this angelic spokesman did Jesus Christ, the substantive author of the book (1:1), commission St. John to be its descriptive author.

THE FIRST VISION AND ITS ASTRAL SYMBOLS

As he heard that voice of authority speaking behind him, St. John turned and saw the first of Revelation's many visions. And at once the solitary worshiper was admitted into the celestial temple seen more fully in Act 2—that now veil-less temple "in the heavens" after whose plan and furnishings those of the earthly temples of the ethnic religions of the Middle East have all been "patterned" (Exod. 25:9,40). He saw seven golden candlesticks, the celestial originals of those that stood in the holy place of the Mosaic tabernacle; and he saw the theophanic presence of the risen and glorified Savior in the midst of these candlesticks, and the seven stars in his right hand. That theophany, then, must be accepted as the mediational divine presence represented by the Shekinah that rested of old on the mercy seat, the throne of the Holy of Holies (Rev. 21:3; cf. John 1:14).

The Seven Stars

The theophanic figure, the divine author of the book, identifies the seven stars held in his right hand as "the angels of the seven churches." Here we have a clue to all the star symbolisms of the Apocalypse: All its "stars" are "angels"; and all its "angels"—that is, all its mystic beings, whether good or bad, its dragons and wild beasts as well as its "living creatures" and "strong angels"—are either stars or star figures.

It is to these star-angels associated with the churches that the letters are directly addressed; and so it must be assumed that they in turn are to read and expound this Christian Torah in the public worship of the several churches. It is natural, therefore, to construe them as the pastors or bishops of the churches of Asia. That this is in accordance with the intention of the author is witnessed by the fact that one of the Semitic words for "star-angel"—and the first one found in the book of Daniel, which is for our author a store-house of apocalyptic precedent—could very properly be translated into the language of Revelation by the original of our word "bishop"—the Greek word *episcopas*. The literal meaning of that word is "overseer, watchman," and this is precisely the meaning of Daniel's first word for "star-angel," the Hebrew word *'ir*, which in our English versions is rendered "watcher" (see Dan. 4:13,17,23).

In Daniel's interpretation of star-angels as "watchers" we find a clue to the astral identity of the star-angels of the Apocalypse. They must be the seven heavenly bodies (Mercury, Venus, Mars, Jupiter, Saturn, plus the Sun and the Moon) known to the ancients as "planets." In the ancient Hebrew cosmology these "planets" symbolized a special cohort of God's angels charged with supervision of the Church and the State, the two fundamental social institutions of earth life. (See Appendix 1.)

The Seven Golden Candlesticks

Identification of the seven golden candlesticks is also provided by the book's divine author. They are the seven churches; and in the heavens they must be represented by the seven zodiacal "houses" of the planets in their religious significance. (See Appendix 1.) These are the constellations Cancer, Leo, Virgo, Libra, Scorpio, Sagittarius, and Capricornus. Taken together they represent the Church as a whole, the institution divinely charged with responsibility for the direction of the religious life of earth.

The Theophany

The great theophanic representation of the Savior is clearly related symbolically to both the stars and the candlesticks.

In the ancient cosmology, as has been noted, the seven planets were interpreted as divine agents influencing developments on earth, specifically with reference to Church and State. Reflecting that concept, the theophanic presence is pictured as holding the seven stars in his right hand as one having authority over them. This reflects the ancient concept that the movements of the planets through the zodiac were to be interpreted as oracles of divine revelation, which were made known by the Euphratean "tablets of destiny" and the jeweled breastplate of the Hebrew high priest with its Urim and Thummim.

Since the theophanic figure is seen walking "in the midst of the seven candlesticks," the astral figure representing it must bear a similar relationship to the zodiacal constellations that represent the candlesticks. This can be no other than the great constellation known by the Greek name Boötes, which lies just north of Virgo and Libra. To the ancient Hebrews this was the celestial figure of the archangel Gabriel, whom we have already recognized as the angel through whom the Savior signified his

21

Revelation to St. John. And so we may conceive of him here as enacting the theophanic role that was peculiarly his, lending himself and his celestial figure to the Savior and beginning in this first vision of the Apocalypse the work of signification assigned to him.

In the drama this theophanic figure serves first to identify the writer of the letters to the churches, for in the first four of them the signature of the Savior consists, not of his name, but of allusions to this vision as it is described by the revelator. Thus the Savior calls himself: "he that holdeth the seven stars in his right hand, and walketh in the midst of the seven golden candlesticks"; "the first and the last, which was dead and is alive"; "he which hath the sharp sword with two edges"; "the Son of God, who hath his eyes like a flame of fire, and his feet are like fine brass."

In this apparition that was "like unto the Son of man" there is also, however, a prophetic symbolism, one that St. John adopts from the Savior's own use of it. The avatar of the figure is to be found in visions of Ezekiel (1:26–28) and Daniel (7:8–10, 13–14), the latter adding also that he saw "the Son of man" coming "with the clouds of heaven." St. John uses this phrase in his initial greeting to the seven churches (1:7), and in the Savior's "little apocalypse" it serves as the final token of his presence as the Mighty-to-Save and the Mighty Avenger of the last great day when he shall come again in his second advent. After great tribulation, he said, there shall appear "the sign of the Son of man in heaven: and then shall all the tribes of the earth mourn, and they shall see the Son of man coming in the clouds of heaven with power and great glory."[1]

St. John's vision of "one like unto a Son of man," the great portent of the last day, serves therefore to define the primary purpose of his Revelation, which is to tell of the Lord's second coming and to foreshadow the course of events leading up to it. It is as if here, at the beginning of the Apocalypse, the seer had caught a sudden glimpse of its end, for this same symbolism, the sign of the "Son of man," is seen in the vision of the Heavenly Harvester (14:14) that closes the story of the inter-advent years as told by the trumpet oracles.

This first vision of the glorified Savior shows him also, however, as a veritable "Son of man" who could say of himself: "I am the first and the last; I am he that liveth, and was dead; and, behold, I am alive forevermore...and have the keys of hell and of death" (1:17–18). Clothed in "a garment down to the foot," clearly to be understood as a high priest's robe for the Day of Atonement, he is our Advocate with the Father, a great high priest who is "touched with the feeling of our infirmities" (Heb. 4:15). And he will continue as the Advocate our present weakness needs until he appears as the Judge symbolized in the book's last theophany (20:11–15).

The purely personal relationship represented here is the principal concern of religion, and therefore of the Church. This feature of the first vision's symbolism therefore gives us to understand that the revelation set forth in the following seven letters is especially concerned with the religious life of the times their foreshadowings cover. There are also, however, some suggestions of interrelationships between Church and State.

The Seven Letters: The Worship Drama's Parashoth

The vision of the glorious theophany is followed by the letters to the seven churches, and in this interpretation of Revelation as a worship drama these letters are viewed as the parashoth, the readings from the law. The traditional Hebrew synagogue service begins with such readings from the Torah, the "law of Moses." In the public worship of the early Christian Church that pattern was retained, but the old readings were of course superseded by readings from the "law of Christ." The earliest and most numerous of the New Testament writings that set forth that law authoritatively were letters written by the Apostles to churches they could not visit in person—letters of admonition, expostulation, exhortation, exposition, as the need might be. By the time this Apocalypse was written it had long been the custom to read such apostolic letters to Christian congregations, as is indicated by St. Paul's instructions to the churches of Colossae and Laodicea (Col. 4:16).

The Christian Church had therefore become accustomed, in its worship services, to giving the New Testament law of Christ the place of honor that the Jewish synagogue gives to the Old Testament law of Moses. With respect to religious tradition, however, conservatism is proverbial; and St. John, who wore a petalon as the legitimate hereditary high priest of Israel (cf. John 18: 15-16), was conspicuously conservative. So, naturally,

23

were the churches most directly under his influence. It is possible, therefore, that both he and they were in need of an authoritative declaration of the complete supersession of the old Mosaic tradition by its fulfillment in the person and work and words of Christ.

Just such assurance is provided by the unique pattern of this first act of the Apocalyptic worship drama. In accordance with the established custom, the drama's readings from the law are letters, but they are not the usual apostolic ones. These are actually dictated by the Master himself and therefore they truly represent the law of Christ. Further, because they include references to St. Paul's epistles,[2] they place them and by implication all of the New Testament in the same category with themselves, conferring on them true cannonical authority. The New Testament scriptures thus verily represent the law of Christ, the law by which we must shape our lives, our work, and our thinking.

At first glance this first act seems to neglect the traditional synagogue scheme of translating and expounding the readings of the day, a pattern that is suggestive of the persistent and prayerful and inspired study we must give these sacred scriptures if we would find their true riches. In fact, even the worshipful reading of these letters in the congregation is omitted, for it is their writing that is represented in the drama and that must therefore serve as the substitute for their public reading. There is indirect provision, however, for their incorporation in the worship of the respective churches. These letters are addressed, as we have seen, to the "angels" of the churches of Asia, who have been interpreted as their bishops or pastors; and it must be assumed that they in turn are to have them duly read, translated wherever necessary, and expounded in the public worship of the several congregations. Each letter individually, then was expected to be the parashah for the contemporary church to whose bishop it was addressed. For us who read the drama today, however, all seven letters form its parashoth or appointed lessons from the Christian Torah.

THE SEVEN LETTERS: THEIR MESSAGES

Since the churches to which these seven letters are addressed were actual contemporaries of St. John, it is impossible that

24

their messages should not have applied to personalities and conditions existing at that time. It is equally impossible, however, that these letters would have been included in this Apocalypse unless they had also a metaphorical meaning regarding the future. In the contemporary churches we see types and shadows of what might be expected in the future development of the general Church and of its relations with the State.

During the times when this Apocalypse was written, and for several centuries afterward, the followers of Jesus were hard beset by the then pagan Roman Empire with its emperor worship. It has often been suggested, therefore, that the purpose of the Apocalypse was to offer support to the early Christians during those difficult times. However, the problems that have really troubled God's peculiar people, whether of the Old Covenant or the New, have never been those that originated in any such opposition from without, and persecutions by pagan Rome were not the evils foremost in the thought of the author of this Apocalypse. In fact, in the letters to the seven churches, primarily contemporary in their application, these evils are suggested only symbolically, and only in the letters to Smyrna and Pergamum. Both times they are mentioned with sympathetic concern only, as evils to be endured and not dangers to be shunned.

For some, of course, such evils did involve the danger of apostasy. For the true Christian, however, and the true church, they were as the pruning hook that but strengthens the vine and makes it more fruitful. Such apostasies therefore brought the churches no problem save only that of restoration of the lapsed. They did not call for special apocalyptic warnings such as those we find in the letters. Those must therefore be construed as concerned with apostasies far less overt, though no less real, and far more subtle in their invasions—such as love of the world and the things that are in it, and pride, malice, guile, greed, envy. It is such froward elements of human nature that so often betrayed Israel of old into treason against the Divine King and that have impeded the progress of Christendom during all its history.

It is against such apostasies that the letters carry messages of condemnation. They carry commendations also, however, together with both admonitions and promises. In them the Divine Author, who is both Lord and Judge of all the earth, lays sevenfold emphasis upon the fact that, in accordance with the promise

25

made when he was still in the flesh, he is coming again to deal with each and all in righteousness. That right dealing will be of two sorts, either reward or punishment. For those whom he finds watching and waiting and ready for his coming it will be reward. This is the glad promise that resounds throughout the book in its glorious antiphonies and choruses and that shines resplendent in its final vision of the New Jerusalem. In the action of the Apocalypse, however, the message stressed is the diametrically opposite aspect that the presence of the Mighty One of the great day of Jehovah will of necessity have for such as are not "of the truth." To them he will come as the Mighty Avenger, who treads the winepress of the wrath of God.

In the following analyses of the individual letters, it will be noted that the names of the cities to which the letters are addressed are each suggestive of a Hebrew root, whose meaning is in keeping with the contents of that city's letter. To Jewish Christians of St. John's day such wordplay would have been so evident that they could not have failed to recognize it, and such Hebrew paronyms are among the apocalyptic devices that aid in interpretation of the text. In some cases the city's name has oracular meaning in the Greek language also.

Ephesus

The letter to the church in Ephesus commends it for rejecting the apostate teachings of the "false prophets" and the "Nicolaitans," which may be interpreted respectively (though there has long been uncertainty about the Nicolaitans) as Church dominance over the State and Church subservience to the State, represented by emperor worship (see the Three-fold Interpretation). On the debit side, however, the Ephesian church has lost its "first love," and it is told therefore that its "candlestick" will be removed from its place. This does not mean that the church itself would cease to exist, but that it would be removed from Ephesus; and we shall find, accordingly, that the spiritually dead church of Sardis, to which the fifth letter is addressed, appears to be a descendant of this church that had lost its first love. Ephesus itself, of course, has long been a desolate ruin, and this fate is predicted in the oracle of the Hebrew wordplay on the city's name. *Epheso*, the name's stem, is the Hebrew particle of "nonentity" or "cessation of existence," coming from *aphes*, "to cease, to fail, to come to an end."[3]

26

The Savior calls on the Ephesian church to repent, and to those individuals who do repent and "overcome" he offers the fruit of the tree of life, that tree which in the ancient cosmology represented the way, the only way, leading up from the top of the earth mountain to the heaven of heavens. (See Appendix 1.) As we know from the symbolic Genesis story, access to the gate of that way is pictured as shut off from the world of humanity by the guardian cherubim of the zodiac. In the signature of this letter, however, the zodiac is represented as being under the authority of the Savior, for he identifies himself as holding the seven stars in his hand and walking among the seven golden candlesticks (2:1). We must remember in this connection that it is as much a function of the guardians of a gate to open it for those who have the right to enter as it is to keep it closed to all others. And we know that the purpose of the Savior's coming is to turn aside the flaming swords of those guardian cherubim and open the way of the tree of life for all who will follow him and overcome with him. By this promise the individual Christian is assured that however unfaithful the church as a whole may be, this is for him but a challenge, a handicap, that he will be able to overcome. Under the leadership of the Captain of our Salvation we can brave the flaming swords and win admission to the way of the tree of life and entrance into the realm of the spirit.

Smyrna

The church in Smyrna was altogether excellent and, like the Master himself, was faced with persecution—slander by the "synagogue of Satan" and a threat of imprisonment that might suggest an effort to exterminate Christianity. The apostasy represented here would therefore seem to be the worship of Antichrist in place of Jesus Christ. But to those who would be "faithful unto death"—the fate such apostasy might demand of those who opposed it—the Savior promised the martyr's crown of life, adding that "he that overcometh shall not be hurt of the second death." Here there is assurance that in the resurrection of the just the victory over death is to be complete and final; and at the same time it is implied that for the unjust there will be an equally complete and final second death.

In keeping with both the tribulations this church suffers and the final promise to the overcomer, the name "Smyrna" suggests the Hebrew *shemor-na* — "keep her safe." To the Hebrew Christian of St. John's day the name would also have brought to mind the familiar name "Samaria," which is *shomeron* or *shomeronah* in the Hebrew scriptures and *shamerain* in the Aramaic. This suggestion shines out in the letter's denunciation of the apostates who "say they are Jews, and are not, but are the synagogue of Satan."

In the church of Smyrna, however, not all were apostates. Some were "good Samaritans," and for them there is a message in the oracle of the city's name in its own Greek language, where it means "myrrh." Since myrrh is one of the essential ingredients of the holy anointing oil of the ancient ordinances (Exod. 30:23, for example), it symbolizes the unction of the Holy Spirit, which is harmonious with the unqualified praise given to Smyrna by the Savior. A further significance of myrrh, however, comes from the Jewish use of it in the burial of their dead, as is noted in the mixture of myrrh and aloes provided by Nicodemus for the Savior's burial (John 19:39). In this sense it is harmonious also with the words by which the Savior identified himself in the letter's signature: "These things saith the first and the last, which was dead, and is alive." It may be noted in passing, also, that these two symbolisms made myrrh one of the appropriate gifts offered by the wise men to the King of kings at his birth in Bethlehem.

Pergamum

The church in Pergamum is commended for keeping the faith in spite of the martyrdom demanded by "Satan's throne," which must refer to the cult of emperor worship, the chief seat of which was located here in St. John's time. Not all were faithful, however, for there was tolerance here of the apostasies represented by the teachings of Balaam and the Nicolaitans, which may be interpreted respectively (see the Three-fold Interpretation) as representing the dominance of the Church over the State and the State over the Church. The Savior rebukes such tolerance and promises to make war against these errors with the sharp sword of his mouth, the feature that identifies him in the letter's signature. The favorable outcome of such a spiritual warfare shines out in the Hebrew wordplay on the city's name, for it tells us *parak-'amô*—"the Lord will deliver his people."[4] The Greek name "Pergamon" is also in harmony with this concept of warfare, for while it first appears in literature as the name of the citadel of Troy, it was later often used as a generic term for "citadel" or "castle," a stronghold in case of war.

To the overcomers in the church of Pergamum a double promise is given. They are to "eat of the hidden manna" and to receive "a white stone" on which a new name is written. That white stone, better described as a white pebble, derives its significance as a symbol from the usage of the ancient courts of justice, one that has long lingered in modified form in the secret ballots of fraternal societies; for in the secret ballots of the ancient jurors a black pebble meant condemnation, while a white one, like the "seal of the living God" in the drama's second act (7:2), meant acquittal and assured protection from agents of retribution. That the holder of such a stone deserves acquittal is evidenced by the "new name" written on it. In the usage of the Bible a person's name was inseparable from his personality—his character and capabilities, his fitness for a calling, and his acceptance in society. This new name must therefore be such as Jacob received when he became Israel—a new name for a new creature. It points to the new birth, the more than adequate substitute for the law's death penalty, and therefore the justification for the verdict of acquittal. It is just such a new creature, born again and become a child of God, who has a right to be admitted to the banquet of the "hidden manna," which can be no other than the fruit of the tree of life, the "bread of heaven."

Thyatira

In the four–four division of the Apocalyptic sevens, presented in the Prologue and considered more fully in Appendix 5, the letter to the church in Thyatira, the middle member of the seven, must be interpreted as telling of conditions at the time of the end, when the Savior returns. And in the letter the faithful church of Thyatira is seen as the "body of Christ" through whom he will prepare the way for his second advent. It is the overcomers of this church who will have "power over the nations" to "rule them with a rod of iron," sharing with the Savior his royal office when he comes as King of kings and Lord of lords. The dawning of that new day of the second advent is glimpsed in the closing promise: "And I will give him the morning star," which is to be interpreted as the Savior himself (22:16). Commendation is suggested also by the Greek wordplay on the city's name. The Greek

29

word *thyos* includes all the fragrant substances used on the altar of devotion, and its derivative *thyetra* means "more incense-like, more fragrant." Here we have a suggestion of the truly devotional nature of this church's works—"charity, and service, and faith, and...patience" (2:19).

In contrast to the church in Thyatira, but found also in that time of the Savior's return, is the unfaithful church of Jezebel, so far gone in error and evil that it was excommunicated and so could not directly receive letters addressed to it. Instead, the Savior's call for its repentance had to be given to the "angel" of the faithful church, to be passed on to the unfaithful one. That the great unfaithfulness of the time was the denial of the deity of Christ Jesus is suggested by the first part of the opening signature of the letter: "These things saith the Son of God." And God's wrath against this apostate church is suggested by the remainder of the signature, describing his "eyes like unto a flame of fire" and his feet "of fine brass." The eyes suggest the King of kings riding forth to the battle of the great day of God Almighty, the day of wrath, for his eyes too were "as a flame of fire" (19:12). And the feet of fine brass suggest the treading of the "winepress of the wrath of God" (14:19).

How deep a responsibility the true church must bear for the continuation of apostasy like Jezebel's is indicated by the Savior's condemnation of the Thyatiran church for "suffering" it. Very evidently the divine Author of the letters has no use for the easy-going tolerance that permits error to go its way unchallenged. It is the church's duty to wield the sword of the spirit against error—to bear witness to the truth whenever occasion offers and to "hold fast."

It is the corrupt church of Jezebel that is characterized by the Hebrew wordplay on the city's name, for it tells us *to'ayah-te'areh*—"the apostate woman will reveal her shame." The full force of this oracle is seen in the Old Testament passage to which it alludes, Jeremiah's pronouncement against Edom: "O daughter of Edom...thou shalt be drunken, and shalt make thyself naked...He will visit thine iniquity...he will discover thy sins" (Lam. 4:21–22).

The entirely contradictory nature of the Greek and Hebrew wordplays on the name Thyatira, the one commendatory and the other condemnatory, emphasizes the contrast between the two churches. Together they serve both to conclude the four-fold

survey of the Church during the inter-advent years and to introduce the four-fold picture of conditions at the end of that period.
The final three letters add to the picture of that final time. This
is in accord with the carpenter's square structure of the
Apocalyptic sevens, as outlined in the Prologue.

Sardis

The letter to Sardis is like that to Ephesus in two ways: in
each one the Savior identifies himself in the signature as he who
has "the seven stars," and for each church, and only for these
two, disaster is predicted. The Sardian church appears therefore
to be a descendant of that early Ephesian church that had lost
its first love.

Our Lord's unlimited knowledge of human nature in general
and of each individual with whom he dealt is witnessed in all
seven of the letters to the churches; but it is especially evident in
the one to the church in Sardis, which had the name of being
alive but which he recognized as spiritually dead. To members of
the true church the Lord's coming at the last great day will not
be a matter of surprise or an occasion for terror (1 Thes. 5:4), for
they will be prepared. To the church in Sardis, however, his coming will be like that of a thief, for its members will not be watching. That these unfaithful ones will have their names blotted out
of the book of life is implied by the Savior's promise not to do
that to the overcomers. Even in Sardis there are a few such
faithful ones, and they will be in white garments, like the white-
robed host of martyrs who are to come down from heaven with
the Savior when he comes as King of kings (6:11; 19;14). It is to
these faithful few that the Hebrew wordplay on the city's name
applies, for the closest possible Hebrew equivoke is *sarad*, which
may be rendered: "A remnant remained" (cf. Joshua 10:20).

Philadelphia

The church in Philadelphia, which in Greek means "brotherly
love," has kept the Lord's word. It has not denied his name—has
refused, that is, to join with those who worship Antichrist; and it
has obeyed his last enjoinments to "love one another" and to
preach the gospel to all the world. It is a truly evangelical,
supremely missionary church, making use of the open door set
before it. It is this great opportunity of the open door that is
emphasized in the Hebrew wordplay on the city's name, for the

Hebrew it gives us is *pile'-dal-pîah*, which may be rendered as "a wonderful door is her portion"—the door of missionary opportunity.

In recognition of its faithfulness the Savior promises to keep the Philadelphians from the hour of trial that is to come upon the earth. And to the overcomers of this church the promise is to share in the Savior's high-priestly calling—to serve as a pillar in the temple and to have the names of God and the Savior and the New Jerusalem written on them. Of course in the ancient temples of the East there were no great supporting columns like those of western structures such as the Parthenon. The temple pillar referred to here must therefore be one of the two, known as Jakin and Boaz, that stood free and clear before the sanctuary's door in Solomon's temple to represent the two trees in the midst of the Garden of Eden. (See Appendix 3.) It is of course Jakin that is intended here—the pillar that stood on the right hand before the door and represented the tree of life. In that tree we have a symbol of the primal quest of religion, for the "way of the tree of life" represents the only way from earth and mortality to the heaven of heavens and life eternal. (See Appendix 1.) When Adam and Eve were driven from the Garden of Eden that way was lost, barred by "cherubim, and a flaming sword which turned every way" (Gen. 3:24). For the overcomer of Philadelphia, however, access to the limitless privileges of the heaven of heavens and to the freedom of the universe is guaranteed by the identification provided by the name written on him—"the name of my God, and the name of the city of my God"—a protection that brings to mind the seal of the living God that protects the 144,000 representing all the tribes of Israel (see Act 2 and Rev. 7:4). He upon whom the names of God and the Savior are written has passed the judgment of the last day and is now found worthy and able to undertake the duties and responsibilities, as well as to enjoy the privileges, of citizenship in the New Jerusalem, the city of the final consummation.

These symbols represent the God-ward half of religion, while the meaning of the city's name in the Greek language, "city of brotherly love," represents religion's concern with right relationships of people with each other.

The signature of the letter reflects doubly the Savior's commendation of the Philadelphian church. The writer is described as "holy" and "true"—an apt description of this faithful church—and as "he that hath the key of David, he that openeth, and no man shutteth; and shutteth, and no man openeth" (3:7). These latter words are taken from an oracle of Isaiah, where they describe one Eliakim, who was to be a true "father to the inhabitants of Jerusalem" in contrast to the unfaithful traitor Shebna (Isa. 22:15–25). In like fashion the Philadelphians are in contrast to the apostate synagogue of Satan (3:9). Clearly they have a priestly function, and it will be the high calling of the Philadelphian overcomers, as they carry on their missionary work, to point to the way of the tree of life that leads to heaven, and to testify from personal experience, saying: "This is the way that directs aright. Walk in it!"

Laodicea

The letter to the church in Laodicea brings a rebuke such as is found in no other of the letters, and it is the only one in which the Savior has included no word of commendation. Because the Laodiceans are lukewarm, neither hot nor cold, the Lord will "spew" them out of his mouth. They had grown rich and self-sat-isfied, content with the temporal advantages of their cultured and prosperous city. Spiritually, however, though they did not realize it, they were poor and in need of a great revival of true religion, that they might cease to follow after the riches of this world and become disciples of the Savior. From St. Paul's letter to Colossae, which he asked to have read also at the nearby city of Laodicea (Col. 4:16), it is evident (Col. 2:8–9) that a major fac-tor in the great unfaithfulness of these cities was the denial of the deity of Christ—the neglect of the fundamental confession of faith in "Jesus Christ, the Son of God, our Savior." This is sug-gested also in the opening signature of this letter to the Laodiceans, in which, by allusion, the Savior emphasizes his identity as the Son of God, calling himself "the Amen, the faith-ful and true witness, the beginning of the creation of God."[5]

Severe as the rebuke to the Laodiceans is, however, with no word of commendation, it is not altogether untempered, for to these spiritually wretched ones, "miserable, and poor, and blind, and naked," the Savior writes: "I counsel thee to buy of me gold...and white raiment...and...eyesalve" that you may "be rich...,be clothed" and may "see" (3:18). And to this he adds a call for repentance. The Lord's stern reproof is therefore in reality a manifestation of unfailing love. "As many as I love, I rebuke and chasten." That is, this love will resort to drastic measures, even to the severest discipline if need be, to save us from ourselves; and this is suggested by the Hebrew wordplay on the city's name—*lavô-dake'ah*. *Lavô* is from the verb *lavah*, "to be joined to, to accompany, to attend"; and *dake'ah* is from the verb *daka'*, which is used repeatedly of corrective chastisement of the utmost severity. The Hebrew oracle therefore tells us that the Laodicean church will be attended by chastisement that will crush it to bring it to repentance. And that this will be just punishment is suggested by the Greek oracle of the name, which is to be read as "justice for the people" (from *laos*, "people," and *dikaio*, "to show justice").

This love is also, however, one that will not let us go, as is evidenced further by the two glad promises that end the letter and that offer the hope of salvation even for the Laodiceans. They are:

1) "Behold, I stand at the door, and knock: if any man hear my voice, and open the door, I will come in to him, and will sup with him, and he with me." This is a reminder that the Lord's work of salvation begins in the realm within and must be completed there before victory can be won in the realm without. The church cannot win the world for Christ, or even make our so-called Christendom a safe place for herself, until her members have individually given themselves to him completely and received in return the full spiritual presence that is to be the inner reality of the *parousia*, the second advent. It is this abiding presence that will make them veritable and truly serviceable members of the Body of Christ, and this is the high privilege the Savior offers freely, but too often the response has been lukewarm. Clearly the lukewarmness of the Laodiceans is merely the outstanding example of a failing common to all Christendom. In this promise to anyone who hears the Master's knock and opens the door, we find complete refutation of the great error of predestination, which means the total negation of all effort on the individual's part and which has been one of the chief causes of Laodicean lukewarmness in the church.

2) "He that overcometh, I will give to him to sit down with me in my throne, as I also overcame, and sat down with my Father in his throne" (3:21 AST). This complements the preceding promise, and taken together the two give us an almost complete exposition of the relation of the Christian to the promised

34

parousia of his Lord. The first, offered to everyone, tells of the inner reality of that second advent. The Savior will make every receptive soul his home, communing there with the master of the house in the full-harvest spiritual presence of which Pentecost was the firstfruits. The second is given to those who have accepted the offer made in the first, who have received the quickening of the greater Pentecost and so have been enabled to "overcome." It tells of the outer manifestation of the *parousia*, for the overcomer is to share in the Savior's work and even in his high prerogatives as the Son of God.

There is no promise here, as there was in the letter to the Philadelphians, to keep them "from the hour of trial" (Rev. 3:10 AST). Instead, in the light of the above promises we must understand the Savior as exhorting the Laodiceans to be ready for the martyrdom that awaits them in that hour.

These promises in the Laodicean letter must be supplemented by the "overcomer" promises to the church in Philadelphia, to remind us that the work of the Savior in the coming age is to be two-fold: (1) As our great High Priest he is to relate our human nature to the divine, to make us and keep us children of God; and (2) as our rightful King, the King of kings and Lord of lords, he is to conform the life of earth, even of those who are not God's children, to the kingdom of heaven. In this latter role he is to rule the nations with a rod of iron, shattering all their institutions that are unserviceable, these being the spoiled pottery of worldly wisdom's perversities. The "overcomers" of the churches are to share in both these high offices. The priestly calling is specifically promised only to the overcomers of Philadelphia; and to those in Thyatira and Laodicea is given the promise that they are to share in the royal prerogatives. But in more general fashion it is repeatedly declared that through Christ and in cooperation with him we are all to be "kings and priests unto God" (1:6; cf. 5:10; 20:6).

"He that hath an ear, let him hear what the Spirit saith to the churches" (3:22).

ATONEMENT AND FESTIVAL SYMBOLISMS

The First Atonement Ceremonial
Among the ceremonials of the Jewish Great Day of Atonement, four were especially for the cleansing of the people as a whole,

three of these being offerings and the fourth being the strange sacrifice of the scapegoat. Each of these ceremonials for the people is represented symbolically in St. John's worship drama, one in each act.

According to Hebrew reckoning the Great Day of Atonement, assigned to the tenth day of the month Tisri, actually begins on the evening of the ninth. The temple ceremonials do not start, however, until the next morning, and so that evening is simply a time of deeply religious soul searching. That is in keeping with the revelator's state of mind and heart at the opening of his apocalyptic drama. His was the inner worship of a solitary saint. In spirit, however, it is as if he were in the very Holy of Holies and before the mercy seat, for that is the figurative site of all true Christian worship; and so in spirit he is not alone but is joined with both the individual and the congregational worship of the manifold Church of the Christian centuries.

More direct allusion to this as the eve of the Great Day of Atonement is provided by the theophanic Presence of the first vision, whose "garment down to the foot" is in its form the vestment of the high priest on the Day of Atonement, but in its substance it is the "white robe" he wears as a "Son of man." That is, the physical human body in which he was crucified has been transmuted into the spiritual body of his resurrection. Just such a robe is to be the spiritual body of our resurrection also, ours to be made white through his atonement.

We see here, therefore, an allusion to the Day of Atonement, for that was the one day of the whole year in whose worship Israel's high priest entered the Holy of Holies. And the ceremonial here suggested is of course one of those by which that high priest, having already made atonement for himself—which this high priest did not need to do (Heb. 7:27)—made atonement for the sins of the people in their two-fold relation to God. First of all, he is their God just as he is the God of all who truly seek him, whether Jew or Gentile; but he was also the God and King, Jehovah of hosts, to whom they had pledged allegiance in their acceptance of his gracious covenant, even as he is now, in the person of Jesus Christ, the rightful King of the spiritual Israel of the New Covenant.

It is clearly the first ceremonial of the Day of Atonement that is suggested here. It stands for absolution from personal sins, those offenses against our Heavenly Father to which St. John

36

refers when he says: "If any man sin, we have an Advocate with the Father, Jesus Christ the righteous; and he is the propitiation for our sins; and not for ours only, but also for the whole world" (1 John 2:1–2). As the analogy of the Advocate, our great High Priest, *on* the throne of the Heavenly Father indicates, this is the ceremonial cleansing of the Holy of Holies in which the seven-fold sprinkling of the reconciling blood of the goat for the sin-offering was made *upon* the mercy seat. The vision's suggestion of this ceremonial is reinforced by the identification of the Savior as "he who hath washed us from our sins in his own blood" (1:5) and by the seven-foldness of the letters that immediately follow it. (See Appendix 3.)

Here, then, and in all later references to ceremonials of the Day of Atonement, the sprinkling of blood is not actually pictured but is suggested symbolically. For Christians the offering of sacrificial animals at the altar in accordance with the Mosaic law has been abolished, for Jesus Christ is now our High Priest, and he "needeth not daily…to offer up sacrifice…for this he did once, when he offered up himself'" (Heb. 7:27).

The Festival of the Passover (Now Easter)

In each of the four acts of this composite drama of worship, one of the four great annual festivals contributes its symbolism to our understanding of the act's foreshadowings, and which one it is to be is indicated by the symbol employed to characterize the seven-fold aspect of the act. Here, therefore, the suggestion of the festival is provided by the seven-fold candlestick or lampstand. Its starry lights represent the light that the Savior's letters of admonition and encouragement gave the seven churches of Asia; and in turn these letters exemplify the light that the scriptures of the New Testament were to provide through the Christian centuries.

It is evident that the festival represented here could be no other than Passover, the spring festival whose primal and worldwide cosmic parable foreshadows our escape from sin and death through the sacrificial intervention of the Prince of Life, the spotless Lamb of God. That this parable of personal salvation has social implications as well is suggested by the great allegory provided by Israel's deliverance from Egyptian bondage, of which this festival became the prophecy-laden memorial.

37

The symbolism of light is employed in many religious ceremonials. The Feast of Tabernacles was marked by a grand illumination of the temple area; and the later Jewish Festival of Dedication won for itself also the name Feast of Lights. From the first, however, "lamps" were peculiarly characteristic of the Passover, and this was of necessity, for the paschal supper, eaten in commemoration of the sudden flight from Egypt and deliverance from its bondage, was the one and only night-time celebration prescribed in the Mosaic law. It was established as a "night of Jehovah, to be much observed of all the children of Israel throughout their generations" (Exod. 12:42 AST). To this day, in the homes of Israel according to the flesh—for the Passover is first of all a festival of that primary social unit, the family—this celebration is marked by the lighting of many lamps, many of which are patterned after the seven-branched lampstand or candlestick seen in this vision. (See Appendix 2.)

In this Christian Apocalypse we should expect the paschal festival to be represented in its antitypical consummation on Good Friday and Easter, and it is clear that these fulfillments of the foreshadowings of Passover were dominant in the background of St. John's thought in this first act. The first evidence is provided by his opening statement that he was in the spirit "on the Lord's day." This new name for "the first day of the week," as it had still been called in the Acts of the Apostles (Acts 20:7), reminds us of the chief reason why the Church had made that day instead of the ancient Sabbath its weekly day of worship. It was on that day that our Lord fulfilled the promise of the wave sheaf—the springtime offering of firstfruits as a promise of the summer and autumn harvests—and rose from the grave, the "firstfruits of them that slept" (1 Cor. 15:20). Further, the words of both the authors of the book, St. John and the Savior, abound with allusions to the two great events of that antitypical Passover—the sacrifice on the first Good Friday of "the Lamb of God, which taketh away the sin of the world," and his resurrection on the first Easter Sunday, which was also the first "Lord's Day." Note for example: "the first-begotten of the dead...that loved us, and washed us from our sins in his own blood" (1:5); "and every eye shall see him," even "they which pierced him" (1:7); "I am he that liveth, and was dead; and, behold, I am alive for evermore, Amen; and have the keys of hell and of death" (1:18); "these things saith the first and the last, which was dead, and is alive" (2:8); "be thou faithful unto death, and I will give thee a crown of life" (2:10).

The conclusion is certified by the symbolism of the outstanding feature of the theophany in which the divine author of the seven letters manifests himself in the vision of this act. As we have seen, his "garment down to the foot," which identifies him as now our great High Priest, reminds us also of the glad assurance that we have in him a high priest who is able to sympathize with us because he is one of us, a veritable "Son of man." At the same time he is altogether able to plead our cause because he is also the Son of God, the only begotten Son. At the Father's behest he came to be the world's Redeemer although it involved the sacrifice foreshadowed by the paschal lamb, and he is now the glorified God-man on the Father's throne.

NOTES

1. Matt. 24:30 and 26:64; Mark 13:26 and 14:62; Luke 21:27; cf. Acts 1:11.

2. In the letter to Laodicea the Savior's signature is set forth, not by reference to his Theophanic presence, as is always done in the other letters, but by a quotation from St. Paul's Epistle to the Colossians (1:15); and there are allusions to other Pauline verses (1 Cor. 4:8, 11:32; 2 Timothy 2:12)..

3. Cf. Isaiah's expression *'ephes makôm*, "there is no place, no room," used (5:8) with sarcastic double meaning in the passage that connects his famous parable of the vineyard that brought forth wild grapes (5:1–7) with his first prophecy of the removal of the Israel of his day from their homeland (5:13 ff.).

4. Cf. Ps. 136:24, which tells us that the Lord "hath redeemed us from our enemies."

5. See John 1:1–3 and 8:14–18; 2 Cor. 1:20; Col. 1:14–20.

II. THE SEVEN-SEALED BOOK
Act 2. The Haphtaroth—Readings from the Prophets

The Setting: The Celestial Temple
  The Heavenly Throne
  The Seven Lamps of Fire
  The Sea of Glass
  The Temple Gates

The Dramatis Personae before the Opening of the Seals
  Archangels
  He Who Sat upon the Throne
  The Four and Twenty Elders
  The Four Living Creatures
  The Lamb

The Action: (1) The Opening of the Sealed Book
  The Seal Oracles: The Worship Drama's Haphtaroth
  The First Four Seals: The Four Horsemen
  The Fifth Seal: The White Robes of the First Resurrection
  The Sixth Seal: The Great Day of Wrath and the Seal of
    the Living God
  The Seventh Seal: Silence in Heaven

The Action: (2) Worship

Atonement and Festival Symbolisms
  The Second Atonement Ceremonial
  The Feast of Pentecost

II. THE SEVEN-SEALED BOOK

Act 2. The Haphtaroth—Readings from the Prophets
(Rev. 4:1-8:5)

THE SETTING: THE CELESTIAL TEMPLE

The dome of heaven and its archetypal temple, of which St. John had a glimpse in the first act, is the setting for this second act. By right the whole orb of heaven is God's throne (Isa. 66:1), and his rightful sovereignty originally extended over all of it. In recognition of the passing phenomena of sin, however, and during their continuance, the celestial sanctuary is conceived as confined to the northern, or supernal, dome of heaven, while its southern hemisphere is conceived as infernal. (See Appendix 1.)

In terms of that symbolism, therefore, it was in the northern heavens that St. John saw an opened door, and it was to them that he was called by a voice saying: "Come up hither, and I will show thee things which must be hereafter" (4:1). And "immediately" he was "in the Spirit." From his new heavenly vantage point he could see the constellations of the whole northern heavens, including those of the zodiac, and these form the celestial background of this act and of all the subsequent acts of the Apocalyptic drama. As the revelator interprets these heavens we see a moving picture in which constellations take on life and stars become angels.

In these star pictures of the northern heavens the inspired imagination of the ancient peoples of the Euphratean tradition saw the cosmic temple of God, humanity's ultimate goal, toward which we are to climb from the northern summit of the earth mountain, following the way of the tree of life. (See Appendix 1.) The description of the celestial temple given in this second act is far from complete, however, and other features will be added in the later acts, as each is needed. Here we see only those

43

required to represent worship—the true worship that is the one essential need of even the most glorious sanctuary if it is to be a real temple of God, a veritable gate of heaven.

Incomplete though the description of the heavenly temple is, we can still recognize in it the major elements of the four-staged tower of Jerusalem's temple, which was a conventionalized miniature of the great temple of the universe, built in perfect accordance with the celestial pattern. Most important of all, at the very summit of the tower, was the Holy Place or sanctuary. Its inner chamber, the Holy of Holies, containing the ark of the covenant with its symbols of justice and mercy, pictured the heaven of heavens, where stands the throne of God. So sacred was this little room, representing the revelation of God's imminent presence behind the outer appearance of unapproachable majesty, that it was entered only once a year, on the Day of Atonement, and then only by the high priest for the first two ceremonies of that day of propitiation. Thus the oracles of Urim and Thummim and all other priestly pronouncements of divine judgment had to be obtained in the antechamber of the sanctuary, separated from the Holy of Holies by the veil of the temple. In this antechamber stood the seven-branched golden lampstand, the golden altar of incense, and the table of the bread of the presence. In the temple's main court were the brazen altar for the sacrifices of burnt offerings, and its associated great "sea" or laver, required for cleansing. And the gold-sheathed gates of the temple were embossed with composite figures of the two cherubim that overshadowed the mercy seat in the Holy of Holies, and the tree of life whose way they guard. (See Appendix 3.)

The Heavenly Throne

The northernmost figure of the heavens, which we prosaically call "the Little Dipper," but which the Norsemen called "the Throne of Thor," is seen in this vision as the throne of God, the celestial equivalent of the mercy seat in the Holy of Holies. The north star of our time, Polaris, is at its top, while that of St. John's day is at its foot. Thus this throne is placed, with notable approximation in view of the axial precession, at the north pole of the heavens in their equatorial construction (see Appendix 1), and it therefore represents the sovereignty of the Divine Author and Ruler of the universe with specific reference to his dealings with earth life.

44

The Seven Lamps of Fire

Burning before the throne were "seven lamps of fire...which are the seven Spirits"—or angels—"of God." These seven lamps were, of course, those of the menorah, the seven-branched lamp-stand or candlestick kept in the antechamber of the sanctuary. In the old temple this Holy Place, as it was called, was separated from the Holy of Holies by the veil of the temple, the barrier sin had interposed between human beings and their Creator. That veil was "rent," however, as Jesus died on the cross,[1] and so it does not appear in St. John's vision. The "seven lamps of fire" are therefore seen "before the throne," rather than separated from it by a barrier.

In Israel's ancient cosmology (see Appendix 1) the seven lamps of the menorah were interpreted to represent the seven brightest "stars" of the heavens, the seven "planets" (the five true planets then known, plus the Sun and the Moon), whose zodiacal houses and pathways along the ecliptic are well to the south from all of civilization's historic points of view. Being heaven's brightest and only moving "stars," journeying tirelessly round and round the earth and through and through the zodiacal representations of earth life's essential institutions, these planets were universally accepted as avatars of mighty spiritual beings deeply interested in earth's affairs and supremely influential in the determination of their developments. In religion's polytheistic apostasies they were accordingly identified with the supreme deities of their pantheons. In the reformed religion of Israel, however, they were interpreted as symbols of a special cohort of God's angels, the seven archangels, charged with the supervision of earth's two great institutions as they are represented in the zodiac—the Church and the State.

The actual positions of the planets are, of course, in the constellations of the zodiac, represented here (see below) by the four beasts or living creatures (AST), and these are far to the south of the constellation representing the throne. It is evident, therefore, that St. John's listing of the items in the vision is in accordance, not with their natural sequence from north to south in the heavens, but with their relation to the throne of the Highest, the mercy seat, in Israel's actual temple. He began by taking us to the Holy of Holies, where we saw the throne of God. With the menorah he brings us to the Holy Place, the antechamber of the sanctuary.

The Sea of Glass

"And before the throne there was a sea of glass like unto crystal"—or ice (4:6). This is the revelator's description of an asterism whose appearance and position were such that it could well be accepted as suggesting the great sea or laver, filled with crystal water, as clear and pure as ice. In the temple's fundamental sacrificial service the laver was a very significant auxiliary of the altar of burnt offerings, providing water for cleansing. Clearly this asterism can be no other than the shimmering disk of Coma Berenices, whose appearance and position render it useful, as we shall see, for several other constructions, all of them harmonious and equally felicitous.

This third item brings us, therefore, from the sanctuary into the temple's court of the priests, where of old the priests of the Messianic people performed the sacrificial rites that were fundamental in all the varied developments of ancient religion. Now, however, the foreshadowings of these rites have been fulfilled, and the altar that was once the one essential furnishing has been done away with, leaving only the great sea or laver that was its temple adjunct.

To St. John, however, this crystal sea was not simply the laver of the Old Testament but also a symbol of the cleansing that is still a prime essential in our Christian religion. This becomes evident when the laver is described in a later vision as "a sea of glass mingled with fire" (15:2), and beside it were the hosts of spiritual Israel of all ages, singing the song that Moses and his Israel sang beside the Red Sea after they had passed through it and been "baptized unto Moses in the cloud and in the sea" (1 Cor. 10:2). Clearly the reference to Moses indicates that the Apocalyptic host of singers seen in this vision had also been baptized, not only with water but also with the fire of the Holy Spirit, whose ruddy gleam was seen mingled with the white sheen of the water. In these Apocalyptic visions, therefore, the ancient laver is transformed into the Christian baptismal font.

The Temple Gates

St. John's description of the temple thus moves from the Holy of Holies to the Holy Place and thence out into the main court of the temple. Nowhere in the vision is there any mention of the temple gates, which would complete the structure. They are represented symbolically, however, for the outer limits of the celes-

46

tial temple are marked by the zodiac, and that great belt of constellations is represented in this vision by the four beasts or living creatures (4:6). This relationship will be discussed more fully in connection with those living creatures.

THE DRAMATIS PERSONAE BEFORE THE OPENING OF THE SEALS

The actors in this second act of the drama are innumerable. Those that are revealed as the seals are opened—the four horsemen and other varied groups—will be considered along with the discussion of that action. Only those introduced earlier—archangels, the formless figure on the throne, the four and twenty elders, the four living creatures, and the Lamb—will be considered at this point.

Archangels

Of the seven archangels, four—Gabriel, Michael, Raphael, and Uriel—were pictured as forming a sort of inner circle around the throne of God. To the ancient Hebrews these were represented in the heavens by the four great man-figures north of the zodiac—Gabriel by Boötes, as already noted, Michael by Ophiucus, Raphael by Auriga, and Uriel by Perseus. (See Appendix 1.) The first two of these appear in Act 2.

The very first player in this second act is the unseen angel whose voice St. John heard saying: "Come up hither, and I will show thee things which must be hereafter" (4:1); and St. John identifies this as the same voice, loud like a trumpet, that had spoken to him from the theophanic figure of the first act. Since that figure has been recognized as the constellation assigned to Gabriel, it is clearly that archangel's voice that called St. John up into the heavens, where he saw the vision of the celestial temple.

A second archangel appears a little later, for when St. John first saw the book sealed with seven seals, he saw also a "strong angel" who cried with a "loud voice," the typical indications in this Apocalypse of an archangel, asking: "Who is worthy to open the book, and to loose the seals thereof?" (5:2). It was this proclamation that served to bring to view the Lamb by whom alone the seals of the dragon-book could be broken. Clearly, then, this was the archangel Michael, for he was said to be the high priest of the heavenly temple; and to point to the Lamb of God, slain once for all,[2] is now the one priestly function in any true temple of God. Another note of identification that assures us this is really Michael is that the proclamation with which he performs his priestly task of introducing the Lamb of God is in the form of a question: "Who is worthy to open the book?" And we remember that the name of Michael is itself a question: "Who is like God?" His question in this proclamation is thus in essence a paraphrase of the question of his name that applies it to God-become-man, and challenges us to find anyone in all the universe like Jesus Christ.

He Who Sat Upon the Throne

He who sat upon the throne is clearly identified as the first person of the Trinity by the worship of the four living creatures and the twenty-four elders, who hail him as the Lord God Almighty who created all things. Further, only the Heavenly Father could commission the Lamb-Lion to open the sealed book of prophecy, thus carrying into effect the second part of his great plan of salvation agreed upon "from the foundation of the world" (13:8)—his plan, revealed in the Messianic prophecies of the ancient scriptures, to give his only begotten Son to be the Savior of the world. Here, then, we see the Supreme Ruler of the universe and the Providence that shapes the ends of even this rebel world of ours, at the top of whose heavens, the terrestrial north pole, the throne of this vision is set.

Very appropriately, however, the divine presence on the throne is formless, only shadowed forth by symbols, the resplendent semblances of precious stones. Being altogether incorporeal, these semblances set forth the truth the Savior emphasized in his conversation with the woman of Samaria, that "God is Spirit." The apocalyptist represents this presence on the throne as one divine personality, the Heavenly Father; but the three resplendent semblances suggest the concordant unity of purpose and yet diversity of operation that necessarily characterize the divine Trinity; and that the Little Lamb is first seen "in the midst of the throne" suggests that the glorified Son was sharing the Father's throne, as the Savior indicated in his letter to the church in Laodicea (3:21). And round about the throne was the rainbow effulgence of the Holy Spirit, which, as the Nicene Creed tells us, "proceeds from the Father and the Son" (cf. John 15:26).

The significance of these three precious stones is clarified when we remember that they were among the stones representing the constellations of the zodiac on the breastplate of Israel's high priest. And their zodiacal symbolisms point to the three persons of the Trinity and their special relationships to earth life.

Jasper is the gem assigned to the constellation Pisces, "the fishes." To the Hebrews Pisces symbolized the temple's cleansing laver or "sea," which stood beside the altar of burnt offerings. The laver was a miniature representation of the primal deep, the realm of vital origins, over which the Spirit of God brooded in the beginning (Gen. 1:2). Further, the fish constellation emblazons on the scroll of the heavens the fish sign that was the token of the early church, representing the early confession of faith in "Jesus the Christ, the Son of God, the Savior" (see page 191).

As an apocalyptic symbol, therefore, jasper stands for the second person of the Holy Trinity, the Divine Son. His primal characterization, *yam-ai* or *yawa*, "the Lord of the great deep," was transmuted by wordplay into *yahweh*, "he who will become (the promised Savior, the Messiah)," and this name, which we mispronounce as Jehovah, was his covenant name with the Messianic people. It was the "ineffable name" for which the reverential awe of later times substituted the honorific characterization of "Lord." Accordingly, we find "Lord" employed as the first divine name of the trisagion, in keeping with the naming of jasper as the first of the three zodiacal semblances representing the Trinity. It is given that first position here because the theme here is salvation, which God the Father has given the Son to accomplish (John 3:16, 35; 5:20 ff.). The searchless sacrifice that was to be his cost of intervening for our salvation is symbolized by the temple's altar of burnt offerings, beside which the laver stood. In the zodiac that altar is represented by the constellation adjacent to Pisces. We know it as Aries, but to the Hebrews it was Toleh, "the little lamb."

God the Father remains, however, both the fundamental and the ultimate in power and authority (1 Cor. 15:24–28), and he is represented here by the sardius stone. The sard was assigned to the constellation Libra, "the balances," the symbol of judgment and of its seat in the temple, the Holy Place or antechamber of the sanctuary, where stood the golden altar of incense. Whereas

49

the adjacent Holy of Holies was entered only on the Great Day of Atonement, the Holy Place was entered daily. It was, so to speak, the audience chamber of the Divine Judge of all the earth, God Most High, whose throne was in the Holy of Holies.

The nimbus of glory that shone around the throne must therefore represent the Holy Spirit. In St. John's vision it is likened to smaragdus, identified in our English translations as "emerald," but which in the breastplate of Israel's high priest (Exod. 28:17–20) is called *baraqeth*, "lightning." In this vision, where it is likened to a rainbow, the diamond seems a more suitable translation. Whatever its physical identity, however, this stone represents the zodiacal constellation Sagittarius, "the Archer." It stands next to Capricornus, which in classical times marked the winter solstice and represented the gate by which the downward way from heaven entered the zodiacal region of man's abode. (See Appendix 1.) The warrior Sagittarius, therefore, armed and mounted and waiting at heaven's exit, represents the might of heaven ready for immediate service in any expedition into earth life that the needs of the hour may demand.

Thus when the precious stone assigned to Sagittarius is used as an apocalyptic recognizance of the Holy Spirit, the latter is identified as the person of the Holy Trinity whose special office it is to go forth "to strive with man" (Gen. 6:3), to be "the spirit of truth" and to "reprove the world of sin, and of righteousness, and of judgment" (John 16:8).

The Four and Twenty Elders

In apocalyptic usage there is no precedent for the four and twenty elders seated on their thrones, arrayed in white garments and wearing golden crowns. Nevertheless, their significance is unmistakable.

Their astral relationships are indicated by their positions "round about the throne." The Greek word here translated as "round about" means more specifically "radiating in all directions"; and since the throne from which they radiate is the celestial marker of the terrestrial north pole, the elders must be positioned on the northern meridians of the throne-centered equatorial circle, marking off on it earth's twenty-four hours of the day and night. The constellations of the northern heavens, though traditionally twenty-four in number, are not positioned

50

so as to lend themselves to practical use as actual evenly spaced markers of the hours of the day. Nevertheless, there are suggestions that the conception of such a representation was not alien to the ancient cosmography to which St. John was heir. The Babylonians, for example, had twenty-four fate-fixing star gods. The later Zoroastrians had twenty-four Yazatas or administrative agents serving their god Ormuzd. And in Ovid's picture of the court of Phoebus[3] the hours are shown arranged at equal distances.

If, then, the twenty-four elders represent earth's twenty-four hours of day and night, such a terrestrial relationship suggests that these elders have to do with earth life—with humanity. And that they represent humanity as redeemed individuals, "kings and priests unto God" (1:6), is suggested by their white garments and the "golden vials full of odors, which are the prayers of saints" (5:8). Indeed, their location near the throne of the Most High and their victor's crowns reveal them as representing the supreme in Christian attainment, the fulfillment of the promise to the overcomer of the church in Laodicea: "To him that overcometh will I grant to sit with me in my throne, even as I also overcame, and am set down with my Father in his throne" (3:21). That each of these twenty-four thrones is also, and primarily, a throne of Christ is made clear in a further and more specific vision of the fulfillment of that promise: "And I saw thrones, and they sat upon them, and judgment was given unto them; and...they shall be priests of God and of Christ, and shall reign with him a thousand years" (20:4–6).

In the dramatic action of the scene we shall see the elders joining with the living creatures in worship (4:8–11). And in their last recorded appearance (11:15–18), immediately after the sounding of the last trumpet, they fall on their faces and worship God because "the kingdoms of this world are become the kingdoms of our Lord, and of his Christ; and he shall reign for ever and ever" (11:15).

The Four Living Creatures

The four living creatures, who worshiped the Lord God Almighty day and night, are identified first by two statements that define their location with respect to the throne. In our translations they are said to be "in the midst of the throne" and

51

"round about the throne" (4:6). These two nearly identical descriptions bring before us the concept of a circle, the first referring to the area, the space within it or "between" its outer points, and the second to a line, the circumference of the circle. A more literal translation of the Greek would be: "and the throne being between them (i.e., somewhere in the area of their circle, but not at the center, for that word is not used), around the throne there were four living creatures." The two nearly synonymous statements concerning the position of the living creatures are far from redundant. Instead, they are just such as to identify these creatures with both the cherubim of the mercy seat in God's temple and the cherubim of the cardinal constellations of the zodiac.

That the description of the throne being "between them" identifies these creatures with the cherubim of the mercy seat is made evident by God's words to Moses concerning the place from which he would issue his commandments as the Divine King of Israel: "And thou shalt put the mercy seat" with its cherubim "above upon the ark...and there I will meet with thee, and I will commune with thee from above the mercy seat, from between the two cherubim which are upon the ark of the testimony, of all the things which I will give thee in commandment unto the children of Israel" (Exod. 25:21–22).

On the other hand, this description of the throne as "between them," together with the synonymous description that puts the throne "within their circle," identifies the vision's living creatures, and also the cherubim of the Mosaic Holy of Holies, with the creatures of the zodiac. The latter's circle is indeed "round about the throne," but it has as its center not the throne's equatorial pole but the ecliptic pole, which is at a distance of 23-1/2 degrees from it. That is, the throne of the vision is not centrally located with reference to the zodiac.

Clearly the revelator had a purpose in using the two almost synonymous descriptions of the location of the throne with reference to the zodiac, for that great belt of the heavens is the celestial symbol of earth life. (See Appendix 1.) Since the zodiac circles the far southern rim of the vision's celestial view, the throne at the far north very properly represents God as over all, *transcendent*. This can very easily be misunderstood, however, and taken to represent God as far away, remote from his earthly creatures. To prevent this misinterpretation the revelator also describes the throne as being "between the cherubim," as it was represented in Israel's Holy of Holies. That miniature of the celestial picture showed only its two extreme and most significant features, the throne and the zodiac, representing God and humanity, and instead of being separated by an incalculable distance they were actually interjoined. The mercy seat, the base of the throne, upheld also the two cherubim that represented the zodiac, and their wings in turn formed the chair itself, thus unmistakably representing God as *imminent*, as most intimately in the midst of his creation.

To return to the Apocalyptic drama, the revelator describes these living creatures as like a lion, a calf, a man, and a flying eagle. Clearly these can be equated with the zodiacal constellations we know as the Lion, the Bull, the Water Carrier, and the Scorpion (here a flying eagle). This unmistakable likeness to constellations supports the interpretation here presented, that all the figures in this vision are star constructions. In the drama these creatures, as representatives of the zodiac, can be interpreted as serving two purposes:

1) As is shown in Appendix 1, the zodiac represents human life on earth and its two great institutions, the Church and the State; and it also tells the story of God's great plan for humanity's salvation, as foretold by the Protevangel. In this vision of the celestial temple, therefore, the living creatures symbolize both organized humanity and divine intervention for its salvation. Human cooperation toward that end is represented by the elders, here interpreted as redeemed individuals.

2) In the drama's picture of the celestial temple the living creatures can be taken as symbolizing that structure's gates, for of the stars in the vision those of the zodiac are furthest removed from those of the throne, just as in Jerusalem's temple the gates were furthest from the Holy of Holies. And in that earthly temple, which was "a copy and shadow of the heavenly things" (Heb. 8:5 AST), the gold-sheathed folding doors or gates were embossed with composite figures representing two cherubim and the tree of life whose way they guarded, according to the Garden of Eden story. The early reports of those doors (1 Kg. 6:33–35) do not describe the cherubim, but Ezekiel (41:18–20, 25) pictures each as having two faces, that of a man and that of a lion, thus clearly identifying them as zodiacal figures.

53

The Lamb

After the sealed book was introduced into the scene, one of the elders announced that "the Lion of the tribe of Judah, the Root of David," had "prevailed to open the book" in the hand of him who sat on the throne and to break its seals (5:1–2). The figure the revelator saw receiving the book from the Heavenly Father was, however, that of a Lamb standing (or placed) as though it had been slain (5:6).

Why was it that of all the beings in the universe none but this little Lamb was found able to open the book and break its seals? To all the wondering hosts of heaven it was evident that this was a genuinely prophetic book, and that its oracles were burdened with a course of events whose consummation would be inevitable if they were "signified"—that is, revealed. This does not mean they would be decreed in accordance with a horribly perverted conception of God's exercise of his divine all-sovereignty, but that they would be the inevitable consequences of all the forces that divine foreknowledge saw involved in them. It was inevitable also that it would deserve to be called a Dragon Book, for its course of events was headed toward irretrievable and unutterably woeful disaster. Since the book was close sealed with seven seals, its course of events was as yet only potential, and Divine Providence could still end it all far short of complete disaster—but far short also of the full attainment of the glorious purpose of the Creator! To break the seals, however, and signify their oracles, meant permitting their potential evils to become actual—unless they were to encounter complete and unfailing countervailance. Thus no one could venture to break the seals unless he was sure he had the power to effect this countervailance; and no one—no, not even God himself—had any such power, for it involved transforming the self-willed children of the earth so as to set them free from the curse of sin and enable them to become what they are intended to be, children of the Heavenly Father. It was in order to have them win just this countervailing power that the Heavenly Father had sent his one all-divine Son to earth to become also, at the countless cost of sacrificing his all-divinity, the Son of David, the Son of man, our Elder Brother, the crucified Nazarene.

It was as the Lamb of the Gospel, therefore—so the "new song" of the elders and the living creatures reveals—that the Lion of the Apocalypse won his power to open the sealed book.

His coming as the Lamb of God to take away the sin of the world made possible the countervailance of the law of sin and death (Rom. 8:2) and the restoration of humanity to its designed heredity.

The Lamb is pictured, therefore, as having made the sacrifice in the first advent, but with its seven horns and seven eyes it is now glorified and ready for the work that remains to be done for the salvation of the world and that is to be consummated in his second advent. The seven horns, representing his seven-fold and therefore perfect authority, reveal him as indeed Shiloh, the one to whom alone belongs the divine right to reign. The seven eyes, which the revelator himself interprets as the seven Spirits of God, represent his seven-fold and therefore complete possession of the divine agencies of the Holy Spirit. In this apocalyptic symbol there is no suggestion whatever of the human figure or any other feature that would indicate a personal presence. This is in full accordance with the teaching of the letter to the church in Thyatira, where we learn that the "rod" of authority the Son of God is to wield at his second advent (cf. Ps. 2:9) will be given into the hands of his church, the "body" of his full incarnation (2:27).

So supremely important in the structure of the Apocalypse is this Lamb-Lion figure that we may confidently expect to find it appropriately represented in the stars. What we must look for is a truly heroic figure that will combine all the qualities of its several titles—the Lamb, the Lion of the tribe of Judah, the Son of David—and we find it in the one celestial figure, other than the glorious Sun itself, that is most worthy in its portrayal of the Savior. Indeed, it would seem impossible to devise any other symbol so complete. It is the figure to which modern astrographers, seeking a classical interpretation, have given the suggestive name of Heracles, but to the ancients it was simply "the man upon his knees." His right "heel" is poised directly over the "head" of Draco, the old serpent of the primordial apocalypse, whose invasion of Paradise had such disastrous results for humanity, and with his hands the man grapples with the spawn of the monster hidden in the foliage of a tree beside him. It is a faithful picture of the Protevangel's two pronouncements, showing the wounded but finally triumphant Seed of the woman.

Draco pictures the serpent in Paradise. It is an S-shaped figure, one end of which winds around the ecliptic pole, represent-

55

ing the Garden of Eden's tree of life, and the other end of which issues from the star Alpha Draconis, which as the equatorial pole star of an earlier time represented the tree of the knowledge of good and evil. (See Appendix 1.) Draco is therefore a vivid picture of the problem of evil that results from the sin for which the old serpent stands, the problem that none could solve save the Lamb of God that taketh away the sin of the world; and that Lamb is also the Lion of the tribe of Judah, who will destroy sin's evil effects, and the Son of David, who is to rule as the Sun of Righteousness and Peace.

Although it might be expected from this ancient parable that Draco would be seen in this vision, he does not appear at all as an actor. His S-shaped figure, however, which suggests a rolled scroll, serves as the astral symbol of the sealed roll of destiny that only the Lamb-Lion can open.

THE ACTION: (1) THE OPENING OF THE SEALED BOOK

The Seal Oracles: The Worship Drama's Haphtaroth

As the scroll is unsealed and read we find that it is truly a "dragon" book, in notable harmony with the evil import universally attributed to Draco. It sets forth the dark shadow of his presence in the history of earth life, and its revelations are without exception very largely evil, some of them such that St. John had to employ "demon" figures to represent them. The book therefore pictures warfare and turmoil, the continuously troubled conditions that were to affect Christendom during the time of its treading down by the draconian forces of Antichrist. And to complement the first act's lessons from the law, which deal with a history of Church developments, the seal oracles of this second act provide an outline of Christendom's civil history, treating of empires and their warring princes, the usual point of view from which history is written. Since in the traditional synagogue service the readings that reinforce the parashoth are known as the haphtaroth, that must be the role of the seal oracles in this Apocalyptic worship drama.

Here, as in Act 1, the pattern of the carpenter's square is evident. The first four seals show the four horsemen of the Apocalypse, fearful figures of a succession of warring empires during the history of Christendom, down to the end of the age;

and the remaining seals elaborate on conditions in that final period. At the breaking of the fifth seal we hear the promise that the blood of the martyrs of those dread regimes will indeed be avenged in due time. The breaking of the sixth seal reveals a picture of the literal fulfilling of that promise, at the coming of the great day of wrath. Still greater evils were apparently revealed when the seventh seal was broken, for it was not "signified," and we learn later that its evils would be countervailed by the hastened return of the Savior in his second advent.

The First Four Seals: The Four Horsemen

At the breaking of the first four seals, the four living creatures call forth the four horsemen of the Apocalypse, riding on white, red, black, and pale or dappled horses. (Cf. Zech. 1:8 and 6:2–8.) In accordance with the interpretation here presented, these first four seal oracles will be translated and expounded by the first four oracles of the trumpets and the bowls of wrath respectively, and this association, which will be discussed in detail in Appendix 5, is supported by the fact that in each series the first four oracles can be related to the four trigons of the zodiac. (See Appendix 1.)

These four horsemen come armed with bow and sword, bring famine and pestilence, and are followed by the hosts of hell, in inverted imitation of the armies of heaven that we shall see later accompanying the King of kings. As caricatures of that King they represent successive heads of the third act's symbol of Antichrist, the beast from the sea. Like it, they are represented in the heavens by Centaurus, the rival and counterfeit of Sagittarius, the astral symbol of the Savior coming down from heaven with his white-robed hosts to take possession of his earthly kingdom. These celestial symbols will be discussed more fully in the later acts.

In these four mounted warriors we see, therefore, attempts of Antichrist to forestall the millennial kingdom of Christ, the conquering King of kings. These pretenders to his throne represent successive imperial forms of temporal power and glory that are worshiped "instead of Christ." This follows the symbolism of Daniel's first vision, in which four great beasts represent the course of empire, as it affects the true people of God, on down to the time when "the saints of the Most High" shall receive the kingdom (Dan. 7:1 ff.). How increasingly virulent such anti-

Christian distemper would be is made evident by the ever-increasing menace of the horsemen's caricature of the King of kings: first a rider on a white horse armed only with a bow, whose parody is notably benign and whose regime is outwardly and acceptably Christian; then the rider on the red horse, armed with a sword, and the one on the black horse, bringing warfare's economic disturbances; and finally a pale or dappled horse whose rider, named Death, is followed by the hosts of Hell and whose desolations only the establishment of Christ's true kingdom can retrieve.

The Fifth Seal: The White Robes of the First Resurrection

In the vision of the fifth oracle we see that coming of Christ as the King of kings with the armies of heaven foreshadowed as immediately imminent. Here is the beginning of heaven's mobilization for the final campaign by which, in the fullness of time, our Lord is to establish his democratic kingdom, the place of which the Dragon's despotic empires have of necessity failed to pre-empt. In answer to the eruption of the demon hordes of the preceding oracle and in accordance with an eager plea for action from the heavenly hosts, we see the mobilization of their vanguard, the corps of the martyrs. They are seen "under the altar" of the heavenly temple, which represents the golden altar of incense that stood in the Holy Place before the Holy of Holies and the throne or "mercy seat" of God. Its zodiacal equivalent is the constellation Libra. To each of these martyrs is issued the "white robe" (cf. 2 Esdras 2:38–41) he is to wear when these armies descend to the field of action (19:14). Those white robes, and the palms in their hands, are tokens of the complete and final victory that is to come, and reassurance of the all-sufficient protection of the great salvation represented by the seal of the living God (see the sixth seal), even in the midst of all the dangers that are foreshadowed.

Clearly, however, those white robes of the "first resurrection" are to be conceived as given not only to the martyrs but to the whole body of the saints of the ages, who had "washed their robes, and made them white in the blood of the Lamb" (7:14), and had been waiting for the coming of this hour. In the vision of the sixth seal we see them as "a great multitude, which no man could number, of all nations, and kindreds, and people, and tongues," standing before the throne and before the Lamb and

58

praising and serving God "day and night" (7:9 ff.). The white robes were given, therefore, to all those "souls" whose life in the "body" had been made a "living sacrifice, holy, acceptable unto God" (Rom. 12:1). The virtue of the martyr's self-sacrifice lies, not in the overt act, but in the spirit it manifests; so that St. Paul could even say: "Though I give my body to be burned, and have not charity, it profiteth me nothing" (1 Cor. 13:3). The apocalyptist is here employing the well-known figure of synecdoche, representing the whole Church triumphant by those of its members who, to earthly vision, stand out above their fellows as having manifestly exemplified the sacrificial suffering of the Savior. For all of them, however, this is an essential characteristic, for it is a necessary qualification for the service into which they are here being mustered—the conquest of the world with the King of kings and Lord of lords, and the establishment of and governing with him of his millennial kingdom. Only those who bear the cross with him are to wear the crown with him.

To the cry of these martyr saints, asking how long they must wait for the day of judgment,[4] the answer is that they must rest "for a little season" (6:11) before that great work can be begun. Here we find some understanding of what seems to us like a long and weary postponement of the coming of Christ's kingdom; for we are reminded that among the many factors involved in the completion of any developmental process, one extremely essential one is time.

The Sixth Seal: the Great Day of Wrath and the Seal of the Living God

In the oracle of the fifth seal, however, a divine reassurance is given to the martyrs of the ages that their blood will indeed be avenged when the necessary time has elapsed—when the number of "their fellow servants" and "their brethren" shall be complete, who were to be killed as they themselves had been (6:11). At the breaking of the sixth seal we see a picture of the literal fulfillment of that promise, for it sets before us the well-known prophetic portents of the great warfare for which the armies of heaven and hell are being mobilized (6:12–17).

The agents of the fearful visitations of that "great day of...wrath," here identified as the "four winds of the earth," are more fully and more specifically described as "demons" in the targums of the trumpets and the expositions of the bowls of wrath. For God's true spiritual Israel these evil demons will bring grave spiritual dangers, and these will be held in check as long as possible by countervailing good influences, symbolized here by the four cardinal angels stationed at the four corners of the earth (7:1)—clearly the four royal stars, Fomalhaut, Aldebaran, Regulus, and Antares, which mark respectively the celestial north, east, south, and west and which represent the four cardinal archangels.

These true servants of God, represented here by the 144,000 of the Church militant, are to be protected by the "seal of the living God." This seal was of course no magic charm, but a symbolism already employed by Ezekiel (9:4–6), who derived it from a judicial procedure of his time. On the forehead of a defendant whom he had tried and freed the judge inscribed his signature, certifying that, if innocent, he had been acquitted; or that, if guilty, he had either paid his debt to the law or been pardoned. In any case he was not to be molested further by any minion of the law. The judge represented in this apocalyptic use of the symbol is of course the Savior;[5] and that it is indeed his signature that constitutes the "seal" is specifically indicated in the vision of the Lamb in the midst of these thousands on Mount Zion, where it is said that they had his name and his Father's name "written on their foreheads" (14:1). This seal is therefore simply the Christian's all-sufficient confession of faith that "Jesus Christ is the Son of God, our Savior." That confession, based on the acrostic of the Greek fish-word *ichthus* (see Appendix 1), was carried by the "fish sign" that was the first token of the Christian church.

Use of this fish sign was derived first of all, of course, from the zodiacal fish constellation Pisces, assigned in ancient celestial heraldry to Israel and therefore representing the Messianic hope of that Messianic people. In the early Christian Church it was represented symbolically either by a picture of two fishes fastened together, which is the figure of Pisces, or as a monogram formed by superposing the first two letters of *ichthus*—*iota* (I) and *chi* (X)—to form a six-sided cross. In the heavens such a cross is formed at the equinoxes by the crossing of three great circles—the ecliptic circle, the earth's equatorial circle, and the meridian circle. Because of the association of the sacrificial paschal lamb with the vernal equinox, this celestial symbol is generally identified as the "cross of the vernal equinox." This is the heavenly figure the revelator would have us see in the hand of the urgent herald who brought the "seal of the living God" from the sunrising.

Following the symbol of the ancient judicial procedure, therefore, this seal, this token of faith in "Jesus Christ, the Son of God, our Savior," indicates that those who wear it on their foreheads have had their sins blotted out by the salvation consummated on Calvary. It is a symbolic equivalent of the blood of the paschal lamb that was sprinkled on the doorposts of the houses of Israel on the night of the first Passover to protect them from the angel of death. Accordingly, those who are thus sealed are accounted "not guilty" and are safe from spiritual molestation by any of the agents and judgments that are to be visited upon the impenitent. Temporal evils they must share with the rest of humanity, and so they must face physical perils, as did their Master, and if need be they must even become his martyrs. Against spiritual evils, however, they need no protection other than this seal, which identifies them as "Israelites indeed." "He that keepeth Israel shall neither slumber nor sleep" (Ps. 121:4)—his Shekinah is ever over them. Truly, only the confession of faith represented by this seal was potent enough to protect those who wore it from the demons that were to ascend from the gates of hell with Antichrist as he attempted to anticipate and forestall the coming of the King of kings and to usurp his throne; and it was potent because it certified the genuineness of their Christian faith. Holding fast to this faith the true Christian could not be deceived by the godless hell-born ideologies with which the demons afflicted the world.

The number thus sealed—144,000—is of course symbolic, representing without diminution or increment the number of the Church militant of every period. This is evidenced by the fact that this is also the number of the true and faithful in whose midst, at a much later period, the Lamb is seen on Mount Zion (14:1–5). They are the militant hosts of spiritual Israel, whose mystical evaluation is *twelve*, the cosmic number, three times four, that represents God's perfect creation. (See Appendix 4.) And so, notwithstanding changing times, bringing neither gains or losses, the twelve tribes of spiritual Israel will always each muster twelve battle units, or "thousands." Here is a foreshadowing of the earthly mobilization of the Church militant in

61

preparation for the final campaign when the Savior comes as King of kings and Lord of lords.

Thus, in the midst of all the dangers that we shall find foreshadowed by the trumpet oracles (see Act 3), we are given assurance of the all-sufficiency of the great salvation represented by the seal of the living God and its simple confession of faith in Jesus the Christ, the Son of God, our Savior.

After this vision of the sealing, St. John leaped into the future (7:9 ff.) to give us a vision of the Church as it is to be in the consummation, when it will include all the saints of the successive hosts of the Church militant of all generations. And he saw "a great multitude...clothed with white robes, and palms in their hands." And "with a loud voice" they said, "Salvation to our God which sitteth upon the throne, and unto the Lamb." They have come "out of great tribulation, and have washed their robes, and made them white in the blood of the Lamb"; and the palms they carry are tokens of their complete and final victory. The Lamb "shall feed them, and shall lead them unto living fountains of waters; and God shall wipe away all tears from their eyes" (7:17).

The Seventh Seal: Silence in Heaven

From this vision of the far future the revelator was called back to the Apocalyptic present by the breaking of the seventh seal, and when the Lamb opened it the appalling danger that was to require the protection of the seal of the living God was revealed. How overwhelming it was to be is suggested by the fact that there was "silence in heaven" for about half an hour, a very long silence in view of the relatively short time required for the enactment of the whole Apocalyptic drama. Evidently the hosts of heaven were able to read the seal's oracle and were astounded by the completeness of the final devastation it threatened.

What it would have foretold is revealed later, when its translation in the seventh trumpet oracle tells of the fearful "third woe." Foreseeing its tribulation the Savior had said to his disciples that unless its days of trial were shortened no human being would survive (Matt. 24:22). He had promised, however, that for the sake of the elect they would be shortened, and so he did not permit the signification and ratification of the seventh seal oracle. Mercifully and justifiably he waited for the fuller devotion of his Church that would enable him to hasten his return, for that would be the one event that could shorten those days of tribulation. Only he could countervail and rescind the otherwise irremediable third woe, even as Jonah's pronouncement upon Nineveh was rescinded. Only he, in the power of his second advent presence, could overwhelm that woe's destructive forces at Armageddon and begin the establishment of his millennial kingdom, as was foreshadowed in the oracle of the fifth seal.

That hastened second advent is to be in answer to the needs, the prayers, of the elect, for in addition to his own great power the Savior needs the fulcrum that a leaven of human devotion can supply. Accordingly, we are told that during the silence in heaven the prayers of all the saints "ascended up before God," together with "much incense" duly offered on the golden altar (8:1–4). The one prayer that above all others is continuously going up to God from the public and private worship of the saints of all creeds and all ages is the one taught us by the Lord himself; and the outstanding petition of that universal prayer, its one intercession, is in behalf of the earth as a whole: "Thy kingdom come, thy will be done on earth as it is in heaven." It is above all to this intercession that the angel prophet, enacting the role of priest, adds the incense that is a memorial of the sacrificial death of the Savior of the world. It is faith in that great salvation, the equivalent of the seal of the living God, that makes the prayer acceptable to God.

That this prayer for the full reclamation of earth life is to be answered favorably is suggested by the final symbolic act of this prophet, when he filled his censer with coals from the altar and hurled it burning toward the earth. The significance of this act is gathered from similar oracles of Isaiah and Ezekiel, whose usage is authoritative for our interpretation of St. John. The import of the fire from the coals of the altar is to be seen in Isaiah's theophanic vision (Isa. 6:6–7), when with the touch of that fire on his unclean lips his iniquity was taken away and his sins were forgiven. This is the significance also of the scattering over Jerusalem of coals taken from between the cherubim of Ezekiel's theophanic vision (Ezek. 10:1–8), for thus a remnant was saved from the doomed city. St. John's use of this symbolism is therefore unmistakably a foreshadowing of the redintegration of fallen earth life.

THE ACTION: (2) WORSHIP

In the midst of the turmoil and strife portrayed in this second act there are recurrent scenes of worship, and certain groups are reported as continuing in worship "day and night."

Worship opens the vision's action, with the living creatures and elders giving glory and honor and thanks to him who sat on the throne. The elders, interpreted here as symbolizing redeemed individuals, bowed down (this is the radical meaning of the Greek word "to worship") and cast their crowns before the throne; and the living creatures, interpreted as representing organized humanity, rested not "day and night, saying, Holy, holy, holy, Lord God Almighty, who was, and is, and is to come" (4:8).

When the Lamb had taken the sealed book, he too was acclaimed with glad songs of praise, and in that joyful worship of the Lamb and of him who sat on the throne the elders and living creatures, the representatives of humanity, were joined by the choirs of heaven and all creation. Among these singers were "ten thousand times ten thousand, and thousands of thousands" of angels, and "every creature which is in heaven, and on the earth, and under the earth, and such as are in the sea" (5:11–14).

Again, after the sealing of the 144,000, all the angels around the throne joined in the praise, as did "a great multitude...of all nations, and kindreds, and people, and tongues...clothed in white robes." And one of the elders explained to the seer that these hosts arrayed in white robes are before the throne of God, and "serve him day and night in his temple" (7:9–15).

Here, then, we have a picture of the true worship Jesus described to the woman of Samaria, when he said: "God is a Spirit: and they that worship him must worship in spirit and in truth" (John 4:24). God on his throne is shown as an incorporeal spirit, and the celestial stage as set for the scene is furnished with no properties that would provide for the regular ritual service of sacrifice except for the laver, which represents the baptismal font and serves here only to account for the white garments of the elders and the heavenly multitudes. The only overt acts of worship, therefore, are the bowing down and casting of crowns before the throne, and the words and songs of praise to him who sits on the throne and to the Lamb. This worship is

64

said to continue day and night, however, and since the elders and living creatures are shown talking and carrying on other overt acts from time to time it is evident that their continuous worship is inward and spiritual, expressive of an abiding attitude of mind and heart and tenor of life.

ATONEMENT AND FESTIVAL SYMBOLS

The Second Atonement Ceremonial

The first atonement ceremonial, the cleansing of the Holy of Holies for absolution from personal sin, required as its background only a celestial picture that would represent the sprinkling of the blood of the goat for the sin offering *upon the mercy seat*. That was provided by the theophanic vision of the Savior himself, whose rightful place is *upon the throne* and who has "washed us from our sins in his own blood" (1:5) and "ever liveth to make intercession" for us (Heb. 7:25).

The second atonement ceremonial, represented in this second act, is the seven-fold sprinkling of blood *before the mercy seat*. It is symbolized by the Lamb seen standing *before the throne* (which represents the mercy seat) "as though it had been slain" (5:6 AST). He is not seen actually sprinkling the blood of a sacrifice such as of old foreshadowed the atonement, for he had already made that atonement once for all "when he offered up himself" (Heb. 7:27). And in their songs of praise the living creatures and elders extol the Lamb because he had "redeemed...to God" by his blood the new and royal and holy humanity of the world-wide Church (Rev. 5:8–10); and all the hosts of heaven give all honor and glory to "the Lamb that was slain" (5:11–12). The action of this ceremonial still takes place in the Holy of Holies, but it was for the cleansing of the whole tent of meeting, and this is what we find in this vision. The whole northern dome of heaven forms the temple background for this act and all the subsequent acts of the drama; and as we have seen, the opening description of the temple includes all its parts, from the Holy of Holies to its outer gates.

In the context of the Apocalyptic drama these first two ceremonials have added significance. Since the first one, for personal cleansing, is here associated with the letters to the seven churches, it can be interpreted as a cleansing of the collective

65

religious life of the people. And since the second, for the cleansing of the whole temple, is associated with Apocalyptic symbolisms of government, it can be interpreted as a cleansing of the collective civil life of the people.

The Feast of Pentecost

The door that was opened in heaven to admit the revelator must be identified in terms of the ancient cosmology (see Appendix 1), which pictured the Milky Way as the "way of the tree of life," arching up across the northern skies and leading up to the heaven of heavens. Coming up from the south, the realm of the underworld, it crosses the zodiac near the constellation Gemini, which was therefore considered the gateway to the realm of life, pictured in the northern skies. The neighboring constellation Cancer was interpreted as the outer gate of this way up to heaven, and Cancer was associated with summer, for in ancient times it marked the place of the June or summer solstice, where the Sun reaches its furthest northing.

Recognizing this celestial gateway as the door through which the revelator could have ascended symbolically into the heavenly temple, and remembering its association with the summer solstice, we must conclude that the seasonal festival represented in this second act of the drama must be the summer festival of Firstfruits. (See Appendix 2.) It celebrated the end of the grain harvest, the fulfillment of the promise of the Passover wave sheaf, which it followed by just fifty days—hence its name of Pentecost, the Festival of the Fiftieth Day.

For the people of the Old Covenant it had a further significance, for it celebrated also Moses' ascent of Mount Sinai to receive "the law," God's covenant with Israel. In the Jewish synagogue that law of Moses is of course read as the parashah, but in the Christian synagogue, whose service is dramatized in this Apocalypse, the books of the Mosaic law are now accounted among the *prophetic* books of the Old Testament, symbolized by the sealed book of the second act's vision.

The New Covenant is celebrated on this day also, for Pentecost marks the birthday of the Christian Church. It was on the first Pentecost after the Lord's resurrection that his disciples were baptized with the fire of the Holy Spirit and went forth as the Israel of the New Covenant to become world conquerors. Just as the grain harvest was only the first of summer's many harvests, leading up to the final ingathering in the fall, so this Pentecostal outpouring of the gifts of the Holy Spirit is prophetic of the mightier baptism, the richer gifts, the full enduement with the spirit of life, that will come in the full ingathering when the Savior returns at the end of the age, as is foreshadowed in this Apocalypse.

NOTES

1. See Matt. 27:51; Mark 15:38; Luke 23:45.
2. See Heb. 7:27; 9:12, 28; 10:10.
3. *Metamorphoses*, Book 2.
4. Rev. 6:10; cf. Zech. 1:12 and 2 Esdras 4:35.
5. Cf. Rev. 1:18; Matt. 16:27 and 25:31–33; John 5:22 and 9:39; and Acts 17:31.

III. THE SEVEN TRUMPETS

Act 3. The Targumim—Translations of the Haphtaroth

The Trumpet Oracles as the Worship Drama's Targumim

The Trumpet Oracles: One through Six
  The First Four Trumpets
  The Fifth and Sixth Trumpets: The First and Second Woes

The Episode of the Little Book Open
  The Theophanic Angel
  The Little Book as Megillah
  The Megillah's Targum: The Seven Thunders
  The Megillah's Exposition: The Two Witnesses
  An Anticipatory Day of Atonement

The Seventh Trumpet
  The Sounding of the Trumpet: Joy in Heaven
  A Conspectus of the History of Spiritual Israel
  The Lamb on Mount Zion: The Second-Advent Presence
    of the Mighty One
  The Communion of Saints
  The Second-Advent Work of Christ and His Church: The
    Three Herald Angels and a Voice from Heaven
  The Final Harvest

Atonement and Festival Symbolisms
  The Third Atonement Ceremonial and the Anticipatory Day
    of Atonement
  Rosh Hashanah and the Great Day of Atonement

III. THE SEVEN TRUMPETS

Act 3. The Targumim—Translations of the Haphtaroth (Rev. 8:6–14:20)

THE TRUMPET ORACLES AS THE WORSHIP DRAMA'S TARGUMIM

In this third act of the Apocalyptic drama St. John employs the trumpets of the New Year celebration to set forth the targums, or free vernacular renderings, of the prophecies of the seven-sealed book.

These trumpet translations, and of course the expositions provided by the bowls of wrath in Act 4, must deal with the contents of the seals they translate and expound, and so they too tell of the political developments of the inter-advent years and the time of the end. But just as in ordinary language synonyms are utilized to discriminate nuances, so St. John makes use of these recapitulations to tell the story from different points of view.

Accordingly, while the visions of the seals foreshadow the political history of the times with which the book of Revelation is especially concerned, the visions of the trumpets give us to see this civil history as it affects, and is affected by, the ecclesiastical history of those same times. While in form, therefore, the trumpet visions translate only the visions of the sealed book, reported in the second act, they nevertheless assume a knowledge also of the history set forth in the first act in the letters to the churches. In reality, therefore, they foreshadow a cultural history in which both Church and State are seen developing, not each by itself as in Acts 1 and 2—the one in a sequence of ecclesiastical establishments and the other in a sequence of civil empires—but both together.

71

These two great institutions share the responsibility for the maintenance and furtherance of the social well-being of earth life and ought to work together harmoniously for the accomplishment of their great task. Instead, perverted and more or less fully conformed to the nature of the dragon, they are seen quarreling and fighting, each seeking to dominate or even destroy the other. And the repeated persecutions of the Church through the ages are reviewed in an interpolation following the sounding of the seventh trumpet (12:1–13:18).

Such conflicts between the Church and the world, here represented by the State, persist throughout the act, and the resulting perversions become "woes" that must end in catastrophe, indeed destroying the earth (11:18) unless they can be swept away. That this is to be accomplished is shown in the closing vision of the final harvest of the earth and the treading of the winepress of the wrath of God. The hastened return of the Savior has countervailed the dreaded third woe, and he has come to reign as the Mighty-to-Save and the Mighty Avenger.

With their messages of perversion and woe, these translations of the seal oracles therefore carry the unmistakable implications of the triple call of the trumpet as it was used in the temple service. Its sound invariably had three parts: a long smooth tone; a shattering, reverberating taratantara or alarm blast; and a final long smooth tone. These targums, which tell of great evils, are therefore well represented by the trumpets, with their note of alarm.

The revelator makes it abundantly clear, however, that all through these times of draconian perversion there will be a saving remnant carrying on the activities of both the true Church and the true State, to such a degree as to enlist divine intervention in their behalf. In the special episode of "the little book open" (10:1–11:13), interpolated between the sixth and seventh trumpets, we see the harmonious co-working of these "two witnesses."

THE TRUMPET ORACLES: ONE THROUGH SIX

As with the seal oracles, the first four trumpets represent a chronological sequence telling of evil conditions during the interadvent years, while the remaining three are devoted to the time of the end—a time potentially threatened by three woes, representing the accumulated perversities of the ages. The first two woes were made known as the fifth and sixth seals were opened and read, and these oracles are translated by the fifth and sixth trumpet oracles. The dire third woe, the subject of the seventh seal, was not made known, however, for it was countervailed by the hastened coming of the Savior as King of kings, and it is of that triumphal second advent, not of a woe, that the seventh trumpet tells. Its oracle is different, therefore, from those of the first six trumpets, and it must be treated separately in a later section.

The First Four Trumpets

In the seal oracles that tell of the four horsemen we have seen a conspectus of Christendom's largely unchristian temporalities during the inter-advent years, foretelling the evils they were to bring upon their times. The targums of these seal oracles, brought by the first four trumpeters, spell out these evils, using two different kinds of symbolism. In all four—symbolized, like the seal oracles, by the four zodiacal trigons (see Appendix 5)—we find well-known conventional expressions of condign punishment, some calling to mind the plagues that befell Egypt. The second and third of these oracles, however, add dire disasters that allude unmistakably to well-known apocalyptic oracles of the Old Testament, both of which make pronouncements against Babylon.

In the second targum's reference to a great mountain cast into the sea, the allusion is to an oracle of Jeremiah: "Behold, I am against thee, O destroying mountain, saith the Lord, which destroyest the whole earth: and I will stretch out mine hand upon thee, and roll thee down from the rocks, and make thee a burnt mountain" (Jer. 51:25). Jeremiah refers here to Babylon, which he pictures as the greatest and worst of the ancient temporal enemies of God's people. The "great mountain" of the second trumpet oracle therefore represents the State, and the vision of it being cast burning into the sea foreshadows a time when the State will be completely subjugated to the Church.

In the third targum there fell from the sky a great star blazing like a torch and its name was Wormwood (8:10–11). The allusion here is to an oracle of Isaiah: "How art thou fallen from heaven, O Lucifer, son of the morning! How art thou cut down to the ground...For thou hast said in thine heart, I will ascend into heaven...I will be like the Most High" (Isa. 14:12–14). This picture of Babylon, the symbol of the State, seeking equality with God suggests the dominance of the State over the Church.

Clearly, then, these targums are concerned with both Church and State, as will be evident also in the later vision of the two witnesses. Here we see a picture of the fearful perversion when either of them dominates the other, and this provides the background for the fifth and sixth seal and trumpet oracles and reveals the causes of the woes they foreshadow.

The Fifth and Sixth Trumpets: The First and Second Woes

Although the first and second woes are identified separately and are introduced by two successive trumpet blasts, in reality they form one complex whole, representing the plagues that are to be inflicted upon the earth at the end of the age. With the sounding of the fifth trumpet came hordes of locust-scorpion demons, suggestive of the locust swarms pictured by Joel (1:4 ff.). They are characterized by iron breastplates, and they rose like smoke from the bottomless pit, led by their king, Abaddon-Apollyon, the Hebrew and Greek names respectively for the "Destroyer." With them came the first woe. The sixth trumpet ushered in three armies of horsemen with breastplates the color of fire, sapphire, and brimstone. With them came the second woe. Taken together, these four armies of breastplated demons represent the hosts of "hell" that follow the rider on the pale horse, a caricature of the heavenly hosts following the King of kings. Here, then, we have the completion of the second act's pervert parody of the Savior's parousia, by means of which Antichrist attempts to take possession of the kingdoms of this world and prevent the establishment of Christ's millennial kingdom.

We must conclude that all of these evil hordes, not just the locust demons, had been held in the bottomless pit mentioned in the fifth oracle (9:2), and that Abaddon-Apollyon, king of the locust demons, was one of the four angels released from that pit (9:14). The separate treatment of his hosts highlights their peculiarly abysmal nature and makes it very clear that these dark demons are an infernal counterpart of the white-robed hosts of the King of kings in the supernal vision of the fifth seal, which they translate. There we saw the first corps of the white-robed armies of heaven that are later to follow the Savior when he comes as King of kings and Lord of lords. In them we see a foreglimpse of the kingdom of Christ, a democratic kingdom in which every saint is both a king and a priest. In contrast, the fifth trumpet vision presents a draconian parody of that martyr corps of saints. Here we see Antichrist's demons, each wearing a crown that "looked like" gold—a symbol of a spurious sovereignty; and there is no suggestion of priesthood. This is therefore a godless pseudo-democracy that cannot long escape becoming a tyranny.

The plagues that make up the two woes brought by the breastplated armies have grown out of the social perversions of the regimes represented in the seal oracles, and like them they can be identified with the zodiacal trigons. (See Appendix 5.) They include both ideological attack and physical aggression. The first woe is evidently only of the former type, for the locust demons had no lethal weapons, being armed only with stings. From this we can conclude that their attacks, which were to torture only those who do not have the seal of God on their foreheads, must be of the propaganda type, perhaps representing atheism. The demon horsemen of the second woe, however, have both types of power. From their mouths they breathe out blasts that inflict the deadly errors of the ideologies represented by the pervert seal regimes, and with their serpent-like tails they inflict wounds that presumably represent material aggression, undertaken for exploitation and self-aggrandizement.

THE EPISODE OF THE LITTLE BOOK OPEN

These fearful foes clearly symbolize visitations of divine wrath that call for repentance and amendment if they are not to eventuate in utter and irretrievable disaster—the threatened third woe. And at this point the orderly progress of the histrionic worship service is interrupted by an angel who brings the "little book open," with its promise of the countervailance of that woe and the remedy that will make that possible.

Free spontaneous interruptions of this sort were characteristic of the early Christian synagogue service, and this one, which comes right after the oracle of the sixth trumpet, is one of the most outstanding examples in the Apocalypse. The "little book" can be recognized as the megillah of the service, a scripture reading sometimes added as a supplement to the haphtaroth, and its translation and exposition are presented. It can also be interpreted as representing an anticipatory Day of Atonement. Thus it almost seems like an additional fifth act of the drama, for like each of the acts it represents both a feature of the worship service and one of the great annual religious observances. Instead, however, it is interpolated between the sixth and seventh trumpets as a special episode in the third act.

The Theophanic Angel

The angel who introduces this episode, a supremely notable figure and one of the most felicitously significant in the Apocalypse, is doubly identified, both by his function in the drama and by his voice. Not only did he come with a little book that is later described as bitter-sweet medicine that must be eaten, but he also "cried with a loud voice," like a roaring lion. He is recognized, therefore, as the archangel with two names, who is usually called Raphael—"God heals, comforts"—but who is also known as Labiel, "the lion of God," symbolic of the Lion of Judah who will destroy the destroyers of the earth.

The astral representations of this archangel are in accordance with his name and with the description of his appearance in this theophany. The cardinal star of the zodiac associated with him is Antares, which leads the stars of the Scorpion-Eagle, the constellation especially auspicious for alchemy and medicine and all "wisdom"; while his celestial picture is found in Auriga, the heavenly shepherd who is seen "arrayed in a cloud" of the Milky Way and carrying Capella, the "little kid," in his bosom, like the Good Shepherd of the Gospel. Clearly it is to these astral representations that the revelator refers when he describes the angel as setting "his right foot upon the sea, and his left foot on the earth" (10:2); for in the language of St. John's apocalyptic symbols the "sea" denotes the water trigon of the zodiac, of which the Scorpion-Eagle is the leader, while the "earth" denotes the earth trigon, whose leader is Taurus, just north of which lies Auriga. (See Appendix 1.)

Raphael-Labiel comes as an eager herald, breaking into the service with an extremely important and urgent message that must be delivered before the last trumpet can announce earth's crisic hour and signify the fearful third woe, toward which more and more disastrous events have been leading. He proclaims God's promise that the Savior's second advent will be hastened,

76

so that the third woe can be prevented. And as a complement of that proclamation he presents the "little book open." Its bitter-sweet medicine will provide just the challenge needed to quicken the prayerful devotion of the Church, thus making possible the hastened parousia and the countervailance of the third woe. The seven thunders and the vision of the two witnesses provide the translation and exposition of the book's message.

The Little Book as Megillah

In contradistinction to the seven-sealed book of prophecy in the hand of him who sat on the throne (5:1), the little book or scroll seen in Raphael's hand is "open" or unrolled. It is described as honey-sweet in its beginning and like drastically bitter medicine in its ending, and the revelator was directed to "eat" it and then to masticate and ponder and make its contents thoroughly his own.

The presentation of this little book as an interruption in the synagogue service immediately suggests that it may serve as a megillah—one of the shorter books of the sacred writings, which on special occasions is chosen to supplement the regular prophetic reading. In the traditional Hebrew usage there are five of these—Song of Songs, Ruth, Lamentations, Ecclesiastes, and Esther—but no one of these answers this little book's characterization as bitter-sweet medicine. As an "open" book, however, it could be no other than a divine revelation already known to all, a book of the accepted Hebrew sacred scriptures. And for this histrionic worship service, in which the religious observances ordained in the Mosaic law are modified in accordance with the usages of the early Christian church, we should expect it to be a scripture that has become a part of the Christian service. This leads us to the Psalms, whose five books early became the five megilloth, or little books of supplemental scripture readings, for the Christians and continue in such use today. And here, in the third book of the Psalms (nos. 73–89), we find the one little book of the ancient scriptures that answers all these specifications.

The historical background of the book is most appropriate, for clearly most of the psalms in this collection were written during the seemingly hopeless period of Israel's Babylonian captivity, out of which Divine Providence delivered them. And its targum and exposition foretell a like period of captivity, seemingly hope-

77

less, for God's spiritual Israel of the New Covenant, out of which they also are to be delivered, and far more gloriously.

At its beginning the book is indeed "sweet," its opening words being: "Truly God is good to Israel" (Ps. 73:1). And in the first two thirds of its psalms we find a mingling of hymns of faith and hope; lamentations and desolations over captivity; confession of sin; exhortations to repentance and amendment; memorials of God's past providence; and supplication and praise. Here we find the outpourings of a faith that is victorious though hard beset. These psalms of ancient Israel provide the later spiritual Israel of the Church with the most effective spiritual antidote to the doubts engendered by the evils of this age, which are to culminate in the worse than midnight hour that is to precede the dawn.

In contrast, the last six psalms are divided into two categories, which are presented alternately, three picturing the Church (nos. 84, 86, and 88) and three the State (nos. 85, 87, and 89). These are the two witnesses described in the little book's exposition (11:1–13), and each of them is set before us three times. In each triad the last psalm ends with an unrelieved picture of utter desolation, suggestive of the trumpet's alarm blast; and in the vision the two witnesses are left dead in the streets of the perverted city, while their foes rejoice over them.

Such an intensely bitter ending seems contrary to the purpose the book serves in the Apocalypse. But we must not be deceived by appearances. The Jews of St. John's day had a rule that has come down to us among the notations of the Masorites, providing that if a scripture lesson ends with a passage of bitter import the reading ought to conclude with a repetition of the next preceding passage of happier character. Applying this rule to the portrayal of the martyrdom of the Church in Psalm 88, we find that the next earlier picture of the Church, the first witness, is in Psalm 86, a "psalm of David." And the experience of this "man after God's own heart" gives a foreshadowing of the glorious resurrection of the Church and her triumph over all her enemies. "I will praise thee, O Lord my God, with my whole heart; and I will glorify thy name for evermore. For great is thy lovingkindness toward me; and thou hast delivered my soul from the lowest Sheol...thou, Jehovah, hast helped me, and comforted me" (vs. 12, 13, and 17b, AST).

The passage of happy import next preceding the martyrdom of the State, in the latter part of Psalm 89, is found in the first eighteen verses of that same psalm. There we read: "I will sing of the lovingkindness of Jehovah forever...O Jehovah God of hosts, Who is a mighty one, like unto thee, O Jehovah? And thy faithfulness is round about thee...Thou hast broken Rahab" (the great red dragon, symbol of the world empires as a whole) "in pieces, as one that is slain; Thou hast scattered thine enemies with the arm of thy strength. The heavens are thine, the earth also is thine...Blessed is the people that know the joyful sound" of thy trumpet; "They walk, O Jehovah, in the light of thy countenance. In thy name do they rejoice all the day" (vs. 1,8,10,11,15,16a, AST).

Here we have suggestions of precisely the imagery of the concluding oracles of the angel's exposition of the little book's revelation—the resurrection of the witnesses, their ascension to heaven in the sight of their enemies, the shaking to pieces of the great city that had come to be called spiritually Sodom and Egypt, the triumph of the God of heaven over all his enemies. And in the psalm, as in the oracles of the Apocalypse, there follows immediately the sound of the trumpet that announces the dawning of the glorious age when "the kingdom of the world is become the kingdom of our Lord and of his Christ," and when his people shall walk in the light of his countenance and rejoice in his name all the day.

Clearly, then, the introduction of the unscheduled megillah into the synagogue service had as its object a repentance on the part of Christendom such as that which saved Nineveh from the doom proclaimed by Jonah. It calls for a revival of true religion in the Church that will make it ready for the saving return of her Lord and so will make its hastening possible.

The Megillah's Targum: The Seven Thunders

Interpretation of the little book as the megillah of the synagogue service makes it parallel, in the Apocalyptic worship drama, with the lessons from the law (the parashoth) and those from the prophets (the haphtaroth). In accordance with the synagogue pattern adopted by the dramatist, the complete unfolding of the little book's revelation therefore requires it to be read in the original, translated, and expounded.

In this case there is of course a complete absence of any representation of the reading, for as we have seen the original text can be identified as a familiar part of the sacred scriptures, open and freely available to everyone. It could well be taken for granted, therefore, that it had already been read, doubtless many times.

The translation also is not set before us in detail but is represented suggestively by the seven thunders, which "uttered their voices" in reinforcement of the lion-like hail, the urgent intervenience, of the theophanic herald, Raphael-Labiel. Like the little book, they are brought forward as "witnesses" to explain the situation at this crisic point in the foreshadowings of the Apocalypse. They are represented as having uttered specific messages, which St. John was about to record when a voice from heaven intervened and said: "Seal up those things which the seven thunders uttered, and write them not" (10:4).

The solution of this enigma is found in the apocalyptist's frequently employed device of using Old Testament oracles as the sources of his symbolisms. For such a use of the ancient scriptures we have the warrant of St. Paul (1 Cor. 10:1–11). After drawing specific lessons from the story of Israel's escape from Egypt and wanderings in the wilderness, he added: "Now all these things happened unto them" by way of example; "and they are written for our admonition" and as "examples" for us. As St. John uses this device it is peculiarly felicitous, since it both contributes to the conciseness of his own oracles and provides keys to their proper interpretation.

For identification of these thunders, then, we must look to the Old Testament. There "thunders" are set forth by the words *ra'am* and *qôl*, whose primary meanings are "noise" and "voice" respectively; and these words are employed in the secondary sense of "thunder" nearly fifty times. It is evident, however, that only the thunders attributable to God himself and pointing to specific divine interventions can answer the requirements of the seven in question and provide precedents promising the fulfillment of the prophecy of the archangel whose lion voice they echoed. Such cases are to be found in Exodus, Samuel (First and Second Samuel having been regarded as one book, even in apostolic times), Amos, Isaiah, Psalms, Jeremiah, and Joel.[1] Accepting these identifications of the seven thunders, it is easy to see why they are sealed up. It would have been impossible to set forth all these passages in the space available; nor was it necessary, for the task of searching them out and construing their revelations is just such as properly devolves upon an interpreter.

The scripture citations of the seven thunders are filled with assurances of divine intervention *in answer to prayers of true repentance*, and in the history of God's ancient Israel it was such divine interventions that enabled them to accomplish their Messianic calling. Here, then, is the lesson for the spiritual Israel of the Christian centuries, who must prepare for the second advent. The crisic hour pictured at this point in the Apocalypse needed the hastening of the Savior's return in order that the threatened third woe might be countervailed, and Raphael's proclamation brought a divine promise of such deliverance. Certain preparations are necessary for the second advent, however, and these devolve upon the Church, God's true and faithful spiritual Israel. If the parousia is to be hastened, these preparations must be intensified, and the Church must be called to a new repentance and more intensive devotion, inspired and empowered by prayer. As in the days of old, divine intervention must be in answer to repentance.

The Megillah's Exposition: The Two Witnesses

From the vision of the two witnesses, which expounds the megillah, we realize that the little book open was introduced to supply the historic-prophetic perspective that will enable us to understand the divine judgments that are to be visited upon the earth.

Just as God's ancient people suffered the Gentile subjugation pictured in the ancient psalms of the little book, so also the new Israel is to endure draconian tyranny. In the Apocalypse this is represented (11:1–13) in a vision of Jerusalem during the "times of the Gentiles," showing the whole of the Holy City being trodden under foot by the "nations." Even the outer courts of the temple are in the hands of the enemy, and that includes the moneychangers' tables, the store-rooms and offices—all the exterior organization and outward show and ceremonial of religion. Apostasy appears to have taken possession of the Church entirely, except for the Holy of Holies and the Holy Place. That inner sanctuary proper and those who worship there are protected from this invasion.

81

In spite of these persecutions, therefore, a true and faithful spiritual Israel, an "invisible" Church, continues to exist, even in the midst of the seemingly universal apostasy of the Church visible. The safe-keeping of that faithful remnant in the hands of Providence is represented by the "measuring" of the sanctuary and the altar, a symbolism borrowed from the Old Testament.[2] St. John is here given the glad assurance, which must indeed have been "sweet as honey" in his mouth, that during all the period of seeming dominance of the persecuting world, God's true covenant people will be inviolate, kept safe and pure. Sweet likewise must have been the assurance that in the end Christ and his Church will altogether prevail over the world. Then at last the twenty-four elders, who represent the life of earth, will be able to sing: "We give thee thanks, O Lord God Almighty... because thou hast taken...thy great power and hast reigned" (11:17). But the trials and persecutions and final martyrdom of the two witnesses are such as to cause great bitterness of soul to the lover of Jesus and his Church.

This spiritual Israel is not represented, however, as merely resting safe and secure in the fastnesses of the temple fortress, waiting for the great power of God to overcome the beleaguering world. No, this faithful Church of the future is seen working and suffering in the midst of a pervert Christendom. Its members go forth boldly into the world and join in the fray, bearing protesting witness concerning the true ideals of earth life. It would be impossible for true worshippers to live in the world and not bear witness to the Lord and Savior. Indeed, this must be the major field of their service as worshippers, and accordingly the major portion of the record of this vision is given to the story of their witness. Their prayerful devotion, quickened by the inspiration of the little book's psalms, will hasten the preparation for the Savior's return.

This testimony is personified by the introduction of "two witnesses" or prophets who stand at the altar, serving there as priests. That they can be identified as advocates of the true ideals of Church and State is made clear by two symbolisms taken from the Old Testament.

First, the two witnesses are called "the two olive trees, and the two candlesticks standing before the God of the earth"—a symbolism found also in a vision of Zechariah (4:2–3). It refers, of course, to the menorah, the two seven-branched candlesticks that stood in the temple's Holy Place, and to the olive trees that provided the oil they needed. In zodiacal symbolism (see Appendix 1) these candlesticks are represented by two overlapping groups of seven zodiacal constellations (the "solar" and "lunar" houses of the planets) that stood for the Church and the State. This is the meaning of Zechariah's vision, which pictured Joshua, the high priest, and Zerubbabel, the governor and heir of David.

Second, the powers ascribed to the two witnesses—"to shut heaven, that it rain not" and "to smite the earth with all plagues" (11:6)—are those of two extremely significant prophets who represent Church and State. They are, of course, Elijah, the champion of Jehovah's religion against heathendom, and Moses, the law-giver and Israel's first ruler.[3] Obviously these two witnesses are not to be taken as actually representing Moses and Elijah, come back to earth. Instead, they bear witness to the truths set forth in the law of Moses and the messages of the prophets. They stand for the testimony of the word of God that prepared the way for the first advent of the Redeemer and that will prepare for his final manifestation.

These two witnesses will be "clothed in sackcloth," as a token of their sorrow at the captive state of the Church in its outer form and as a protest against the imperial splendor of the usurping world power enthroned in the court of the temple. They are represented as becoming a torment to those who dwell on the earth, for they will persistently proclaim the truths of the religion of Jesus. Unwelcome though this may be, it will nevertheless be salutary and most effective for all who will listen, even at last for the seemingly unheeding but really tormented world; for the witnesses are to institute reformations in the apostate Church and instigate democratic revolutions against the despotism of the draconian State. At last the State in its final form, the beast rising out of the bottomless pit, is to make war against them and overcome and kill them.

This martyrdom, it should be noted, foreshadows, not the destruction of the true Church but the suppression of her public testimony by the wild beast's ruthless and totalitarian police State. Such testimony is "dead" when for any reason it no longer makes any appeal—perhaps because it has become the merely nominal confession of a dead Church, or on the other hand because those to whom it is addressed no longer have hearing ears and are themselves "dead." The "death" of the two witnesses is attributable to the latter cause, for they were slain by the beast from the abyss. In the midst of all the worldly organizations that call themselves churches, there is still a faithful spiritual Church whose members bear testimony to the truth. Owing, however, to the influences that emanate especially from the realm of the beast from the abyss, the world as a whole no longer takes any stock in such testimony. It discounts the credentials of the witnesses, laughing to scorn their appeals to the supernatural and their old-fashioned moralities.

The little book itself was so written as to end with the martyrdom of the two witnesses; but its exposition rearranges and amplifies its oracles so as to conclude with their resurrection and glorification. The triumph of the beast and his minions is soon to be reversed, for overruling Providence can make even the wrath of man to praise him. After only three and a half days during which their foes rejoiced and made merry over their dead bodies, "the breath of life from God" entered into the two prophets, and "they stood upon their feet; and great fear fell upon them that beheld them" (11:11 AST). In other words, this persecution will arouse the Church, as has always been true in her history, to new and deeper devotion, even such as to make possible the full outpouring of the Holy Spirit promised in the oracles of the prophet Joel (2:28–29), and foreglimpsed at the first Christian Pentecost (Acts 2:17–18). Thus endued and emboldened, the saints of the true Church will no longer be silenced by the beast and his followers but will rise up to testify anew and with unprecedented success.

The two prophets then "heard a great voice from heaven saying unto them, Come up hither." And in the sight of their foes they went "up to heaven in a cloud," a prophetic anticipation of the spiritual "rapture" of the millennium (see Act 4), when the saints of the true Church are "caught up...in the clouds, to meet the Lord in the air" (1 Thes. 4:17)—that is, when their increasing spirituality draws them into closer and closer relations with the unseen realm of heaven.

Thus in the midst of a pervert Christendom we see a faithful Church and State, or rather faithful remnants of religious zeal and civic virtue. And these two witnesses testify against all the oppressors of God's people and bring a promise of the end of captivities.

84

An Anticipatory Day of Atonement

Near the end of ancient Israel's pilgrim journey through the wilderness, Moses declared that from the time they had left Egypt they had been "rebellious against the Lord" (Deut. 9:7); and it was because of their apostasies that the great annual fast of the Day of Atonement was decreed, to call the people to repentance. Provision was made also for a special day of atonement, to be held at any time during the year when it was discovered that "the whole congregation of Israel" had erred (Lev. 4:13–17). On such an occasion the seven-fold sprinklings were made for the cleansing of the people as a whole, not for individuals.

The foreshadowings of St. John's Apocalypse make it clear that the New Israel of the Christian centuries would follow all too closely in the footsteps of its type, the Old Israel, and would have continuing need for repentance and amendment and for the intercessions of our Great High Priest. In recognition of this need St. John made the ceremonials of the Day of Atonement part and parcel of his composite pictures of worship in this apocalyptic drama, representing one of its chief ceremonials in each act.

The need became acute, however, as the increasingly fearful disasters of the first and second woes were revealed and as the time approached for the coming of the dire third woe, toward which humanity's apostasies were leading. That woe could be countervailed by the hastened second advent of the Savior, but to make that possible there must be a great revival of true religion, cleansing humanity of its apostasies. In the regular religious calendar the annual Day of Atonement occurs right after the New Year celebration, the Feast of Trumpets, represented by this third act of the drama, but there was not time to wait for that. A special anticipatory day of atonement was needed, and this is what we find in the episode of the little book, introduced so urgently by the Archangel Raphael.

To interpret this episode as such a special day of atonement is not at all in conflict with the concept of it as the megillah of the worship service. As the megillah, a supplemental scripture lesson, it had to be translated and expounded, and the message thus revealed gives full support to the atonement concept. The seven thunders, it will be recalled, point to Old Testament examples of divine intervention in answer to repentance. And the vision of the two witnesses, penitents clothed in sackcloth, pic-

85

tures the fearful conditions under which they struggled, which called for a special day of atonement, and shows their salvation by divine intervention when they were resurrected by the breath of life from God.

Such a special day of atonement, needed for the full unfolding of St. John's revelation, fits naturally into this third act rather than any other. The background setting for this act's regular atonement ceremonial is, as we shall see, the antechamber of the sanctuary, and this is also where the ceremonial of the special day must take place. Moreover, following as it does after the sixth trumpet's oracle, which at first seems to complete the third act and therefore the New Year celebration it symbolizes, it comes at roughly the proper time for the annual Great Day of Atonement, which falls ten days after New Year's day. Thus this megillah provides also recognition for that Great Day as a whole, in approximately its proper place in the sequence of the year's five major religious observances. Each of the other four is represented by an entire act, and to complete this drama of worship some comparable representation of this fifth observance as a whole is needed, even though its major ceremonials are suggested individually, one in each act.

The sponsor of this episode, the archangel who introduces it, is most appropriately Raphael-Labiel, whose two-fold name symbolizes the two-fold nature of both the Day of Atonement ceremonies and the divine intervention by which the evil days are to be shortened. As Raphael, the heavenly shepherd and the angel of healing, he calls to mind the first three sprinkling ceremonies of atonement, which bring, to those who are repentant and faithful, the assurance of full cleansing from sin and reconciliation with God. This is the *at-one-ment* made possible by the intervention of the Son of God as the Lamb of God that taketh away the sins of the world, foreshadowed in the sacrifice of Passover and now commemorated on Good Friday. As Labiel, the Lion of God, he represents the ceremony of the scapegoat (see Act 4), which was a warning that only a hopeless retribution could be expected by unrepentant continuance in sin and contumacious rejection of the salvation offered at such great cost. Raphael-Labiel is therefore the angelic symbol of the Lamb-Lion of the Apocalypse. If the third woe is to be countervailed there must first be the atonement made possible by the sacrificial Lamb of the first advent. Then, and only then, can he return in his second advent

86

as the Lion of the tribe of Judah, who will cut short the third
woe by cutting off its would-be perpetrator.

THE SEVENTH TRUMPET

The oracles of the seventh trumpet would normally have been
the translation of the revelations of the seventh seal, which were
too fearful to be made known to St. John and which caused
silence in heaven for about half an hour. Certainly these revelations would have had as their theme the third woe, just heralded
as imminent by the angel whose two previous proclamations of
woe had announced invasions from the bottomless pit by civi-
lization-destroying and world-wrecking demons. But because
that third woe had not been revealed to St. John when the seventh seal was opened, it had not been "signified" to him as one of
the inevitable predictions of the seven-sealed book. It was to be
countervailed by the Savior's hastened return. And so instead of
a vision of that woe we learn of the joy caused by its countervailance, by which Divine Mercy answered the repentance and
amendment brought about by the intercession of the archangel
with the little book open.

There follows then a conspectus of the history of Christendom
from advent to advent—a symbolic representation of the birth of
the persecuted Savior, a picture of developments of both Church
and State leading up to his return, and finally a vision of his second-advent presence and activities. It is the whole story of the
Savior's two-fold, his Lamb-Lion, intervention for humanity's
salvation, which will not permit any "woe" to be more than a corrective scourge for those who will so accept it.

Here, then, is a representation of the exceedingly significant
two-fold foreshadowings of the festival of the winter solstice,
which tell both of the Savior's birth as the Sun of Righteousness
and his return to "bring back the age of gold." (See Appendix 2.)
That festival was necessarily omitted from the Torah and the
annual observances it established, but its foreshadowings were
abundantly set forth by Israel's prophets and psalmists, and its
celebrations figured largely in the social life of the Roman world
that was to become the Christendom whose developments St.
John's Apocalypse was to foretell and appraise. He was therefore
not content to leave the festival of the winter solstice unrepre-
sented and unutilized in his composite worship drama; and since

it had no place in the established Jewish ritual, he was free to employ it in whatever way his Apocalypse required and its own nature permitted. Accordingly, he found it just what would serve to represent the desperately needed intervention of the Savior's hastened return, foretold by the Lord himself (Matt. 24:21–22).

The Sounding of the Trumpet: Joy in Heaven

The intervening archangel who brought the little book "lifted up his hand to heaven" and swore that "in the days of the voice of the seventh angel, when he shall begin to sound, the mystery of God should be finished" (10:5–7). The hastened return of the Lord to save his "elect" is therefore to be conceived as taking place when the seventh angel was about to sound his trumpet—indeed, just as he had finished making his final proclamation: "The second woe is past: and behold, the third woe cometh quickly" (11:14).

The revelator does not describe that return, but a three-fold assurance of its accomplishment is given us immediately after the sounding of the seventh trumpet. First come great voices in heaven, acknowledging the full establishment on earth of the kingdom of God and of his Christ. Then the twenty-four elders, also accepting this development as an established fact, join in a prayer of thanksgiving for the deliverance of the saints and the destruction of them that would destroy the earth. And in token of the unfailing divine promise that will bring this to pass, we are given a vision of the ark of God's covenant in the sanctuary of heaven.

A Conspectus of the History of Spiritual Israel

The final objective of the revelations of the seventh trumpet is therefore the glorious reversal of fortune that our Lord's second advent is to bring in the age-long warfare of the moral and spiritual forces affecting earth life. The forces of evil are now to mobilize for the last phase of that warfare, and a full understanding of the evils of that struggle requires a knowledge of what has preceded it. Accordingly, in chapters 12 and 13 St. John gives a picture, partly historical but mostly prophetic, of the outstanding developments of the Church during the centuries of Christendom leading up to the second advent. This is a substitute for the targum of the unsignified oracles of the seventh seal, which would have told of the third woe were it not to be countervailed by the special day of atonement heralded by the archangel. It tells instead of the age-long conflict between the invading hosts of hell and the intervening hosts of heaven, a conflict that is now to close with the hastened final intervention of the Captain of our Salvation, and we are given a promise of its imminence in the vision of the Lamb on Mount Zion.

In this retrospective we see a symbolic portrayal of the continuous struggle between the Church, represented by "the woman," and the world spirit represented by the great red dragon and his minions and manifested in the State.

That dragon, the great enemy and oppressor of the Church, represents of course the same spirit of evil that arrayed itself against ancient Israel, for it is further identified as "the old serpent" who is "called the Devil, and Satan," the deceiver of the whole world (12:9). In this figure we see a representation of the spirit of utter and incorrigible evil—of falsehood and perfidy, of rapacious greed and exploitation, of senseless wrath and heartless cruelty, and of self-exalting and God-denying pride. His "seven heads" suggest that he is represented here as incarnate not simply in the world as a whole, but in a succession of murderously conquering and ruthlessly exploiting world powers that manifest his malignant evil spirit.

The "woman" is a generic symbol of the faithful and loyal of God's covenanted people, ideally the same throughout the ages but actually embodied in a different way in every generation. In Old Testament times she was the faithful of Israel and was called "the spouse of Jehovah";[4] and as we see her here in her first appearance in the Apocalypse (12:1–2) she is still the faithful of Judaism, whose culminal personality was the virgin mother of the Messiah. But as we find her represented in the later verses that tell of her flight from the dragon and her escape into the wilderness, she is the faithful of the Church of Christ. This she is also, of course, in the later visions in which she is called "the bride of the Lamb" (19:7-8; 21:2,9). But in another of the later visions, at a time when the Church of Christ is seen as unfaithful and apostate, the woman who represents it is pictured as "Babylon the great, the mother of harlots" (17:5), with reference to the supreme symbol of heathen apostasy.

Against the Church the spirit of the world has always been arrayed in bitter hostility, and it has always been more or less active in its hostility just in proportion as the Church herself has

89

been more or less active in her championship of the righteousness that the world hates. And so it will always be until the
world is finally overcome by the man-child now introduced into
the vision. He is the Seed of the woman, and it is he who is to
crush the head of the old serpent, the spirit of evil now incarnate
in the world. The birth of this man-child is therefore of supreme
interest to the great enemy, for the Church when it becomes
Christian will become active as never before against all the evils
fostered by the old serpent. Accordingly we see him, represented
here as the great red dragon standing before the woman waiting
for the birth, that he may "devour" the child. But in accordance
with the promise memorialized by the ark of the covenant, mentioned in the immediately preceding passage, God continues to
keep his Church, as it were, in the hollow of his hand. The child
"was caught up unto God, to his throne. And the woman fled
into the wilderness, where she hath a place prepared of God"
and where she will be nourished (12:5–6).

The child is of course the Christ, pictured not simply as the
Babe of Bethlehem but as the first-born among many brethren,
for "the rest" of the woman's seed, which can only be the Church
of which Christ is the head, are mentioned later as the real
objects of the dragon's wrath (12:17). The first six verses of the
chapter sweep through the entire course of the Christian centuries, telling of the birth of the Christ; his ascension as our
Elder Brother to be our Advocate at the throne of grace; the continuing presence of his Holy Spirit "nourishing" his Church; the
implacable hostility of the world-spirit and its persecutions of
the Church; and God's unfailing providence over her. There is
even a glimpse of the second advent, when he is "to rule all the
nations with a rod of iron."

The revelator's use of astral symbols to portray his story is
here brought forcefully to our attention, for the woman and the
dragon are both introduced as "great signs in heaven." We must
therefore pause to identify these astral figures.

The woman is described as "clothed with the sun, and the
moon under her feet, and upon her head a crown of twelve stars"
(12:1). Any astral figure that meets this description must therefore be on the ecliptic, one of the zodiacal constellations, and it
can be no other than Virgo, which symbolized both God's
covenanted people and the temple's Holy of Holies. Just above
Virgo is the gleaming starry mist of Coma Berenices, symboliz-

90

ing the Shekinah that rested on the ark of the covenant in the Holy of Holies to represent God's presence in the midst of his people, and that was the column of fire by night and cloud by day that led Israel in her flight from Egypt. It was to this Shekinah that St. John referred when, in the prologue of his Gospel, he described the Christ as the Word that became flesh and dwelt among us and was "the light of men."

The great red dragon, with seven diademed heads and a tail that sweeps down a third of the stars of heaven, is of course the great infernal constellation Hydra, one of the astral representations of Satan. Its serpentine form parallels the ecliptic south of Virgo and three adjacent zodiacal constellations—four of the twelve.

In the remainder of Chapter 12 and all of Chapter 13 the revelator sets forth the salient features of the age-long contest between the Church and the State. Just as the world spirit symbolized by the great red dragon arrayed itself against ancient Israel, so that same old adversary is seen persecuting and trying to debauch the Church, the New Israel. In St. John's visions the Church is sometimes victorious, but it is defeated when the State is dominated by the old serpent's evil spirit. The story falls naturally into three parts.

The Gospel's first glorious triumph over the world spirit is described as "war in heaven," in which Michael and his angels cast the dragon and his angels out of heaven—a struggle described in terms of the ancient cosmic story read in the stars. There the constellation Ophiuchus represents the archangel Michael, while Satan is represented by Serpens, another of his celestial figures. Satan is here no longer shown as the seven-headed monster of his successive terrestrial incarnations, but as the spiritual malignity that has always obsessed and largely possessed each of them. In these astral figures Michael is interpreted as grasping the old serpent with both hands and casting him over the equator and so out of the supernal heavens of the northern skies and into the infernal regions of the south.

In the picture of Heracles and Draco we have seen the wounding of the heel of the hero, the Protevangel's foreshadowing of the crucifixion of the Savior at his first advent, and the persecutions of his Church that are to continue until the victory of his second advent. Such persecutions have just been symbolized by the celestial figures of Virgo and Hydra. Now, in the Ophiuchus-

Serpens vision we see the victorious aspect of the Protevangel, with the head of the serpent under the conquering heel of the hero. The fulfillment of this aspect of the foreshadowing is of course not to reach its consummation until the final victory has been won by Christ and his Church at his second advent. It was begun, however, even during his first advent, in the victories won by the Savior himself over sin and death; and it has continued down through the centuries in victories won by the Church, not only in despite of the persecutions of the dragon but even in consequence of her steadfastness in enduring them.

Even in this vision of Michael and his angels, which pictures a contest in the spiritual realm, we see the role played by the Church on earth, for a loud voice from heaven announces the victory won by the faithfulness and valor of its persecuted saints, who conquered "by the blood of the Lamb, and by the word of their testimony" (12:11). Thus we are reminded that while the work of social salvation on earth cannot be accomplished without the intervening assistance of Providence, represented here by Michael and his angels, it must be done by humanity itself. And as we shall see in Act 4, the Savior's own work of social salvation in his second advent is to be done in collaboration with and through his Church. It is the saints who are to wield the "rod of iron" with which he is to shatter the draconian "nations" (2:27), and they are to sit with him on the throne of his democratic kingdom (3:21; 20:4–6).

Even though the dragon is pictured in this vision as having been cast down to earth, he continues to persecute the "woman," and with even more violence than before. And so the next campaign (12:13–16) shows the Church now on the defensive. The ancient lore that is the source of apocalyptic warns of such ever-threatening recrudescence of chaos when it tells of the dragon of the primordial deep ever eager to return and overwhelm the incipient earthly cosmos, as in the flood of the apocalypse of Genesis. In St. John's vision the Church (the "woman") is pursued by the dragon, who sends forth a flood to sweep her away. Since apocalyptic employs "waters" to stand for "peoples, and multitudes, and nations, and tongues" (Rev. 17:15), this flood might represent invasions of alien peoples and hostile faiths. In this attack the Church suffers defeat and is compelled to flee from her adversary. It is only a partial victory for the dragon, however, for the Church is carried to a safe asylum where she is to be nourished. Angered by this, the dragon goes off to make war on "the rest" of the woman's children—those who "keep the commandments of God" and bear testimony to Jesus—the third phase of the campaign.

In this connection we must remember that Satan is always conceived as having two characteristic methods of warfare—attacks from without and from within. Whenever opportunity offers he goes about "as a roaring lion...seeking whom he may devour" (1 Pet. 5:8), and it is this sort of open hostility we see in the second aspect of his campaign, described above. With the Church protected in her safe asylum, however, such open attack is no longer possible, and Satan must use his other method, that of boring from within. In his subtlety as the old serpent he can disguise himself as an angel of light and deceive even the very elect, a procedure most congenial to his nature as the father of lies. This is what we see in the third phase of the campaign, symbolized by the visions of the two wild beasts that rise from the sea and from the land. They picture the State and the Church as they were to be more or less perverted by the insidious evil spirit of the dragon.

In the first beast, rising from the sea with its ten crowned horns, we see a picture of the State, for the horn is the apocalyptic symbol of authority, and the crown represents fully independent and sovereign power. It is an apostate State, however, exercising dominion over the Church, such as developed when Saul presumptuously assumed the priestly functions of Israel's religion (1 Sam. 13:8–12). This beast is shown blaspheming God and making war on the saints; and because of its temporal power and glory and its material riches the people worship it instead of Christ, the meek and lowly. It even poses as a manifestation of Christ, appearing to have been slain and come to life again, like the little Lamb that St. John saw in the throne room of heaven. And while that Lamb had seven horns and seven eyes, this wild beast has ten horns and seven heads—three more horns and twice as many eyes. So does this Antichrist, like all others, over-reach and betray himself.

Here, then, is a veritable reincarnation of the dragon, a despotic power that exploits and despoils the peoples of the earth. It is evident, however, that the stellar picture on which this vision is based is not to be sought in any figure that presents an outward suggestion of the serpentine form of Hydra, and this is indicated also in the further description of the beast, which is likened to a leopard, a bear, and a lion—symbolisms that may be construed as partaking of the same significance as the well-known beast imagery of Daniel's seventh chapter. These considerations point to Centaurus, which from the southern shore of the island of Patmos would be seen rising "out of the sea," and here again we have a counterfeit of Christ. This warrior riding on a horse is the southern or infernal perversion of the supernal warrior on a horse, Sagittarius. As we shall see later, in Act 4, that zodiacal constellation is the astral symbol of Christ coming down from heaven as the victorious King of kings, riding on his white horse.

The second wild beast, which rose out of the earth and had two horns "like a lamb," must be construed as standing for the Christian Church, which is supposed to be like its Master, the Lamb of God. There is no doubt, however, about the real nature of this beast. Like Jacob, the proverbial "supplanter" and deceiver of old, he is betrayed by his voice, for he "spake like a dragon." Like the first beast, therefore, this one is also a counterfeit of the Savior, a wild beast masquerading as a lamb, and it "deceiveth them that dwell on the earth." Instead of worshiping the meek and lowly Nazarene it worships as its ideal the imperial State represented by the first beast; demands that all acknowledge allegiance to that power and bow down to it; and puts its "mark" on those who comply, in imitation of the protective "seal of the living God."

In this draconian usurper we see, however, only the outward form of the Church, its hierarchical organization—the outer courts of the temple that were to be trodden underfoot by the Gentiles (11:2). There were still true and faithful worshipers, like the two witnesses of that earlier vision, and like them they were subjected to persecution and death when they refused to worship the beast.

In the heavens this beast is well represented by a southern, and therefore "infernal," figure that was in St. John's day called Therion, "the wild beast." We now know it as Lupus, "the wolf." From the southern shore of Patmos St. John would have seen it rising up from the southeastern extremity of the island, and it would therefore have seemed to come up "out of the earth."

In the fourth act we shall meet this second beast as the false prophet, the equivalent of the great harlot, or Babylon the great.

The Lamb on Mount Zion: The Second-Advent Presence of the Mighty One

After these foreshadowings of the Church's history in the inter-advent years we return again to the promised parousia, the second-advent presence of the Savior that was hailed with rejoicing at the sounding of the seventh trumpet; and it is presented in two different visions, the first a picture of the Lamb on Mount Zion and the second a theophanic representation of the Savior on a white cloud at the final harvest.

The "Lamb" seen here on Mount Zion is clearly to be taken as identical in every respect with the symbol seen in the vision of the heavenly throne room of the Divine Ruler of the universe (5:6), where we noted that he is represented in the heavens by the constellation Heracles, the stellar version of the Protevangel (see Act 2). That there is to be a change, however, in the Lamb's relationships and activities with respect to earth life is apocalyptically represented by the removal of the symbol of his presence from heaven to Mount Zion, the poetic term for Jerusalem. This, the earthly seat of spiritual Israel, symbolized here by the hundred and forty-four thousand bearing the seal of the living God, is a foregleam of the New Jerusalem that is to come down from God out of heaven.

We have here, therefore, an unmistakable foreshadowing of the promised return of our Lord; for he is seen manifested to his Church on earth in the very same presence in which he is seen in heaven. As the Lamb that was slain he has made the sacrifice involved in the first advent and is now glorified and ready for the work that remains to be done for the salvation of the world. He must therefore still have the seven horns that represent his seven-fold perfect authority, his divine right to rule over all the earth; and now, returning to the earth, he is actually to take his "great power" and reign (11:17). He must also still have the seven eyes that represent his seven-fold limitless possession of all the agencies of the Holy Spirit, on which depends his exercise of the authority symbolized by the horns and from which the Church will receive the final full and lasting enduement of spiritual power of which Pentecost was but the firstfruits (John 7:38–39; Joel 2:28 ff.).

What, then, would seem to be the teaching of this vision concerning the nature of the Savior's presence at his second coming?

During the Christian centuries he has been manifested to his Church only as a spiritual presence, mediated through the Holy Spirit. At the second coming, however, his presence will be a personal one, analogous to that of the first advent but not identical with it. As we have seen, his presence on Mount Zion is the same as his glorified presence in heaven, while in the first advent he had laid aside that heavenly glory and had taken upon himself the human form of a servant. It was therefore only his humanity that was immediately manifest at that time, but at his second coming he will be revealed in his unity with both humanity and the God-head, the Father and the Holy Spirit. It will be, therefore, both a personal and a spiritual presence. It will of course affect all of earth life, but it will be "manifest" only to his Church, to those who are sufficiently like him to see him as he is (1 John 3:2). This can come to pass only in the consummation, of which St. John gives us but a far-off and altogether mystical glimpse in his vision of the New Jerusalem, the holy city "coming down from God out of heaven" (21:2).

The Communion of Saints

As we have seen, Mount Zion is the holy city of earth life, in the fortress sanctuary of whose temple there was to be kept secure a saving remnant of true worshipers (11:1). The hundred and forty-four thousand of this vision are evidently representatives of that true Church, and they are found watching and ready when the bridegroom comes. They "follow the Lamb whithersoever he goeth," and they "were purchased from among men, to be the firstfruits unto God and unto the Lamb" (14:4 AST). In other words, they are the earnest of the new humanity of which our Elder Brother will be the head. They are also those whom we saw sealed on their foreheads with the seal of the living God (7:2 ff.; cf. 9:4 and 3:12). In accordance with the custom still followed in the east, that seal gave both the Lamb's own name and that of his Father, and it represented the true Christian's confession of faith that "Jesus is the Christ, the Son of God, our Savior."

These sealed thousands are not a host of peculiarly choice spirits from among the countless multitudes of the redeemed in heaven, but are the Church on earth, their symbolic number of 12,000 from each of the twelve tribes of Israel representing the sum total of the true servants of God to be found at any one time in all the different religious groups of the earth. They are the Church militant mobilized for aggressive action under the Joshua of the New Covenant. It is they whom the Lord will find waiting and watching for his coming, and it is through them that he will gather all humanity—all save such as are hopelessly perverse—into the world-wide Church of the second advent.

As St. John saw the Lamb he heard "a voice from heaven...of harpers harping with their harps: and they sung as it were a new song before the throne" and before the living creatures and the elders (14:2–3). This "choir invisible," symbolized by the constellation Lyra, is evidently not yet known to the seer, but it is revealed in his vision of the next chapter. There it is seen as the innumerable company of all those who have come off victorious from all the temptations of the world and are standing by the sea of glass "having the harps of God" (15:2). These are the newly resurrected saints of the fifth seal vision, who have received their white robes (6:9–11), the spiritual bodies representing their righteous deeds. Thus, in this vision of the Savior's promised presence on earth again with the hosts of the Church militant, we find the Church triumphant present also, unseen but manifest, singing a "new song" of thanksgiving and rejoicing to celebrate their resurrection, the "first resurrection" of the just that will come at the beginning of the parousia. They are teaching this song of the new day to the ranks of the Church militant, the only ones on earth who can learn it. No one else could share in its rejoicing, for no one else was to share in the resurrection it celebrated. That spiritual host of the choir invisible, seen already exerting a mighty influence on the thousands of the Church still incarnate, is waiting only for the drying up of the water of the great river. Then, as the armies riding with the King of kings (see Act 4), they would be able to intervene irresistibly in the affairs of earth life.

We have here, therefore, a representation of the communion of saints. The Church is one, whether in heaven or on earth, for the saints of the Church triumphant were first of all soldiers of the hosts of righteousness on earth; and the saints on earth, each in his turn, will be called to join the choir of heaven.

It is unmistakably of the Church and of the period represented in this vision that St. Paul is speaking when he tells us of the "rapture" of the saints to meet their returning Lord and the hosts of the resurrected Church triumphant "in the air."[5] It is also clearly to this same feature of the parousia that St. John himself refers in his description of the rapture of the two witnesses at the end of the seemingly unsuccessful testimony in behalf of the truth during the whole period of the great falling away (11:11–12), for they went up to heaven in a cloud—an expression that clearly connotes the second coming of the Lord. Now the "coming in the clouds" is of course theophanic, while the two witnesses are certainly mystically representative, as we have seen, not of personalities but of institutions, the Church and the State. We must regard as equally mystical St. Paul's expression "in the air." Indeed, we can understand it only as equivalent to St. John's expression, "in the spirit."

Accordingly, the "rapture of the saints" as set forth by St. Paul must be seen as the spiritual rapport between earth and heaven pictured in this vision of St. John. The "change" of which St. Paul tells us in connection with it is not to come to the dwellers on earth until some time after the resurrection, the full "clothing upon," of the Church triumphant. It is that which will enable it to enter into fuller communion with saints on earth, as evidenced in the vision. We must conclude, therefore, that it is the final mutation of earth life. Like every other leap in the evolution of organic life it will come suddenly—"in a moment, in the twinkling of an eye" (1 Cor. 15:52); but it can come, nevertheless, only after a due period of inner growth, at the end of the intensive spiritual development that must go on during the period represented by this vision.

The qualities that will make the Church militant ready for this change can be seen in the description (14:4–5), itemized below, of the hundred and forty-four thousand seen in this vision and applicable to the saints of all ages:

(1) They "were not defiled with women; for they are virgins." That is, they are free from spiritual harlotry. They have not been beguiled by Jezebel (2:20) or by any of the Midianitish emissaries of spiritual idolatry sent forth by the Balaams of Antichrist.[6] This first declaration concerning these true Christians is obviously an allusion to the Israelites of old and their temptations to idolatry as they were led out of Egypt and up to Canaan. What it means in terms of the imagery of these apocalyptic visions is obviously that they have not worshiped the beast or received his mark on their foreheads and hands, for the apostates who have done so are threatened with the final wrath

98

of God (14:9–10); and in the next vision it is said of the church triumphant that they have come off victorious from the beast and from his image (15:2).

(2) These are they who "follow the Lamb whithersoever he goeth"—down through the dark valley of humiliation and up to the heights of his glory!

(3) "These were redeemed from among men [to be] the firstfruits unto God and to the Lamb." As we have seen, it is the Church—born at Pentecost, the Feast of Firstfruits—that constitutes an earnest of the new humanity that in the coming age is to inhabit the new earth wherein dwelleth righteousness; and these hundred and forty-four thousand represent the members of that Church whom the Lord will find watching and ready when he comes.

(4) Of these samples of the new humanity it is said further: "And in their mouth was found no guile; for they are without fault before the throne of God." Mistakes on this earthly plane they will inevitably make, and weaknesses and the besetments of old habits and old ideas they will still have to fight; but there is neither hypocrisy nor self-deceit about their endeavors to follow the Lamb in all things. They are therefore blameless, worthy to be sealed on the forehead with the signature of the Judge of all the earth in token of their acquittal at his bar of judgment, the true sign of absolution.

The Second-Advent Work of Christ and His Church: The Three Herald Angels and a Voice from Heaven

Following the vision of the Lamb and the redeemed who can sing the "new song" come the messages of three herald angels, breaking into the prescribed ritual of the synagogue service, as was permitted in early Christian worship. Their proclamations warn the world of the imminence of the warfare that will mark the beginning of the parousia, the advent of the Lamb who is also the Lion of the tribe of Judah, the Mighty Avenger. They tell of portentous developments, call for repentance, and cite the dire consequences of godless contumacy and of the apostasy symbolized by Babylon the great. Clearly they foreshadow the spiritual activities of Christ and his Church for the bringing about of the new order of affairs on earth, of which his coming is the promise.

The first angel specifically announces the coming event, emphasizing the imminence of God's judgment and bringing a gospel message to those who dwell on earth. This is not the familiar glad tidings that offer eternal life, not a pleading call to repentance, but a stern demand for obedience: "Fear God, and give glory to him; for the hour of his judgment is come; and worship him that made the heaven, and earth, and the sea, and the fountains of waters" (14:6–7).

This is no new gospel, but simply a new social application of the old gospel, and so it is proclaimed, not to individuals, but "to every nation, and kindred, and tongue, and people"—a world evangelization, which the Savior noted as a sign of "the end" (Matt. 24:14). It is therefore the gospel "for the age"—the new age whose beginning is pictured here. Those whom love cannot bring to glad obedience to the laws of righteousness, whether they be men or nations, must now be compelled to obey. Where love cannot prevail, fear must and will intervene. The world is to be made safe, not only for democracy but for righteousness, good will, and innocency in all their forms. And woe be unto the man or institution that stands in the way, that persists in exploitation of any form or degree.

This is the burden of the second angel's proclamation: "Babylon is fallen, is fallen, that great city, because she made all nations drink of the wine of the wrath of her fornication" (14:8). That supreme example of the dragon spirit stands for all the ruthless exploiters who from time immemorial have battened upon the misfortunes of their fellows and have made even the offices of religion the field of their exploitations. Morally and spiritually they have fallen beyond redemption, and this will finally and inevitably lead to their ruin in every respect.

In the message of the third angel we find a new emphasis on the old gospel call for repentance, for it describes the fate of those who do *not* repent—those who share Babylon's apostasy, worshiping the beast and receiving his mark. They "shall drink of the wine of the wrath of God" and "shall be tormented with fire and brimstone...and the smoke of their torment ascendeth up for ever and ever; and they have no rest day nor night" (14:10–11).

If this call to repentance is based on fear to a degree that seems to us extreme, let us recall that this was indeed an insistent note in the evangelism of former years. Perhaps a consideration of the relative ineffectiveness of the evangelism of our own day may suggest the advisability of our enlisting under the banner of this third angel, joining him in the old call to flee from the wrath to come. Here too, so the angelic evangelist assures us, is to be found an effective influence for maintaining "the patience of the saints," those who "keep the commandments of God, and the faith of Jesus" (14:12).

This angel's warning, the most fearful in all the word of God, does not refer to the worshipers of the beast as members of any particular religious organization or as believers in any particular creed. It is for such as are possessed and dominated by the spirit of which the mark of the beast is the supreme token. This is the spirit incarnate in all the old earth-devastating world powers, which with its subtle serpent nature creeps insidiously even into the Church. The "beast" represents, therefore, the archenemy the Church is commissioned to conquer, and it is to those guilty of the supreme treason of harboring his spirit that the third angel utters his hopeless pronouncements of eternal doom.

In contrast to the messages of the three angels, which tell of the Savior's coming as the Mighty Avenger, the message that immediately follows them tells of his coming as the Mighty-to-Save. Brought by a voice from heaven, it is clearly intended to relieve the gloom of these unprecedented pronouncements; and the Church is right in accepting it as a message of consolation for all ages, rather than as a prediction applicable only to the time of the second advent. This is indicated by the fact that the revelator is particularly enjoined to put it in his book, so that through all the Christian centuries it might be seen and read. It presents the other side of the picture, showing the fate of those who do *not* worship the beast, those who have lived in the light of the Savior's ideals and who die trusting in his salvation. Of these the angel says: "Blessed are the dead who die in the Lord." And to this glad reassurance the Holy Spirit hastens to add his confirmation, together with an added note that brings the thought back to the theme in hand—the second-advent work of the Church. They are blessed, he says, in that they are entering into the rest that remains for the people of God,[7] a rest symbolized in Israel's history by the conquest of the Promised Land. They are to enter into that rest, however, without the distresses of a toilsome pilgrimage, for their works are following with them, even now as the time has come for the final ingathering of all the fruits of all labors. That is, they will immediately come

101

into possession of the white robes of their spiritual bodies, made strong by their works. These are the same blessed ones seen when the fifth seal was opened (7:9 ff.), the martyrs who had come "out of great tribulation."

Our Lord's second coming is to be marked by two resurrections. At its beginning will come the resurrection of the just, which we have already noted as represented by the saints making up heaven's choir invisible, and which is further represented in the pronouncement of the voice from heaven. The other, the general resurrection, will be associated with the judgment of the last day of the age (cf. 20:11 ff.), and so it is unmistakably represented here by the two harvest visions that follow the vision of the Lamb on Mount Zion.

The Final Harvest

The harvest vision, like the first theophanic vision of the Apocalypse, employs the initial "sign" of the second advent foretold by the Savior himself—the Son of man coming on the clouds of heaven;[8] and again the archangel Gabriel lends the Savior his celestial figure, the great constellation Boötes. The crown on the Savior's head, represented by Corona Borealis, suggests his second-advent victories (11:15–18; cf. Heb. 2:9), while the sickle, the constellation Ursa Major, is ready for the final harvest of the earth. And the white cloud is Coma Berenices.

At the word of command sent by a heavenly messenger direct from the Father's throne room in heaven, the Savior swung his sickle and "the earth was reaped." All the fruits of the labors of the Savior and his followers, of all creeds and regions through the ages—the souls redeemed, the characters transformed, the personalities refined, the minds developed, the treasures of the heart stored up—all have been kept and matured, and the golden harvest is now gathered into the garner. This vision pictures, of course, the meaning of the Lord's return for his own people, the final salvation of the redeemed.

There is another meaning, however, of the coming of the King of kings, the Judge of all the earth, for the rebels whom he must pronounce guilty, even such as the Savior himself had painted in his parable of the wheat and the tares (Matt. 13:24 ff.). These rebels have refused the salvation he came to purchase, at such great cost, as the Lamb of God that takes away the sin of the world. They have proved themselves to be immovably fixed in their perverse determination to seek their own at the expense of the common good. In the end they would "destroy the earth" (11:18). Their fate is symbolized by the last of the ingatherings of the harvest, that of the vineyard; and we see the righteous judgments visited upon the wicked represented by the cutting of the "vine of the earth" and the treading of the "winepress of the wrath of God," pictured by the constellation Krater. The cutting is done by another archangel, who came out of the heavenly temple holding a sickle. This must be Gabriel's companion Uriel, whose name means "the fire of God." The star assigned to him is Regulus, the bright star of the constellation Leo, the zodiacal "house" of the Sun. (See Appendix 1.) He was directed to use his sickle by an angel messenger "who had power over fire," evidently the herald angel of the Sun, which in St. John's time was counted as one of the "planets." And just under the sickle of Leo, in the trailing vine-like figure of Hydra, a group of its seven brightest stars provides the revelator's symbol of the cluster of grapes ripe for cutting.

In this two-fold harvest vision, then, we see the two-fold nature of the Savior's return. To his true followers, reaped and garnered, he will come as the Mighty-to-Save—as the Shekinah, the divine imminence represented by the white cloud of Coma. To those who reject him, and who are therefore thrown into the winepress of the wrath of God, he will come as the Mighty Avenger, the Lion of the tribe of Judah, represented here by the constellation Leo.

ATONEMENT AND FESTIVAL SYMBOLS

The Third Atonement Ceremonial and the Anticipatory Day of Atonement

Just before the blowing of the trumpets began an angel stood in the antechamber of the sanctuary at the golden altar, and upon it he mingled much incense—a memorial of the Savior's sacrificial death—with the prayers of the saints. And from that altar he took fire and threw it upon the earth to cleanse it (8:3–4). This scene, at the end of the second act, provides the setting needed for the third act's third ceremonial of the Day of Atonement. Its seven-fold sprinklings of sacrificial blood on the golden altar of incense represented earth life's worshipful relations with God. As we have seen, in this apocalyptic drama the

103

first and second ceremonial sprinklings can be interpreted as representing the cleansing of the religious and civil life of the people collectively. This third ceremonial is for the cleansing of the people individually from all the sins of which they have truly repented. In this third act such cleansed and redeemed individuals, those marked by the seal of the living God, play significant roles. It is they who make up the faithful remnant of spiritual Israel, kept safe in the inner sanctuary of the temple while its outer courts were trampled down by "the nations." And it is they who make up the hosts of the Church triumphant and the Church militant, who together sing the "new song" that is to hail the Savior's second advent and the beginning of a new era.

How desperately such individual cleansing and atonement are needed is revealed by the introduction of a special anticipatory day of atonement, the ceremonies of which took place also in the sanctuary's antechamber. Only the spiritual revival and reformation brought about by such at-one-ment with God could make possible the hastened second advent of the Savior and the countervailing of the dreaded third woe.

Rosh Hashanah and the Great Day of Atonement

The great sign in heaven of a woman clothed with the Sun and the Moon under her feet is an unmistakable pictorial representation of the skies of the autumnal equinox. (See Appendix 1.) In St. John's time the autumnal equinoctial "crossing of the line" passed through Virgo, the astral representation of that "woman;" and the associated new Moon, just out of combust and far enough from the Sun to be visible, marked the beginning of the month Tisri. The first day of that month is celebrated as Rosh Hashanah, the New Year day of the Hebrew civil year; and because it is characterized by much sounding of trumpets it is known also as the Feast of Trumpets.

In the days of the ancient Hebrews, however, the autumnal equinox was marked by the constellation Libra, which was the zodiacal representation of the Holy Place, the entrance room of the temple's sanctuary. This was the audience room of Israel's divine King, whose throne room behind the veil in the Holy of Holies was represented by the adjacent constellation Virgo. In this antechamber, the setting of this third act, offerings of incense were made on the golden altar, and here the priest, equipped with the breastplate of judgment, "enquired" of God's judgments by means of the Urim and Thummim (Num. 27:21).

This weighing of evidence and rendering of just judgments is suggested by the name of the constellation Libra, "the balances." The New Year day of the autumnal equinox was therefore thought of also as a Day of Judgment, and it is this aspect of the day that serves as an introduction to the period of penitence ending ten days later with the Great Day of Atonement. As in all the other acts, that great fast day is represented here by one of its ceremonials; but in this act it is represented also in its entirety, this being one of the symbolic functions of the special day of atonement brought by the episode of the little book open.

This element of judgment is very evident in this third act, which is concerned with the accumulated evils and woes inflicted by the hosts of hell, the demon hordes of Antichrist. And the beginning of a new year, a new era, is marked by the great spiritual renewal that makes possible the Savior's hastened return and the judgments of the harvest visions.

NOTES

1. See Exodus 9:23–34, 19:16, 20:18; 1 Samuel 2:10, 7:10, 12:17–18; 2 Samuel 22:14; Amos 1:2; Isaiah 6:8, 29:6, 30:30–31, 66:6; Psalms 18:13, 77:17–18, 81:7; Jeremiah 10:12–16, 51:15–19; and Joel 2:11, 3:16.

2. Cf. Jeremiah 31:39; Ezekiel 40:3, 47:3; and Zechariah 1:16, 2:1 ff.

3. Regarding Elijah and Moses, see respectively 1 Kings 17:1 and Exodus 7:1a.

4. See Jeremiah 2:2; Ezekiel 16:8; Hosea 2:19–20.

5. See 1 Corinthians 15:51–52; 1 Thessalonians 4:13–18.

6. See Numbers 25:1 ff. and 31:16; Revelation 2:14 ff.

7. See Hebrews 4:9; cf. Psalm 95:1.

8. See Matthew 24:30; Mark 13:26–27.

IV. THE SEVEN BOWLS OF THE WRATH OF GOD

Act 4. The Derashoth—Expositions of the Haphtaroth

The Church Triumphant in the Heavenly Temple

The Bowls of the Wrath of God
   Divine Retribution
   The Bowl Oracles: The Derashoth of the Worship Drama
   The Symbolisms of the Bowls

The Second Advent: The End of the Old Age
   Babylon, the Great Harlot, and Her Fall
   Songs of Victory
   The King of Kings and Lord of Lords
   The Great Day of God Almighty

The Millennium: The Beginning of the New Age
   A Time of Transition
   The Final Conquest of Evil
   The Last Judgment

The New Jerusalem, the Bride of the Lamb: The
Consummation of the New Age
   Cosmological Symbolisms
   The New Jerusalem's Promise

Atonement and Festival Symbolisms
   The Day of Atonement: The Ceremony of the Scapegoat
   The Autumnal Festival: Full Ingatherings and
     Tabernacles

IV. THE SEVEN BOWLS OF THE WRATH OF GOD

Act 4. The Derashoth—Expositions of the Haphtaroth (Rev. 15–22)

THE CHURCH TRIUMPHANT IN THE HEAVENLY TEMPLE

Throughout this fourth act there are numerous spontaneous testimonies and extra-ritual revelations, as was the custom in the early Christian synagogue, and one of these introduces the act.

After a brief but emphatic notice of the coming vision of the bowls of wrath, the revelator turns aside abruptly and sets before us a picture of the Church triumphant, those who "had gotten the victory" over the beast, his image, and his mark. These were the martyrs who, in response to their plea, were given white robes (6:11; cf. 7:13–17), spiritual bodies that enabled them to enter fully into the activities of heaven. Here, therefore, we find them singing the song of final triumph, for they have arrived at the goal of human destiny. They make up the heavenly choir that was heard but not seen in Act 3; and accompanied by harps of God they sing the song of Moses and the Lamb, extolling the righteousness of God (15:2–4).

These heavenly singers are seen beside a sea of glass, represented in the heavens by the hourglass figure of Cygnus, which suggests the temple's great "sea" or laver and its pedestal. In the glass there is also the appearance of fire. Thus it is evidently a composite picture of Israel of old, who escaped across the Red Sea with its waters like glass ("congealed," in Exodus 15:8), and of the Hebrew children who passed safely through the fiery furnace (Daniel 3:25).

By these symbols we are reminded of the wickedness of Pharaoh and Nebuchadnezzer, archenemies of God's people and examples of all the tyrants of the world, all of whom are incarnations of the evil spirit represented by the mark of the beast. Until the world has been purged of all these incorrigible Egypts and Babylons it cannot be made safe for the commonwealth of Israel—for righteousness, lovingkindness, gentleness; and these singing saints, many of them martyrs in the extreme sense of the term, are indeed witnesses to that fact.

Included in this vision of martyrs, we must conclude, are not only those whose cry was heard from under the altar when the fifth seal was opened but "their fellow servants also and their brethren, that should be killed as they were" and for whom they were to wait (6:9–11). The seer is shown the whole glorious company of the martyrs of all ages, whose blood demands and is to receive vengeance. Similarly, just retribution is not to fall only upon the final generation of evil men, worthy heirs though they may be of those who killed the prophets. No, it is to be meted out to all the persecutors and murderers of successive generations.

Here, therefore, in this vision of the martyr throng standing beside the "sea of glass mingled with fire," we see the ground for the unreserved condemnation and unmitigated punishment poured forth from the bowls of God's wrath.

THE BOWLS OF THE WRATH OF GOD

After the song of the Church triumphant, "the temple of the tabernacle of the testimony in heaven was opened" (15:5); and from it came forth the seven angels who are to receive and pour out on the earth the bowls of the wrath of God, the "seven last plagues." They are arrayed in priestly vestments and wear the ephod of the high priest.

Divine Retribution

The "testimony" thus referred to is the broken law. After the first tables of the law, written by the finger of God on Mount Sinai, had been broken, new ones were written and placed in the ark of the covenant under the mercy seat.[1] These new tables were therefore a testimony against Israel, a testimony covered up by the mercy seat, on which stood the cherubic symbols of the divine government of the world. There it was to remain, covered and unremembered, as long as the mercy seat was sprinkled with the blood of the atonement. This could be done effectively, however, only as the concomitant of true repentance. But as the seven angelic priests come forth from the sanctuary, the Holy of Holies where the testimony was kept, bowls of the wine of the wrath of God are given them, in token of the fact that where no atonement for the broken law has been made, where there is no repentance, the outpouring of the wrath of divine justice must follow.

The oracles of the seven-sealed book, the seven trumpets, and the seven bowls of the wrath of God all picture such divine retribution and the spiritual consequences of good and evil. Retribution follows hard upon the heels of evil, not only as a natural consequence of overt deeds but also in proportion to the moral and spiritual guilt involved, and we see the final doom of all the ungodly and unsaved. On the other hand, we see also that righteousness will finally triumph, and in the end the meek will indeed inherit the earth.

In these three sets of oracles, however, the pictures of divine retribution are progressive. When the sixth seal is broken, the visitations of wrath are represented as foreshadowed both in the foreboding heart of nature and in the guilty conscience of humans; but the Judge himself makes no pronouncement. There is merely the finding of the jury, and no sanctions of any law are brought to bear. Under the soundings of the trumpets the penalties inflicted are those demanded by disobedience to the law of natural religion. The bowls of God's wrath, however, are poured out because of sin against the full light of the Gospel, sin that involves the deliberate crucifixion of the Lord anew. The astral figure of the living creature who gave the angels the bowls of the wrath of God must therefore be the constellation Scorpio, the supreme symbol of divine retribution.

The Bowl Oracles: The Derashoth of the Worship Drama

In the third act we have seen the plagues and woes of the trumpet oracles summoning Christendom more and more insistently to the repentance that will make possible the hastening of the Savior's second advent. Now in the fourth act these trumpet oracles, along with the readings of the sealed book, are expounded by the bowl oracles, which form the derashoth or sermons of the Apocalyptic worship drama.

These bowl oracles provide seven further forewarnings setting

111

forth the pronouncements of divine justice concerning the inevitable consequences of refusal to learn the lessons of those chastenings of divine mercy—of refusal to heed their calls to repentance. Note, however, that though the need is urgent the penalty is not to be visited immediately and irretrievably upon these unrepentant sinners. The angelic priests, who could not pour atoning blood upon the mercy seat because there was no repentance, received from the heavenly cherub not one great mixing bowl but only little bowls of divine wrath, seven of them, the all-sufficient number. (See Appendix 4.) These are to be poured out one by one in order that, if possible, erring humans might yet be led by these chastisements to repent of their sins and follies.

Among the apostates upon whom these bowls of God's wrath are poured we see those who have bestowed the Lord's worship and authority upon an Antichrist, for they "had the mark of the beast" and "worshiped his image." There are those also who "shed the blood of saints and prophets" in an effort to exterminate the Lord's true disciples, and those who "blasphemed the name of God" and "repented not." (These are named in the first, third, fourth, and fifth oracles, 16:2,6,9,11.) This same unrepentant heart is suggested also by the analogy of Pharaoh's hardness of heart, for the "sores" of the first oracle, the water turned to blood in the second and third, and the "darkness" of the fifth clearly allude to the similar plagues visited upon Egypt.[2]

For the offenses against which these bowls are poured, there can be no excuse. Justification for God's wrath, and for the final exaction of the full penalty of the broken law, is voiced by the angel of the waters on which the third bowl was poured: "Thou art righteous, O Lord, which art, and wast, and shalt be, because thou hast judged thus." And a voice from the altar agreed, saying: "Even so, Lord God Almighty, true and righteous are thy judgments" (16:5–7).

The fifth bowl is poured out upon the very throne of apostasy, the "seat of the beast," and in the later section on the fall of Babylon we shall see this to be the constellation Corvus, throne of that great harlot. The sixth dries up the great river Euphrates, symbol of the influence of that same harlot over the minds of the people; for the many waters of that great river, represented by the constellation Hydra, are later (17:15) identified as "peoples, and multitudes, and nations, and tongues"—vast

112

populations that acknowledged the harlot's absolute authority. The drying up of her influence prepares the way for the coming of "the kings of the east," the conquering hosts of the King of kings and Lord of lords, with their promise of the sunrise of a new day.

Finally, after the pouring out of that sixth bowl, the apostates, far from repenting, listen still further to the emissaries of the trinity of evil (the dragon, the beast, and the false prophet), and gather themselves together to make war against the King of kings. Thus, by their challenge, they bring upon themselves the irretrievable and utter destruction that is to come in the final war of the "great day of God Almighty," the battle of Armageddon.

In the midst of his account of the preparations for that great battle, the revelator pauses to let us hear the unannounced proclamation: "Behold, I come as a thief. Blessed is he that watcheth, and keepeth his garments, lest he walk naked, and they see his shame" (16:15). That is, beware lest you have no spiritual body, no spiritual white robes made of your own righteous acts, wherewith to meet the Lord and the hosts of the Church of the firstfruits "in the air"—that is, in the spiritual realm—and so be left outside when the Bridegroom comes, like the five foolish virgins who had no oil for their lamps.

When the seventh bowl had been poured out, "there came a great voice out of the temple of heaven, from the throne, saying, It is done" (16:17). The pronouncement of the Judge had been made. And the picture of mighty convulsions that follows indicates the last judgment, which is set forth more fully later (20:11 ff.). The testimony of the broken law could no longer remain covered under the mercy seat.

The Symbolisms of the Bowls

In the bowls of the wine of the wrath of God two symbolisms can be recognized, that of the vintage and that of the scapegoat.

In the vintage symbolism that ends the third act, the vine of the earth is cast into the winepress of the wrath of God. It is obviously as a sequel to that vision that these bowls of God's wrath foretell the final woes that are to come upon the wicked world, the retributions that sin brings on those who will not repent. And this vintage symbolism is recalled after the pouring of the seventh bowl. There we find Babylon, the supreme exam-

113

ple of apostate offending, remembered in God's sight, "to give unto her the cup of the wine of the fierceness of his wrath" (16:19).

Note that the penalty is not to be visited immediately and irretrievably upon God's unrepentant sinners. The angelic priests, who could not pour atoning blood upon the mercy seat, received from the heavenly cherub not one great mixing bowl but only little bowls of divine wrath, seven of them, the all-sufficient number. (See Appendix 4.) These are to be poured out one by one in order that, if possible, erring humans might yet be led by these chastisements to repent of their sins and follies.

There are, however, perverse iniquities in human life that neither the persuasions of the Gospel nor the chastisements of Providence can correct. Those guilty of such iniquities are incorrigible. They will not repent, and on them the final visitation of wrath is promised. The only salvation is the coming of the Mighty One himself, in accordance with the prophecies of his two witnesses, to cast the beast and the false prophet into the lake of fire and to imprison the old serpent himself in the bottomless pit (19:20; 20:3). Only then will the rest be "affrighted" and give "glory to the God of heaven" (11:13), and the authority of the Judge Eternal over human minds will be restored.

The emphasis of the bowl oracles on such unrepentant hardness of heart suggests the scapegoat ceremonial, described fully in the last section of this act. Upon the scapegoat's head were placed all the sins of Israel, and it was turned out to wander in the desert to its own destruction, as the embodiment of sin, a symbol of that for which there is no atonement. So also is there no atonement for the victims on whom God's wrath is poured, for they will not repent. Like the scapegoat they will go to their own destruction, self-offered sacrifices to their own false god, the world, to whose lusts they have already devoted themselves.

The pouring out of the bowls of wrath is followed by a survey both of the evils it is necessary to destroy and the ultimate and glorious excellence these judgments will enable earth life to attain. The findings are summed up in the two contrasting pictures shown to the revelator by two of the bowl angels—on the one hand the apostate Church, symbolized by Babylon, the great harlot (17:1 ff.), the persecutor and would-be supplanter of the Bride of the Lamb; and on the other hand that Bride herself, the New Jerusalem (21:2 ff.). These two symbolic cities represent respectively the end of the old age and the consummation of the promised new age.

THE SECOND ADVENT: THE END OF THE OLD AGE

Chapters 17–19 of the Apocalypse provide elaborations of the oracles of the sixth and seventh bowl angels, which tell of the end of the age. The revelator has already presented, in Act 3, the general outline of the dragon's warfare against the "woman," the symbol of the Church of the centuries, and of her fleeing from his wrath "into the wilderness" (12:14). It was against this Church in the wilderness that he then sent forth his destroying floods; and it was against the rest of her seed (12:17), those who had escaped these floods, that he sent the two beasts, fearful emissaries of his wrath, described in the thirteenth chapter. And we have seen the dragon's triumph over the Church and the wrath to be poured out upon him, in all his manifestations, in his final defeat when the crucified Lamb of God returns in glory. Here, in Act 4, we have a fuller account of the supreme crisis in that campaign and of the Redeemer's victory over the great draconian oppressors of his Church in the battle of the Great Day of Jehovah. First, however, there is a close-up view of Babylon the great, symbol of the wickedness upon which sentence is now to be passed, and a prophecy of the doom that is to lay her waste. This view (chapters 17 and 18) is essential to a full understanding of the visions of the Word of God, the King of kings and Judge of all the earth (chapters 19 and 20), for Babylon is the great usurper that must be dispossessed to make way for the coming of the New Jerusalem.

Babylon, the Great Harlot, and Her Fall

One of the bowl angels now carries the revelator away into the wilderness to see "the judgment of the great whore that sitteth upon many waters"; and when he saw her, a woman sitting on a scarlet beast, he marveled greatly (17:1–6). In astral figures the scarlet beast can be pictured as the constellation Hydra, one of several celestial representations of the old serpent. On its back, forming a seat for the woman, the great whore or harlot, is the little constellation Corvus.

This vision of the beast-enthroned harlot thus represents the mutually debauching union of the apostate Church and the pervert State. To understand the symbolism here we must recall the two beasts of Act 3. As we have seen there, the first of these represents the State persecuting the Church and setting itself up as an Antichrist, to be worshiped in place of Christ. The scarlet beast of this fourth act is clearly to be identified with this first beast, for both have seven heads and ten horns (13:1 and 17:3). The second beast, the one with "two horns like a lamb" (13:11), represents the Church become apostate, led astray by the evils of the heathen world around it and causing men to worship the first beast—a seeming triumph of the dragon over the Church. In apocalyptic and prophetic symbolism apostasy is always represented by harlotry;[3] and so it is evident that the third act's second beast, the symbol of apostate religion, is pictured here by Babylon the great, the great harlot (17:1). This identification is indicated also by the way in which the vision was revealed to St. John; for to see it he was carried "into the wilderness," the place to which the "woman," symbol of the Church, had fled from the dragon. And in this identification we find the reason for St. John's great amazement when he saw her—so familiar, so like the true Church, but so sadly different in character.

Babylon the great represents, therefore, the most dangerous of all the great enemies of the Church, the enemy within. Fearful and unalleviated condemnations are pronounced against her. These consist of three parts—the indictment (18:1–3), the pronouncement of judgment and the sentencing (18:4–20), and the symbolic execution of the sentence (18:21–24).

To deliver the indictment against Babylon, an angel came "down from heaven, having great power," so that "the earth was lightened with his glory" (18:1). He may be thought of as heaven's prosecuting attorney, and the charge he brings against Babylon is that she has become irremediably evil—she has "fallen." This declaration is no mere proleptic prophecy of the great city's fall into physical ruin, but a forensic plea charging her with a moral and spiritual fall. As evidence of this meaning there is a further charge that this fall of the great harlot has by its spiritual contamination caused also the fall, again clearly moral and spiritual, of all the nations of the earth. Thus the harlot is far worse than an ordinary wanton. As Babylon of old was the mother of the sorcerers of the east, so this later and greater

116

and far more guilty Babylon is "the mother of harlots and abominations of the earth" (17:5). "All nations have drunk of the wine of the wrath of her fornication, and the kings of the earth have committed fornication with her, and the merchants of the earth are waxed rich" by the power of her wantonness (18:3).

The judgment is now pronounced upon her by a "voice from heaven"—clearly the voice of the Divine Judge himself—which prefaces its words of doom with an exhortation to all God's true people to "come out of her" that they "be not partakers of her sins," and that they "receive not of her plagues" (v. 4). She is then declared guilty as charged, "for her sins have reached unto heaven," and although she confidently expected not to "see...sorrow" because she sat as a queen, nevertheless her complete destruction is decreed. It is to come all at once, "in one day," and it is to be meted out in accordance with her evil deeds, not only measure for measure but even in double recompense (vs. 6–8).

Following the announcement of these judgments against the harlot, there are lamentations by all her former paramours, and by the merchants and mariners who had profited by catering to her excesses (vs. 9–19). In heaven, however, there is a call to those who have suffered so much from her, saints and apostles and prophets, a call to rejoice, for they are avenged. God has given judgment against the great whore (19:1–2).

Full execution of the sentence of destruction is presented later, in the description of the battle of Armageddon on the great day of God the Almighty, but a symbolic picture of it is given here, immediately following the judgment scene. "A mighty angel took up a stone like a great millstone, and cast it into the sea, saying, Thus with violence shall that great city Babylon be thrown down, and shall be found no more at all" (18:21). And the hopelessness of her doom, complete and eternal, is emphasized by the listing of all the activities that are to cease: there shall be no more harpers and minstrels and flute players and trumpeters, no craftsmen, no sound of a millstone, no light of a lamp, no voice of the bridegroom and bride (vs. 22–24).

In conclusion, the justice of the judgment is indicated. By her "sorceries were all nations deceived. And in her was found the blood of prophets, and of saints, and of all that were slain upon the earth" (18:23b–24). She was the consummate incarnation of the great dragon that has cursed the world from the beginning of time.

Songs of Victory

Throughout the Apocalypse the songs of the heavenly choirs have given continual assurance of the final victory over evil, and at this point there are two mighty hallelujah choruses of this kind. The first is a spontaneous outburst of joy by the choirs of heaven, praising God for the final deliverance of the earth from the evil works of the harlot (19:1–4). The second is an exultant anticipation of the "marriage of the Lamb," the imminence of which was made certain by the fact that his bride—the Church, no longer misguided and divided by an apostate hierarchy—had "made herself ready," and she was to be "arrayed in fine linen, clean and white" (19:5–8). Here we see recognition of the two aspects of the Lord's second advent. The evil system that had enslaved God's true people has been completely overthrown by the Savior in his role as the Mighty Avenger; and this has made room for a new social order, a new and better world, under the Savior's leadership as the Mighty-To-Save.

The King of Kings and Lord of Lords

After these songs of victory comes the vision of the Savior's return as King of kings and Lord of lords, the seventh bowl angel's exposition of the seventh trumpet's vision of the Lamb-Lion in the midst of the Church militant on Mount Zion. Seated on a white horse, and armed with the sword of the mouth and a rod of iron, this King, whose name is the Word of God, rides forth to final victory over the wrongs of earth life. In the apocalypse of the stars this is the glorious figure of Sagittarius, the celestial horseman, and he follows the Milky Way, the shining way that leads from heaven to earth, on down to the zodiacal gateway of Capricornus, through which all who descend from heaven must pass in order to come forth upon the earth.

Following the King, also on white horses, are the hosts of heaven, the white-robed martyrs whom we saw first in the second act, at the opening of the fifth seal (6:11); and at that time we were told that these saints had "washed their robes, and made them white in the blood of the Lamb" (7:14). Now we learn that the substance of the clean white linen in which they are arrayed, which represents their glorious resurrection bodies, is made of their good works, for "the fine linen is the righteous acts of the saints" (19:8 AST). This was revealed earlier also by the

Holy Spirit, who said of the blessed dead who die in the Lord that "their works do follow them" (14:13). Here, then, we find faith and works in their true relationship. The white robes of heaven will be garments made by good works during the life on earth, and worn and stained there; but through faith in the work of our Redeemer they will be washed and made white in the blood of the Lamb.

This King on a white horse followed by the armies of heaven is the figure that was imitated in inverted form by the four horsemen of Act 2, who were followed by the hosts that came up from hell. And in Act 3 it is imitated by the beast from the sea, the Antichrist who attempted to displace Christ as ruler of the world. Now the forces of Antichrist are to be faced and overcome by the hosts of heaven, riding forth with their King.

The two weapons of this King and his heavenly army are the sword of the mouth and the rod of iron that breaks the heathen enemy nations as a vessel of the potter is broken. In this world these represent the only possible means of conquering.

The sword of the mouth, the sword of truth, is the really constructive weapon, for it destroys error in the mind and allows the truth of the Gospel to be established there. Would that it were possible for the proclamation of the Gospel to make the world what it ought to be! But the Bible gives us to understand that some people refuse to be converted. The divine intervention for our salvation offers a way of escape from sin and death, but it cannot compel its acceptance. Each person is sovereign over his own life, and God, the Almighty and All-wise, cannot invade that personal sovereignty. He allows every human being, created in his likeness, to decide for himself, for if we were good only because God forced us to be, we would be nothing but sponges and oysters, instead of personalities sharing the divine nature.

As we have noted, however, some persons will not choose the Savior as their King. It is upon such sin against the light that the bowls of wrath are poured out by the angels of the heavenly altar. And against such hopelessly perverse neglect and rejection of the great salvation the other weapon must be used, the rod of iron that will destroy the wrong. Its purpose is not to dictate to the minds and hearts of the incorrigibly unconverted and unrepentant to make them good, but to keep them from dictating to the rest of the world and overwhelming it with their evil. They that would destroy the world must themselves be destroyed.

119

It was this weapon, the rod of iron, that Jesus used when, foreshadowing the last great battle, he drove the malefactors out from the temple after his triumphant entry into Jerusalem. And he has been continuing this fight ever since through his Church, whenever it lifts up its voice and hands against wrong. It is through his Church, too, that he has continued to use the sword of the mouth. And the fight must go on, using both weapons, until the King of kings finishes the last battle, which we see now in the Apocalypse, in a vision that looks into the future further than human eye can see.

The Great Day of God Almighty

A foreglimpse of the consummation pictured in this vision of the King of kings is found in the letter to the church in Thyatira, with its promise of the "rod of iron" (2:27). So also the enigmatic promise of the "morning star" in the next verse finds its fulfillment in the omens of final and sweeping triumph set forth in the proclamation of "an angel standing in the sun" (19:17–18). The planet Mercury, often the morning star and the herald of all the mythologies, furnishes the only possible and altogether harmonious interpretation of this angelic herald. And seen also in the early morning sky are Aquila, the "eagle," and Cygnus, the "swan," which represent "the fowls that fly in the midst of heaven," the guests that the angel invites to "the supper of the great God."

The great battle that follows is called also "the marriage supper of the Lamb" (19:9), the great battle of Armageddon (16:16), and the "great day of God Almighty" (16:14).

The "day of Jehovah" is the prophetic equivalent of the flood, the no longer permissible figure employed in the cosmogonic apocalypse of the Torah's prologue (Gen. 9:8–17) to represent the cleansing judgments of Providence. The course of history is seen, not as a continuum, but as a succession of changes, just as the Savior noted in one of his parables of the growth of the kingdom: "First the blade, then the ear, after that the full corn in the ear" (Mark 4:28). But unlike those stages in the development of the full corn, the changes in our sin-cursed world must sometimes be remedial. In the social life of our fallen humanity so many things go wrong that progress is made possible only by repeated visitations of the day of Jehovah—cataclysmic crises and destructive revolutions that sweep away society's old incrustations and thwarting evils, allowing hidden ideals and aspirations and purposes to flower.

In the Old Testament the prophets noted successive crises of this sort, and always they looked forward to a last great day of Jehovah, a "day of wrath" (Zeph. 1:15) that will "burn as an oven" (Mal. 4:1). Its cleansing, by fire instead of water, would be so thoroughly effective that it would be followed by the glad consummation for which the ages have been longing, when "the wolf...shall dwell with the lamb...the calf and the young lion and the fatling together" and when "the earth shall be full of the knowledge of the Lord, as the waters cover the sea" (Isa. 11:6–9).

In St. John's picture of that last great battle we see the final visitation of the wrath of the Lamb upon the great harlot and all her company. The forces of Antichrist are faced by the Word of God, the King on his white horse, followed by the white-robed hosts of the Church triumphant. And the beast and the false prophet are taken and cast into the "lake of fire burning with brimstone." And the rest "were slain with the sword of him that sat upon the horse," the sword that came forth "out of his mouth" (19:20–21); and "he laid hold on the dragon, that old serpent, which is the Devil, and Satan, and bound him a thousand years, and cast him into the bottomless pit, and shut him up" and sealed him in, "that he should deceive the nations no more, till the thousand years should be fulfilled" (20:2–3). Thus is enacted the second promise of the Protevangel. He who came first as the Paschal Lamb, whose heel was bruised by the serpent, will come again as the Lion of the tribe of Judah, to crush the serpent's head. In the heavens this is represented by Ophiucus, interpreted as a mighty man struggling with Serpens, the symbol of Satan. One of the hero's feet has been hurt, and the other is poised ready to crush the serpent's head. This picture of Ophiucus and Serpens is the companion piece and complement of the great picture of Heracles and Draco. (See the second act.)

Here we see the work of the Redeemer as the Mighty Avenger of the great day of Jehovah, destroying all the evils that would otherwise destroy the earth and make impossible the establishment of his kingdom of righteousness. He must be the Mighty Avenger in order to be the Mighty-to-Save. The symbolism with which this work of destruction is pictured is naturally that of the most terrible warfare; but when we come to consider it closely we discover that in reality it is a warfare of truth against error. The law of sin and death, represented by the dire tribulations of the third woe, will be countervailed by the law of the life-giving spirit of holiness in Christ Jesus.

THE MILLENNIUM: THE BEGINNING OF THE NEW AGE

The second-advent presence of the King of kings and his victory over the forces of Antichrist in the great battle of Armageddon mark the beginning of a new dispensation in which, under the leadership of the Savior as the Mighty-to-Save, heaven and earth are to be reunited. Its first phase, the millennial imprisonment of Satan, will end with his final overthrow and the last judgment. Then the King of kings will usher in the new earth seen in the vision of the New Jerusalem.

Like all other time units in St. John's Revelation, the thousand years of the millennium must of course be taken symbolically rather than literally. This number must be evaluated in the light of the relative aspect of time to which St. Peter called our attention when he noted that "one day is with the Lord as a thousand years, and a thousand years as one day" (2 Peter 3:8).

This symbolic period must therefore be conceived as representing not a mere literal duration of time but rather a period of progress. The millennium will be the beginning of a new era, the second advent of the Savior, in which he will serve both as the King of kings and the great Judge of all the earth. Although it is often spoken of as the consummation of human development it will not be that, for it will be marked by many lingering reminders of the old era. It will instead be a time of transition toward that consummation of our social salvation—the cleansing and reorganization of our social life—that is to bring about a new world "wherein dwelleth righteousness" (2 Peter 3:13). It is toward that end that the Savior will serve as Judge, separating the good from the evil, and as King, leading the forces of good in the final overthrow of Satan and the establishment of his own earthly kingdom of righteousness and peace, pictured in the vision of the New Jerusalem. This will begin with the great battle of Armageddon, which will imprison Satan for a thousand years. Then, during those years that are unvexed by the exploitations of the old serpent, there will be the peaceful developments of the millennial reign of Christ and the saints of the first resurrection. And the final gloriously triumphant campaign at the end of the millennium will deliver the whole earth from the blighting dominance of the old enemy.

Special attention must therefore be given to the millennium as **a time of transition**, and to **the final conquest of evil** and **the last judgment** that will mark its close.

A Time of Transition

The outstanding feature of the coming age, of which the millennium will be the first period, will be the second-advent presence of the Savior in the midst of the Church militant. This will be a spiritual presence of full-harvest rather than Pentecostal power, in which he is accompanied by the saints of the Church triumphant. In the corresponding trumpet oracle with its vision of the Lamb on Mount Zion, the glorified Redeemer is represented by a symbol, and the saints of the first resurrection are a choir invisible. The present vision, however, is conceived on the plane of the natural and literal; and so the glorified Redeemer is not seen even in symbolic form. Nevertheless, his presence is not only implied by reference to it, but is specifically indicated by the name given to the holy city of this period, a city that is in the process of becoming the New Jerusalem. Here it is called the "beloved city"—clearly an allusion to the only occurrence of the term in earlier Hebrew sacred literature, its use by the son of Sirach in his personification of wisdom (Sirach 24:11). There wisdom, which thus personified has always been accepted as the *Logos*, the Word of God, is represented as finding in the "beloved city" his long-sought rest, his final dwelling place among the children of men.

It must not be thought, however, that the Savior, returning as King of kings, will sit in person on a throne and rule. Instead, he will rule through his people of the Church militant and the Church triumphant. It is through a declaration concerning the latter that the nature of the millennium's social organization is revealed. These saints of the first resurrection, those who have not worshiped the beast or received his mark, are to be "priests of God and of Christ and shall reign with him a thousand years" (20:6). Clearly these are the "overcomers" to whom the Savior promised that honor in the fourth and seventh of the apocalyptic letters to the churches. They will not be royal presences that ordinary earth life can recognize but will be "souls," clothed in the white robes of their spiritual bodies and therefore altogether invisible to mortal eyes.

The revelator naturally stresses the presence of these psychic hosts of the good of all generations, but he does not fail to indicate the presence also of the saints of the Church militant who are still in the flesh. They are the 144,000 with the Lamb on Mount Zion, who will be watching and waiting, mobilized and ready to greet the Lord when he comes (14:1). To the physical eye of the world, the governance of its peoples and the protection of the beloved city against the forces of Gog and Magog will still be carried on by human beings in the flesh. Only the discerning eye of spiritual vision will be able to see their psychic fellow workers and mentors.

To the world at large, therefore, the second coming of the Redeemer will be manifested through his Church, which will be his appointed agent. Its members will be the kings of whom he is King, the lords of whom he is Lord. It will be their hands that are to wield in his name the rod of iron with which he will rule the nations (21:26–27); and in their priestly function it will be through their voice that the sword of the mouth will "smite the nations" (19:15). Like the unseen saints of the Church triumphant, the members of the Church militant will each be a sovereign and a priest in his own right; but in this commonwealth of priest-kings, a true unity of Church and State, each will be utterly dependent upon the great High Priest after the order of Melchizedek and utterly devoted to him as King of kings.

To the Church itself the millennial kingdom of Christ and his saints will be a time of intense and growing spirituality, marked by a seven-fold or full and supreme enduement of the Holy Spirit that will make the baptism of Pentecost seem as only the firstfruits. In the figurative words of St. Paul (1 Thes. 4:17), the members of the Church militant will be "caught up" to meet the returning Lord and the saints of the Church triumphant "in the air." That is, they will enter more and more fully into the realm of the spirit. Thus this "rapture" of the saints cannot be interpreted as meaning that they will be removed from the earth, from the Church militant. Rather it must mean that, because of their increasing spirituality, they will become a link between earth and heaven—between the seen and the unseen, the natural and the supernatural. During the millennial transition these two worlds will be drawn closer together as the Savior establishes his kingdom on earth more and more firmly and widely, and with the elimination of evil that kingdom will finally become world-wide. The veil between earth and heaven will be broken through and there will be a new earth, an earth reunited with heaven.

The Final Conquest of Evil

The conception presented here of the relation of the Church militant to the millennial kingdom of our Lord and to the Church triumphant limits that kingdom and its social progress to Christendom. The Master himself specifically indicated that his coming in his second advent as King of kings was not to wait until all the nations of the earth had become nominally Christian, but only until they had all been evangelized (Matt. 24:14). And so at the end of the millennium there will still remain, evangelized indeed but worse than unchristianized, the "nations which are in the four quarters of the earth, Gog and Magog." And Satan, released from his thousand-year imprisonment, is seen leading them in battle against "the camp of the saints" and the "beloved city." We are assured, however, that under millennial conditions swift and final retribution will overtake this recrudescence of the old leaven of unrighteousness (20:7–10). At first glance that would seem to mean complete annihilation of the hosts of Gog and Magog, for they are to be "devoured" by "fire from God out of heaven." Surely, however, we must consider this as an example of extreme apocalyptic hyperbole that is really an emphatic metonymy. It must mean, therefore, not the complete elimination of these numberless hosts but rather the complete eradication from their hearts and minds of the ideology of the dragon, leaving them easy converts to the teachings of millennial Christendom—the Church militant, with its increased spiritual power, led by the King of kings and reinforced by the Church triumphant. We must conclude, therefore, that when Christendom becomes what it ought to be, it will not be long in winning much of the rest of the world. For Satan, however, and those who will persist in following him, the end will be complete elimination for they will be cast into the lake of fire and brimstone, as the beast and the false prophet had been.

The word here translated as "lake" may be accepted as mean-

125

ing originally a salt lake or marsh left by the sea. Accordingly, in the cosmological symbolism of the Apocalypse it suggests some outlying remnant of the great deep of the primal chaos, one that will still remain somewhere in the void beyond the bounds of the final cosmos. This etymological interpretation of the lake of fire agrees also with the revelator's references to it as existing somewhere outside the otherwise finally all-inclusive city of God, the New Jerusalem (21:18; 22:15).

The Last Judgment

The final destruction of Satan is followed by the vision of the last judgment before the great white throne (20:11–18), represented in the heavens by the zodiacal constellation Libra, the "balances" of the unseen Judge of all the earth. The ancient Egyptians called this constellation the "mountain of the Sun," while in the old Euphratean cultures the month associated with it was called "the month of the resplendent mound." It is in accordance with these ancient interpretations that St. John beheld it as a great throne.

Before that throne appear all the dead, not only the great and the small but also the good and the evil—the "sheep and goats" of the Master's parable of the last judgment (Matt. 25:32–33). Judgment is to be based on two opened books, the one in which the "works" of the dead have been written, and "another book...which is the book of life" (20:12). As St. Paul states it, on the basis of the first book, which records what each person has done, judgment is to come "upon all men to condemnation" (Rom. 5:18), for we are all debtors, unprofitable servants. "All have sinned, and come short of the glory of God," the divine likeness that is the pattern of our creation. If any are "justified" it is only "through the redemption that is in Christ Jesus" (Rom. 3:23–24). That is, all who have accepted that redemption and have become new creatures in him will have their names written also in that other book, which is elsewhere called "the book of life of the Lamb slain from the foundation of the world" (13:8; cf. 3:5, 17:8). Their debts, recorded in the first book, are now covered, blotted out, through his blood, and they have opened up new accounts in which they are accepted on the credit of the Savior and on the promise of their new purpose.

That our destiny is thus to be determined in this life is indicated also by the order in which the vision marshals the dead (and the living) before the great white throne: "And the sea gave up the dead which were in it; and death and hell delivered up the dead which were in them" (20:13). The abodes from which these three great companies come suggest that they are respectively (1) the righteous dead of the ages; (2) the contemporary generation living on the earth, both the good and the evil, whom physical death must release from his dominion; and (3) the wicked dead of the ages.

The first of these three identifications has been obscured by failure to realize that the sea here equated with death and hell cannot be the material sea, which the Apocalypse properly equates with heaven and earth in the ancient three-fold division of the cosmos. We must look for an apocalyptic sea of the same symbolic order as death and hell; and we find it in "the sea of glass like unto crystal" that St. John saw before the throne in his vision of the heavenly temple (4:6). It was by this "sea," the laver of the temple, that he always saw and heard the saints of the Church triumphant waiting in their heavenly abode for the consummation (7:9–17). They were the choirs of heaven (14:2–3; 15:2–4; 19:1–8); they were the white-robed hosts riding with the King of kings and Lord of lords in the great battle of Armageddon (19:14); and they are the blessed ones of the first resurrection at the beginning of the millennium—the martyrs and all those who have not worshiped the beast and who do not have his mark (20:4–6). It is they who, upon their resurrection, represent the final full harvest of which the resurrected Savior is the firstfruits, the wave sheaf. To these saints of the ages must be added those of the contemporary generation whose names are written in the book of life. It is evident, then, that the sea or laver of St. John's astral picture of the heavenly temple is his apocalyptic representation of the "mansions" or "abiding places" of the Heavenly Father's house (John 14:2) in which the souls of the righteous are to rest in God's keeping until the resurrection.

While the resurrection of these saints is described at the beginning of the millennial period, it is evident that they too must have stood before the great white throne that is pictured in the final scene, and judgment must therefore be construed as extending through the entire period of the millennium. Not until the end, however, do we learn the fate of those others, the still wicked former denizens of death and hell who have rejected the great salvation. Upon these hopelessly perverse ones the King of righteousness, coming in his "lion" advent, visits the death penalty. They are cast into the "lake of fire," the "second death," because they were "not found written in the book of life" (20:14–15). These two distinct phases of judgment, of the righteous saints at the beginning of the millennium and the unrepentant wicked at the end, are pictured in the two distinct judgment visions of the seventh trumpet, and there the continuity of the process is obvious. Between the early summer reaping of the wheat harvest (14:14–16) and the fall cutting of the grapes, which were cast into the winepress of the wrath of God (14:17–20), there would be a succession of other harvests throughout the summer. The so-called first and second resurrections are therefore not two distinct transactions with an age-long void between them, but rather the two extremities of a continuous process, beginning with the resurrection and judgment of those whose full and unequivocal acceptance of the offer of salvation made possible their own full acceptance at the beginning of the Lord's parousia, and ending with the resurrection and judgment of those whose contumacious rejection of salvation made them hopeless.

It is not only individuals that are to be judged, however, but earth life as a whole, when the Word of God sits as the Judge inexorable for the final adjudication. Both the majesty of his appearance and the effect of his judgment are represented by the apocalyptist when he says that from his face "the earth and the heaven fled away; and there was found no place for them" (20:11).

It is evident that we have here not a literal statement concerning the physical world but a symbolic representation of the profound significance of the events being foreshadowed. The cataclysmic picture employed here is essentially identical with that found in the oracles of the sixth seal (6:14) and the seventh bowl of wrath (16:20) and in each of these the context shows that the physical universe is to remain unaffected. This is therefore another example of the metonymous hyperbole noted in the vision of the battle with Gog and Magog (20:9); and it is such a familiar usage in the Old Testament[4] that there ought to be no possibility of its ever being construed literally.

What is pictured by these symbolic expressions is of course a moral and spiritual rather than a merely physical renovation.

The old principle has been cast out, for the millennium is ushered in by the imprisonment of Satan in the bottomless pit, but old practices and institutions have to be discarded as they are brought under condemnation by a progressively fuller understanding of the new principle. It is not, then, the present orderly physical world that is to flee away from before his face, but the present disordered human world. Only such terrestrial things and institutions as are part and parcel of the old evil order of human affairs are to be abolished utterly (cf. 2 Peter 3:10).

THE NEW JERUSALEM, BRIDE OF THE LAMB: THE
CONSUMMATION OF THE NEW AGE

Always the processes of growth and evolution manifest themselves in changes, the more radical and significant of which come forth with relative suddenness as a leap, a mutation. Just so the second advent will manifest itself in the mutations that accompany the cataclysmic upheavals of the last great day of the Lord, when the warfare of the King of kings and his hosts will result in the chaining of the old serpent and his imprisonment for a thousand years. The changes that will come at the end of the millennium are likewise represented as climacteric. We see the last of the cataclysms earth life is to suffer on account of evil—the vast but transient and futile rebellion of Gog and Magog and the final destruction of Satan and the wicked ones of the second resurrection. And so marked is the change when all evil is finally banished that it is as if there were a new heaven and a new earth (21:1).

In the last vision of the Apocalypse St. John sees this newness in the form of "the holy city," the New Jerusalem. It is not in some far-off region of the heavens, but comes "down from God out of heaven, prepared as a bride adorned for her husband" (21:2), to stand upon the summit of the earth mountain. "The nations...shall walk in the light of it: and the kings of the earth do bring their glory and honor into it" (21:24). Earth and heaven have at last been reunited.

Clearly this holy city is the exact antithesis of Babylon, the harlot city. In Babylon we see a picture of the seeming triumph of the world over the Church, as was set forth in the earlier vision of the holy city and the court of the temple given over to be trodden under foot of the Gentiles (11:2). In the New

Jerusalem, however, we see a picture of the final victory of the Church over the world, made possible when the crucified Lamb of God returns in glory.

In astral symbols also the two cities are antithetic. As has been noted, Babylon the great is represented in the heavens by the little constellation Corvus, whose quadrilateral form is a parody of and precisely antipodal to the great square of Pegasus, the symbol of the New Jerusalem (see below).

Cosmological Symbolisms

In the vision of the New Jerusalem the emphasis is of course on newness, but we would misinterpret its meaning, if we were to conclude that the old has been entirely superseded by something completely new. The old has not lost its identity, for the vision is a blending of Mount Zion, the poetic name for the temple hill of old Jerusalem, and the Garden of Eden. Like Zion and all the temples of the ancient Middle East, this new city is in full accordance with the primitive cosmological concept of a heaven-piercing world mountain. (See Appendix 1.) Its conventionalized four-square pyramidal structure, like that found in the temples of the ancient Middle East, is clearly indicated, for we are told that its length and breadth and height are all equal, each measuring 12,000 furlongs. This is commonly interpreted as representing a cube, but that it is instead a pyramid is indicated by its bordering wall, only 144 cubits in height and therefore much lower than the height at the center. Like the old Jerusalem it also has gates and a street. Here also is Eden's river of the water of life, and the tree of life that grew in the midst of the garden (Rev. 22:1–2; Gen. 2:9–10). In Old Testament symbolism the paradise of the Garden of Eden, at the top of the northern world mountain, represented the goal of earth life. Through age-long struggle up that mountain the goal was once reached, only then to be lost. In the New Jerusalem we see this paradise not only restored but developed into a glorious city covering the whole earth and uniting it with heaven. Indeed, it is the very vestibule of heaven, with its tree of life—the ecliptic axis (see Appendix 1), the one true axis of the universe—leading up to the heaven of heavens and signifying full and free intercourse between earth and heaven. The new ideal pattern of the consummation is therefore represented in terms of earlier earthly symbols of right construction—Zion and Eden.

In terms of astral symbols this four-square city, which is described further as "a bride adorned for her husband," is represented by the great square constellation of Pegasus and its adjacent constellation Andromeda. That celestial picture of a maiden has been interpreted as representing the Church, the "bride of the Lamb." The street of the city is the Milky Way, the way of the tree of life, which leads from Cancer, the zodiacal guardian of the gate of the summer solstice, on up to the heaven of heavens, and then descends on the other side to Capricorn, the winter solstice gateway back into the realm of earth life or on down to the underworld. (See Appendix 1.)

Other aspects of the early cosmology are also helpful in this study. It attached great significance to the zodiac, and zodiacal symbolisms are important in the description of the New Jerusalem. That great band of twelve constellations was pictured as surrounding the earth and marking the utmost bounds of the world of the living. It had a protective role also, for it was thought that as the planets moved through its constellations they supervised the earthly affairs of Church and State. This relationship was symbolized in the encampment pattern of the ancient Israelites as they journeyed through the wilderness. In each camp's center was the tabernacle, on the curtains of which were pictures of the cherubim associated with the twelve zodiacal constellations. Arranged around this in a square were the twelve tribes of Israel, three on each side, each tribe being associated with one of the zodiacal signs. The whole encampment thus became a picture of God's universe as it ought to be, earth and heaven united, and we find the same pattern in the New Jerusalem.

That four-square city is surrounded by a wall consisting of the disciplined hosts of spiritual Israel of all the ages. The wall's height is said to be 144 cubits, which is in Hebrew 144 *amat* or, by paronomasia, it can be interpreted to mean 144 nations; and this gives us to understand that the 144 "thousands" or clans of the twelve tribes of spiritual Israel have so multiplied through the generations that each has become a whole nation.

The twelve gates of the wall confirm this interpretation; for, being called by the names of the twelve tribes, they identify the wall with the hosts of spiritual Israel. It is a living wall. At each gate there is an "angel." Presumably these angels are the zodiacal cherubim again, standing guard around the city as the zodiac was thought to surround the earth; and this interpretation is supported by the precious stones that adorn the foundations of the wall, for these are the symbols of the zodiacal constellations and of the twelve tribes associated with them. And since the zodiac was thought to mark the utmost bounds of the world of the living, it follows that the four-square city must symbolize the whole earth.

St. John's list of these precious stones has one peculiarity that seems, at first glance, to be altogether inexplicable. It is just the reverse of the order found in our almanacs for the signs of the zodiac, which these stones represent. On second thought, however, the significance of this reversal becomes perfectly clear and most gloriously appropriate. The order in our almanacs represents the sequence of the months and years, while the order in St. John's description of the New Jerusalem is that of the precession of the equinoxes. It symbolizes the truth that in this city the months and years of mortal time have given place to the ages of eternity.

The New Jerusalem's Promises

The New Jerusalem is therefore not a picture of heaven, as is so often assumed, but of the earth, surrounded by the zodiac. It is a new earth, however, for with the last judgment the old order, the world of sin and sorrow, will indeed flee utterly away from before the face of him who sits upon the great white throne. "God shall wipe away all tears from their eyes; and there shall be no more death, neither sorrow, nor crying, neither shall there be any more pain; for the former things are passed away" (21:4). And it will be an earth purged of all evil. "There shall in no wise enter into it any thing that defileth," but only "they which are written in the Lamb's book of life" (21:27). For them there is universal and unhindered access to the tree of life, for the gates of the city are never closed.

For them these gates have another meaning also, one that is revealed by a form of word play. Each gate is made of a single glorious pearl, and the Greek word for pearls, *margaritai*, suggests the Hebrew word *margehroth*, the plural of *margehrah*. This poetic word for "rest, repose," is derived from the verb *raghar*, which means "to return to rest after wandering." It is this "rest unto their souls" that the weary and heavy laden, who have been wandering in the wilderness of sin, will find when

132

they hear and heed the voice of the Savior. And so these pearly gates represent the "sabbath rest" that remains for the people of God.

No longer, then, must the Lord's kingdom be limited in extent, as it was during the millennium, when the unconverted forces of Gog and Magog remained outside the fold. There was still a chance then, of course, for them to change their allegiance, and the overcomers of the church of Philadelphia continued their evangelistic efforts to win them, following the Master's great commission to make disciples of all nations (Matt. 28:19); and the possibility that many of them might be won has been suggested earlier. At the time of the last judgment, however, final decisions had to be made. All who had accepted the pleas of the Philadelphian evangelists were sealed with the seal of the living God, which vouches for their worthiness to enter through the gates into the holy city. All who had not heeded those pleas and who continued to be allied with Gog and Magog will have chosen to shut themselves out, and they will be thrown into the lake of fire. Not until the last judgment's inexorable confirmation of these decisions can the holy city, the New Jerusalem, be established on earth, with a world-wide domain. The realm of the southern earth mountain, with the sea that dominates it, will no longer be infernal, as it was conceived to be in the ancient cosmography; and therefore the sea as a symbol of evil will be "no more" (21:1); and the whole earth will be the Lord's.

Here we see why, in his vision of that city, St. John saw no temple. There will no longer be any need for the evangelistic work of the priests of the order of Philadelphia, for everyone in the city will be listed in the Lamb's book of life. Salvation, the grand objective of the old order of God's providence, will be an accomplished fact, and its symbols will find no place in this vision of the new earth—except for the Lamb of God, which suggests the altar.

This does not mean, however, that the city is unsanctified. The revelator would have us understand that, though there is no official temple here, God's presence gives the whole city the sanctity of the temple's innermost sanctuary, "for the Lord God the Almighty and the Lamb are the temple" thereof (21:22). In further support of this interpretation we note the golden color of the city and its street, which are said to look like both pure gold and clear glass. This combination suggests chrysolithos, the "golden stone" that is assigned to the constellation Virgo, the zodiacal symbol of the temple's inner sanctuary.

In this vision of the holy city, therefore, there is nothing hierarchical, sacerdotal, sacramentarian, or ritualistic, for all of these require a temple with its altar. Far better than anything of this sort, there is true worship in all things, filling the city. The symbolism here suggests, in even more comprehensive and exalted fashion, the picture presented in Zechariah's description of the golden age that is to fulfill the foreshadowings of the Feast of Tabernacles. In that age, Zechariah tells us, "shall there be upon the bells of the horses, HOLINESS UNTO THE LORD"; and "every pot in Jerusalem and in Judah shall be holiness unto the Lord of hosts"—altogether acceptable equivalents of the "bowls before the altar" in the Lord's house (Zech. 14:20–21). The worship of this ideal city of God, here set before us as a pattern for our own age, is clearly in the same high plane as that commended by the Master himself in his conversation with the woman of Samaria.

God's presence in the city is further emphasized in both the opening and the closing words of the vision. When St. John first saw the holy city he heard a great voice from heaven saying: "Behold, the tabernacle of God is with men, and he will dwell with them, and they shall be his people, and God himself shall be with them, and be their God" (21:3). And in his closing description of the city he tells us that "the throne of God and of the Lamb shall be in it...and there shall be no night there...for the Lord God giveth them light" (22:3,5).

This closing statement reinforces the earlier revelation that in the holy city there is no need for the sun and the moon, "for the glory of God did lighten it, and the Lamb is the light thereof" (21:23). Here, as in all St. John's visions of the throne of God, there is no picture of God himself (cf. 4:3). We see only the glory of God. This relationship between the invisible Godhead seated on a throne and his visible revelation in Christ Jesus is explicitly set forth here in this final vision, for while it is the glory of God that lights the city, it is from the Lamb in the midst of the throne that the glory shines forth as from a lamp. Or, as the term signifies apocalyptically, it shines forth as from a heavenly luminary, a star or the orb of day itself, which indeed furnishes the most ancient, the most universal, and the most perfect of all the metaphors that represent divine Providence.

Accordingly, just as the Shekinah manifested God's providential presence with the ancient Israelites in the wilderness, so here in the holy city we see the presence of the Mighty-to-Save in the midst of his people. And his people are shown as both priests and kings. "His servants shall serve him: and they shall see his face; and his name shall be in their foreheads" and "they shall reign for ever and ever" (22:3–5).

The vision St. John saw when he was carried "away in the spirit to a great and high mountain" (21:10) is not only the pattern for the upbuilding of the New Jerusalem of the consummation, but the pattern also of every right construction of earth life through the ages, past and future. It is the ideal of earthlife. To be sure, some of its features can be realized only in the consummation. Only then can paradise be restored, transcended, and extended so as to include the whole earth. Only then will evil be done away with altogether, and night be abolished. And only then can we see God face to face, for as St. John tells us in his First Epistle, we shall be able to see the glorified Savior "as he is" and share his glory only when "we shall be like him" (1 John 3:2), and that will not be until the consummation. Even so, the revelator points to some measure of realization of the ideal in the nearer future. Having told of how the city is lit by the glory of God, he adds: "And the nations of them which are saved shall walk in the light of it: and the kings of the earth" shall "bring their glory and honour into it" (21:24). Clearly, notwithstanding their captivity to the perversions of gentile Babylon, the commonwealths of Christendom have sometimes walked in this light and progressively fashioned their institutions according to the city's pattern as they understood it. In his earlier apocalyptic visions, also, St. John had seen foreglimpses of this ideal in the beloved city of the millennium, and he had recognized some of its features, even though in crude and badly marred form, in the "holy city" of the times of the Gentiles (11:1–2). Although that city was trodden under foot by those conquerors even to the outer courts of the temple, its inner sanctuary and altar were still true to the pattern, and it was not without the saving features of the true Church and the true State, as represented by the two witnesses. Now, in the New Jerusalem, the promise of those earlier forms is fulfilled, and we see the ideal in all its perfection. Its personification as the Bride of the Lamb, made ready for the coming of the King (19:7–8), reveals its true nature; for

135

just as the white robe of each individual saint is fashioned of his own righteous acts (3:5,18; 7:14), so the Bride's "fine linen, clean and white," is described as "the righteousness of the saints." The holy city, therefore, represents the divinely supervised collective social effect of all the righteous acts of all the saints of the ages.

The Day of Atonement: The Ceremonial of the Scapegoat

On the Great Day of Atonement the ceremonials began with the presentation of two goats at the door of the tabernacle. By the casting of lots one of these animals was chosen "for the Lord," to be slain as a sin offering, and the other became the scapegoat.[5]

While all Israel fasted and made humble confession of their sins, the high priest, on that day only, entered the Holy of Holies to sprinkle the mercy seat with the atoning blood of the sin offering, the goat devoted to the Lord. That seven-fold sprinkling of the mercy seat symbolizes our great High Priest's "sacrifice of himself ... once offered" (Heb. 9:26,28), and when his sacrifice is accepted with confession and genuine repentance, its atoning power is all-sufficient.

After the ceremonials of the atonement had been completed, the high priest placed his hands on the remaining living goat—an act of "devotion" like the pouring of a libation—in token of its "devotion" to sacrifice. . Upon its head were put all the iniquities and transgressions and sins of Israel, which the high priest confessed in their name, and sin and its embodiments are doomed, "devoted," to their own undoing. In the symbolism of the Day of Atonement this goat—'Az, the "wanderer"—was devoted to 'Azazel, the demon who "causes to wander." He was, by his wandering unprotected in the wild, to offer himself as a victim to the evil spirit that causes all unredeemed and untransformed goat-natures to wander. This represents contumacy's final self-chosen and self-inflicted doom.

The scapegoat is indeed a symbol of the inevitable self-destructive effect that follows every sin, a result from which there is no self-deliverance and for which mere forgiveness can furnish no cure. We would all have to die the death of the scapegoat were it not that we are enabled to countervail sin's devolution by a new inbreathing of more abounding life from without,

136

from above—the divine life of the Son of God. In a sense he can be said to have become the scapegoat in our place when for all eternity he became man, making the supreme and eternal sacrifice of sharing our nature and our life, that we might share his life. As a natural consequence, of course, he shared our death also, and in his human death on the cross, which in its essential nature it is ours to share, he symbolizes the sacrifice offered on the altar, whose blood sprinkled the mercy seat. This is the significance of St. John's picture of the Savior as the Lamb standing as though it had been slain, a symbolism that was foreshadowed by the paschal lamb.

For humanity in its weakness and sin, its proneness to wander, this atonement through the blood of the Lamb is the only hope, offered freely to those who genuinely repent of their sins. Those who refuse, however, to repent, and thus to avail themselves of this hope, will suffer the fate set forth in the apocalyptic symbolism. It is simply the natural out-working of their own evil nature that is finally to uproot the very vine of their existence and cast them into the winepress of utter ruin. On the other hand, the outcome is very different for those who accept this atonement. Responding to the appeal of the Savior's love, they turn from their old estate and identify themselves with him as their ideal, the goal of their aspirations; and it is these whom the Son of God imbues with "life"—his own divine life.

The Autumnal Festival: Full Ingatherings and Tabernacles

The great autumnal festival involves two interrelated symbolisms, the seasonal and the memorial. In the seasonal sense it marks the final full ingathering of the harvest, whose primary significance is the confirmation of spring's seedtime hope. But just as the spring celebration of seedtime was supplemented by the memorial Feast of the Passover, which recalled Israel's deliverance from bondage in Egypt, so the fall harvest festival is supplemented by and is indeed largely overshadowed by the Feast of Tabernacles, a commemoration of the completion of Israel's forty years of wandering in the wilderness. These two great festivals are not only memorial, however, but also prophetic, looking forward to the two advents of the Savior proclaimed by the Protevangel. Passover's symbolisms and foreshadowings of the first advent have of course been fulfilled literally. And if the parity of these two seasonal festivals is to be completed, we must

137

expect a second advent that will prove to be just as literal a fulfillment of the foreshadowings of the Feast of Tabernacles.

The seasonal and memorial-prophetic aspects of these vernal and autumnal celebrations combine to teach great moral truths; and again the two festivals complement each other. (See Appendix 2.) Taken together they represent God's two-fold plan for our salvation. The primary lesson of the Passover is that the supreme formulation of the law of love is the law of sacrifice, and we see love and sacrifice writ large in the Savior's incarnation: the advent of the Son of God as the Babe of Bethlehem (the life of heaven planted in the soil of earth), and his death and resurrection. Just so the autumnal festival sets forth the sanction of the law of love and sacrifice: the law of righteousness, that will not permit love's sacrifice to be in vain. In the symbolisms of St. John's Apocalypse we see foreshadowed the law of truth and justice writ large in the second advent, when that divine-human life will be glorified and multiplied in its maturity at the harvest, just as is true of the grain that is sown in springtime. But we see also, alas, the final revelation of the utter futility of life that is not developed under the law of sacrifice, and the worse than futility of every attempt to challenge the law of righteousness. This is in harmony with the Savior's own promise that in due time he would return in glory to judge the world—to cast out the tares and gather the wheat into the garner, just as must be done at each fall ingathering of crops. The implication of judgment is inherent in the nature of the harvest itself, and it is significant in the immemorial symbolism that associated the harvest month with the zodiacal constellation Libra, the scales of justice, the celestial symbol of the Judge of all the earth. It was set forth also in the ancient ceremony of the scapegoat on the Day of Atonement, just preceding the harvest festival.

To recognize how the Feast of Tabernacles contributes to St. John's apocalyptic symbols we must recall the outstanding features of that festival. In it the people of Israel looked back in grateful remembrance to the providentially shepherded march of their forefathers through the wilderness toward Canaan, the Land of Promise—the rest that remains for the people of God (Heb. 4:9). On that journey through a fruitless and waterless desert, pathless and hostile, their only hope was in the guidance and support of Divine Providence—the Shekinah presence of Jehovah himself, the manna he sent from heaven, and the water he caused to flow from the flinty rock. And so, in memory of that time, during the week of the festival the people lived in booths or tabernacles, as had been necessary in the wilderness, and carried out great ceremonies of lights and outpourings of water that recalled God's guidance and care.

This memorial symbolism is evident in many aspects of St. John's apocalyptic visions. He calls the bowls of wrath "plagues" (15:1; 16:9), and most of them do allude to the plagues that were inflicted upon the Egyptian oppressors of Israel. He alludes also to the escape across the Red Sea in the vision of the saints of the Church triumphant, who are seen standing by the sea of glass (15:2); and in the song they sing we hear echoes of the song of triumph sung by Moses and the children of Israel on that occasion. Indeed, the song of the apocalyptic vision is called "the song of Moses the servant of God, and the song of the Lamb" (15:3). Still further, it is to the time when Israel finally arrived within sight of the Promised Land that St. John alludes in his description of the 144,000 who are seen standing with the Lamb on Mount Zion; for it is said of them that they are altogether innocent of the harlotries with which Balaam taught Balak to tempt the followers of Joshua of old as they camped in Moab just east of the Jordan. And so it is clearly in the crossing of that host from the east over the river Jordan, the "great river" of Palestine, and the beginning of their conquest of Canaan, that we find the clue to the significance of the sixth bowl, which was poured "upon the great river Euphrates; and the water thereof was dried up, that the way of the kings of the east might be prepared" (16:12).

In its prophetic sense, the Festival of Tabernacles looks forward to see the same all-glorious presence leading Israel, the redeemed of the Lord, to the final victorious recovery of humanity's rightful heritage. That great migration of old has come to symbolize the pilgrimage of earth life out from the bondage of sin, through the wilderness of temptation and tribulation of the world as it is, and into the marvelous liberty of the children of God—into the Land of Promise where every Canaanitish abomination will be smitten and the world will be made what it ought to be. Here again is the implication of judgment, associated with the harvest festival and represented by the sign of Libra.

The closing visions of St. John's Apocalypse picture the end of that journey, when he who, as the Paschal Lamb, made possible its beginning is to come again as the Lion of the tribe of Judah to make possible its consummation. And the prophecy of the all-sufficient Mighty-to-Save in the midst of his people is set forth in the picture of the New Jerusalem coming down out of heaven from God—the holy city in which the Shekinah of God is with men and of which the Lamb is the light. This is in accordance with the Savior's own elucidation of the festival's feast of lights, for it was while he was in Jerusalem at the time of his last attendance upon these ceremonials that he said: "I am the light of the world: he that followeth me shall not walk in darkness, but shall have the light of life" (John 8:12).

Thus the autumn festival of olden times looked forward to the consummation of earth life. It pictured the end of this age of the seeming triumph of evil, of which the wilderness wanderings were a type, and the development of a new and truly spiritual Israel. As the final full harvest is greater than the firstfruits of Pentecost, so will the spiritual power of the new age far exceed the outpouring of the Holy Spirit at that festival. The new Messianic people will have gathered the full harvest of the fruits of the spirit, and, following the Joshua of the New Covenant, they will lead humanity into the promised land of the New Jerusalem—into possession of the Sabbath rest that remains for God's people, when earth shall become the vestibule of heaven.

NOTES

1. Deut. 10:1–5; cf. 31:26–27.
2. Exod. 7:17–21; 9:9–11.
3. See, for example, Isa. 1:21; Jer. 2:20 ff.; Ezek. 16:15 ff.
4. See Ps. 68:8, 97:5; Isa. 34:4, 54:10; Jer. 4:23-24; Ezek. 38:20; Mic 1:4; Nah. 1:5.
5. Lev. 16:5–10, 15,20–22.

A THREE-FOLD INTERPRETATION:

REVELATION AS A FORESHADOWING OF DEVELOPMENTS WITHIN AND BETWEEN CHURCH AND STATE

REVELATION AS A FORESHADOWING OF DEVELOPMENTS WITHIN AND BETWEEN CHURCH AND STATE

I.   Surveys of Church and State Separately
   (Acts 1 and 2 of the Drama)

   The Church

   The State

II.   Conflicts Involving Church and State
   (Act 3 of the Drama)

   Astral Symbolisms of Such Conflicts

   The Apocalyptic Visions of Such Conflicts

       War between the Pervert Church and
       the Pervert State

       The Testimony of the True Church and
       the True State

       Persecutions of the True Church

       The Lamb–Lion in the Midst of the Church Militant

III.   Church and State United
   (Act 4 of the Drama)

   The Ideal of Such a Union

   A False Union between the Pervert Church and the
   Pervert State: Babylon the Great, the Harlot City

   The Promised Union between the True Church and the
   True State: The Bride of the Lamb, the City of God

       The Millennium of Mobilization

       The New Jerusalem

REVELATION AS A FORESHADOWING OF DEVELOPMENTS WITHIN AND BETWEEN CHURCH AND STATE

As we have seen, the Revelation of Jesus Christ, signified to St. John by the angel to show things that must shortly begin to come to pass, can be interpreted as a worship drama portraying the synagogue service of the early Christian Church, with its readings from the law, the prophets, and the sacred writings. It is concerned with just one theme—the moral and spiritual warfare involved in earth-life's salvation from its own perversities. Here we read, therefore, of the problems that will beset the religious and civic life of Christendom, represented by the Church and the State, and the developments that will lead finally to the promised return of the crucified Lamb of God as the Lion of the tribe of Judah, the King of kings and Lord of lords.

As a histrionic synagogue service this drama can be divided into four acts. These have been discussed in detail in the preceding section of this monograph, and it has been shown that each act sets forth the theme of the Apocalypse, but that in each one that theme is seen from a different point of view. Thus the pattern of the synagogue service makes possible the recapitulation that is such a striking characteristic of the book.

It is possible also, however, to divide this Apocalypse into three equal sections. This can be done when it is considered as a foreshadowing of developments within and between Church and State, the two chief protagonists of the drama and the two great social institutions divinely ordained for the ordering and development of human society. Again each section surveys the whole grand movement, from apostolic times to the end of the age, and again in each one the point of view is different.

145

The following brief outline of these three sections will serve as a summary of the book. Here specific mention will be made only of those visions and oracles that are direct foreshadowings of the future. It must be understood, however, that the other visions and oracles not noted here are significant supplements to these predictions, adding portents that will mark their fulfillment, the background necessary for their understanding, and other helpful matters. Clarification of the interpretations presented here can be found in the corresponding parts of the drama.

I. SURVEYS OF CHURCH AND STATE SEPARATELY
(Rev. 1–7; Acts 1 and 2 of the Drama)

Here both Church and State are presented separately and objectively, and each one is shown to be a composite of good and evil.

The Church (Rev. 1–3)

The letters to the seven churches of Asia foreshadow the history of the Church's development as an institution, or a series of institutions, pointing out both good qualities and shortcomings.

On the positive side recognition and approval are given, for example, concerning hard work, charity, and faith. Some churches are praised for patient endurance of poverty, tribulation, and suffering, and some for having rejected certain evil teachings.

At the same time some of these churches are charged with various faults. Among these are the failing love of Ephesus; the lack of vigor with which Pergamum and Thyatira wielded the sword of the Spirit against error; the spiritual inertia of the dead church of Sardis; the lukewarmness of the Laodiceans. These are negative faults, for which the condemnation is "inasmuch as ye did it not."

Looming darkly in the background of the letters, however, there are other evils that are positive and even aggressive in their nature, apostasies of perverted elements in the Church that have deserted the King of kings and transferred their allegiance to an Antichrist. In the letters these evils are represented by the teachings of Balaam and the Nicolaitans, both of which are soundly condemned; and from all the evidence that has come down to us we can conclude that they are both employed in the

Apocalypse as symbols of apostasy. In the case of the Balaamites that is made evident by reference to the Old Testament story of Balaam, "who taught Balak to cast a stumbling block before the children of Israel, to eat things sacrificed unto idols, and to commit fornication" (2:14). Idolatry and immorality are stereotypical characterizations of apostasy in prophetic literature.

In their historical sense, then, these teachings appear to symbolize social perversions. A hidden meaning, referring to the book's recurring theme of Church-State relationships, may be derived, however, from the etymology of the words. *Balaam* is a Hebrew word that can be broken down into the verbal element *bal*—"to devour," or by wordplay *ba'al*, "to master"—and a nominal element *'am*, "people, nation, state"; and the nominal element must be interpreted as the object of the verbal element. *Nicolaitan* comes from the Greek and is made up of the verbal element *nikao*, "to conquer, master," and the nominal element *laos*, "people, nation, state." In this case the nominal element may be construed as either the subject or the object of the verb. Since these terms are used in the letters to the churches, the Church can be understood as the antagonist of the State (*'am* or *laos*), and so the teachings of Balaam can be interpreted as the Church dominating over the State, while those of the Nicolaitans might represent the opposite, the Church dominated by the State.

Thus, while the letters focus on the Church they contain also a hidden suggestion regarding perversions of the right relationship between Church and State, perversions that will be pictured more specifically in the following sections. It is evident, of course, that the well-being and proper evolution of society would require the true and faithful and wise cooperation of these divinely ordained institutions. Any failure on their part to work together properly, especially any antagonism between them or any wrong done by one to the other, would therefore be injurious or even disastrous for society as a whole.

The State (Rev. 4–7)

The oracles of the seven-sealed book survey the development of the State. Here we see the four horsemen of the Apocalypse, representing four successive forms of civic power—warring empires that are progressively more and more infernal counterfeits of the King of kings and Lord of lords (seals 1–4). Here too we see the effects of their despotic and ruthless rule—the martyred saints who are to make up the hosts of heaven following the Savior when he returns (seal 5). We see also the fearful visitations that are to afflict the earth on the great day of God's wrath (seal 6). The section closes with a vision of the 144,000 persons sealed with the seal of the living God—the Church militant mobilized in preparation for the Savior's return and protected from the spiritual evils resulting from the conflicts described in the next section.

II. Conflicts Involving Church and State
(Rev. 8–14; Act 3 of the Drama)

After concerning itself with Church and State on essentially separate terms, the Apocalypse becomes a cultural survey of both of these institutions as regards both their ideal forms and their perversions. Here we are shown the pervert Church and State warring against each other in jealous hostility, but cooperating unfailingly in their deadly enmity against the true Church and State. We see also the persecutions to which the latter are subjected, and the final coming of the Lamb-Lion to avenge their wrongs and destroy their enemies.

The Astral Symbolisms of Such Conflicts

In the heavens the interrelationships between Church and State and the influences under which they must carry on their work are represented by the zodiac. In ancient Hebrew thought that great belt of the heavens represented human existence, and its twelve constellations were arranged into two overlapping and therefore interrelated groups of seven each—the solar and lunar "houses" of the seven "planets"—to represent earth-life's two major social institutions, the Church and the State. These are the two "witnesses" of the Apocalypse, described as "the two candlesticks standing before the God of the earth" (11:3–4), presumably seven-branched like the menorah. And that the life of earth and its institutions is subject to competing influences of good and evil is pictured in the heavens by the zodiac's position between the celestial or supernal agencies represented by the constellations of the northern heavens and the satanic or infernal agencies represented by the dragons and wild beasts of the southern heavens. (See Appendix 1.)

148

The Apocalyptic Visions of Such Conflicts

In the Apocalypse this competition between good and evil influences is set forth in the visions of the trumpets and the exposition of the little book open, which is interpolated in their midst. Essentially it is pictured as a struggle of the Savior against draconian foes that are to invade human society, incarnate as apostasies. The Church is represented as continuing to respond in large part and in many respects to the high and holy and helpful influences pictured in the supernal heavens. Nevertheless, both Church and State are seen at times estranged from heaven and conforming in some very important matters to the "world" whose ruler is the evil spirit of the dragon. In such situations Church and State become mutually injurious and pervert, with the Church sometimes subservient to the State and sometimes dominating it.

These visions are of the following four types:

War between the Pervert Church and the Pervert State.

War between pervert forms of these two great institutions is set forth in the visions of the first six trumpet oracles and is shown, not in its entirety, but in outstanding illustrations of its results.

For the principals themselves these struggles bring the doom of destruction, for the visions of the second and third trumpets suggest respectively the fall of the false State dominated by the Church and the fall of the false Church dominated by the State.

For Christendom at large, too, these pervert institutions and the warfare between them bring trouble. The two woes of the fifth and sixth trumpets, with their four demon hosts, foreshadow the exaggerations and negations of religion and statecraft that have plagued and still plague Christendom. And the associated social despotisms make slaves of the children of God and leave no opportunity for the full development of the personality of each individual in the likeness of the Heavenly Father. (Rev. 8 and 9).

The Testimony of the True Church and the True State..

Clothed in sackcloth, the true Church and the true State (the "two witnesses") testify against the pervert Church and State and are martyred in the "hour" of the world's final saturnalian madness. At the end of that hour they are resurrected and

149

ascend to heaven, a symbolic representation of their increased spirituality that will enable them to serve as the priest-kings of the parousia. This is set forth in the exposition of the little book open (Rev. 11).

Persecutions of the True Church.
Following the seventh trumpet, persecutions of the true Church by both the false Church and the false State are reviewed. These recapitulations include the visions of the woman pursued by the great red dragon and of the two beasts that represent the apostate State and the apostate Church. (Rev. 12 and 13.)

The Lamb-Lion in the Midst of the Church Militant.
While the song of the choir invisible, the Church triumphant, is heard from heaven, the Lamb-Lion is seen on earth on Mount Zion, coming to save and avenge his elect, who would otherwise be destroyed by their enemies, the false Church and the false State. This vision of the Lord's parousia in the great day of his long-awaited return is the dynamic revelation of the seventh trumpet. The results of that great day's events are given here, however, only in the proclamations of the Savior and the Holy Spirit reassuring the saints; and in the dramatizations of the final harvest and vintage of the earth. (Rev. 14.)

III. CHURCH AND STATE UNITED
(Rev. 15–22; Act 4 of the Drama)

The vintage symbolism is continued in the pouring out of the bowls of the wrath of God upon unrepentant apostasy (Rev. 15 and 16), after which we see two contrasting visions of a union of Church and State.

The Ideal of Such Union
Such a union is a return to the pattern of patriarchal times, when the care of humanity's spiritual and temporal interests was in the hands of the family rather than of society as a whole, acting through Church and State. It assumes, therefore, that society as a whole has become one great family, whose head, because his is the birthright of the eldest son, is both priest and

chief; or who, as in the city-state of the settled tribe, is the priest-king. For us, the outstanding example of such a leader is Melchizedek. As the priest-king of ancient Jerusalem, or Uru-Salem, "the city of peace," he is the type of the Lord Jesus—our Elder Brother, our rightful King, and our great High Priest, the King of kings and Lord of lords.

St. John's revelation foreshadows, as its great promise, the actual return of society to this idyllic condition, which it is to attain and maintain by the help of the sovereign power and mediatorial work of our Lord, peculiarly present in the age to come. The book shows us also, however, a worse than vain attempt to establish a like union of the pervert Church and the pervert State. Glimpses of both the true and the false union are given throughout the Apocalypse. In this third section of the book they are set forth fully in the visions of two cities, Babylon the great and the New Jerusalem.

A False Union between the Pervert Church and the Pervert State: Babylon the Great, the Harlot City (Rev. 17–19)

First comes the vision of Babylon the great, seen as a great harlot seated on a scarlet beast. She herself is drunk with the blood of the martyrs of Jesus, and she is making the nations of the earth drunk with the golden cup of her abominations. In this apocalyptic picture of the union of the pervert Church (the harlot) and the pervert State (the scarlet beast), the latter is dominant. The great harlot is shown worshiping the beast and his image, the Antichrist of imperial grandeur, and yet she assumes all the authority of Christ Jesus as both priest and king. Her reign is a parody of the millennial kingdom of Christ, for she has impudently forestalled the Bride of the Lamb and usurped her place. She is judged, however, and convicted as the chief enemy of the true Church of Christ, and she is to be dispossessed forthwith when the Bridegroom comes.

The execution of that judgment is foreshadowed in the nineteenth chapter, which tells of rejoicing in heaven over the prospective casting out of the usurping harlot; the restoration of the Bride of the Lamb to her rightful place; the return of the Bridegroom as King of kings and Lord of lords, to overthrow the usurper and establish his own true millennial kingdom; the proclamation of the bridal supper of the Lamb-Lion; and the great battle of Armageddon. The victory of the King of kings at that final battle of the warring age will bring about the utter destruction of the false State and the false Church.

The Promised Union Between the True Church and the True State: The Bride of the Lamb, the City of God (Rev. 20–22)

That great victory of the King of kings will usher in the kingdom of heaven on earth, Christendom as it ought to be, which is represented here by the holy city, the City of God.

In the Apocalypse the realization of this ideal is presented in two stages, a millennium of mobilization and an eternity of progress in the New Jerusalem. Both are marked by a continued and increasing influx of the heavenly influence and by the second advent spiritual presence of the Savior, working through the Church, his larger incarnation.

The Millennium of Mobilization.

The millennium begins with the conclusion of the climactic crisis of the great day of the Lord, when Satan is bound and imprisoned for "a thousand years"; and it ends with the last of the cataclysms earth life is to suffer on account of evil, the rebellion of Gog and Magog. With the failure of that final effort of Satan, he is cast into the lake of utter perdition, and the final judgment is pronounced upon all evil (Rev. 20).

In the millennium society will become the family it ought to be, the household of faith whose head is the King of kings and great High Priest. As a commonwealth of priest-kings, members of the body of Christ who do his will, it will represent the true unity of Church and State. Instead of being destructive, as when such unity is established by the collectivism and totalitarianisms of the world's present social organizations, this unity conserves and enhances the total personality of the individual and speeds it on its way toward the beauty of the divine likeness. And when, as individuals and finally as the whole Church, we come to be like him, we shall be able to see him as he is; and the consummation of earth life will have been won.

The New Jerusalem

That consummation, the New Jerusalem, follows after the elimination of all evil from earth life at the close of the millennium. It is personified as the Bride of the Lamb "arrayed in fine linen, clean and white," and the revelator explains that this fine linen is "the righteousness of the saints." The holy city, therefore, will be the divinely supervised collective social effect of the righteous acts of all the saints, just as the white robe of each saint is fashioned from his own righteous acts as an individual.

It is evident, however, that St. John saw the earth life even of the consummation still but "a copy and shadow of the heavenly" (Heb. 8:5). The saints of this vision are still living in the "beloved city" of the millennium; but because it is no longer besieged by the wicked they can, without such hindrance and with the help of God, keep making it more and more completely new, building it up into ever fuller accordance with the ever more clearly discerned "pattern" coming down from God out of heaven. This eternity of progress is in accordance with the declaration of him who sat on the throne, for he said: "Behold, I make [am making] all things new" (21:5).

It is, however, only in ever closer conformity to the plan already adopted in the millennium, in ever fuller exemplification of the spirit it implies, that the social organization of the City of God in the consummation can be said to be new; for the millennial plan of social solidarity in the true unity of Church and State—a rule of priest-kings acknowledging glad fealty to the King of kings and Lord of lords—finds no suggestion of amendment in the final vision of the glorious ideal pattern of earth life.

The New Jerusalem is a great symbol of the unity of the universe. It is a unity, not of substance or entity, but of understanding and heart and will—a moral and spiritual unity that only sin could destroy and that only the Savior's great salvation can restore. Such unity is supremely and unconditionally exemplified in the Creator's triunity and the Creator would share it with all his creatures. It is shared now by those who have accepted the great salvation offered by the Lamb of God that taketh away the sin of the world. It will be shared by the whole world, the whole universe, when the work of the Lion of Judah, foreshadowed in these visions, is at last completed—when the old serpent and all his perversions are cast into the lake of utter destruction and the New Jerusalem covers the whole earth.

153

THE MESSAGE
FOR
TODAY'S CHURCH

THE MESSAGE FOR TODAY'S CHURCH

The Ideal: What Earth Life Ought To Be

The Promise of Divine Help: The Lord's Second Advent

The Challenge to the Church
   Renewal within the Church
   Renewal of the World at Large

When Will This Be?

THE MESSAGE FOR TODAY'S CHURCH

"Blessed is he that readeth, and they that
hear the words of this prophecy, and keep
these things which are written therein: for
the time is at hand" (Rev. 1:13).

These words follow immediately after St. John's introductory
statement about the nature of his Revelation, and they challenge us to study the book thoroughly, in order that we may find
in it a message for our own time. The main body of this present
study has been directed toward the first part of that challenge,
for it endeavors to provide new understanding of the book's
structure and symbolisms. Such understanding must not be
viewed as an end in itself, however, but as a means toward
meeting the second part of the challenge, a means of discovering
the book's message for the Church militant of today.

Those who read the book toward these ends are "blessed," so
the first words of the verse tell us, and while this is true, of
course, for all the books of the Bible, it is peculiarly true for St.
John's Revelation. That book, the most curious and wonderful
one ever written, sets before us, as no other does, the social
ideals toward which we must work. It shows us what is wrong
with earth life and what it ought to be and will be when heaven
comes down to earth in the New Jerusalem.

The processes of change and growth proceed by mutations, as
Jesus pointed out in his parable of the growth of God's kingdom—"first the blade, then the ear, then the full corn in the ear"
(Mark 6:26 ff.). And so, after a period of providential shepherd-
ing of Israel of the Old Covenant, the way was prepared for such
a mutation, the advent of the Son of God, who came to overcome
the sin and death of the world by the law of his own life-giving
spirit of holiness and to make possible the personal salvation of
those who will accept him. The Gospels and the New Testament
epistles are concerned chiefly with such individual relations
with God, showing us Christ as the pattern we must follow in

159

our own lives. St. John's Revelation, however, is concerned with our lives together as a human society and with the salvation of that society. It helps us to understand that it is not enough merely to save our own souls and rescue a few other brands from the burning city, as did Bunyan's pilgrim. No, it is our business to save the city, no matter what the cost may be, even at the cost of our own lives. It is not enough merely to ameliorate the evil conditions that plague our world. Instead, we must strike at the roots of such evil. It is only a thorough cleansing and reorganization of our human society that can save it and make possible the new earth pictured in Revelation; and while we, the Christian Church, are charged to work toward that goal, we cannot reach it by our own human efforts. Such a regeneration of our earth life will again be a mutation that will require divine intervention, this time by the second advent of the Savior. Such social salvation will be the work of his royal office as King of kings and will be the objective of his second advent.

St. John's Revelation, then, gives us a picture of the ideal pattern for human society on this earth; a promise of the Lord's second coming that will bring it to pass; and a challenge to the Church, the spiritual Israel of the New Covenant, to prepare the way for that coming and to be the Lord's agents through whom his work will be accomplished.

The Ideal: What Earth Life Ought To Be

The beautiful vision of the New Jerusalem, so often and so wrongly interpreted as a picture of heaven, is instead a picture of earth life as it ought to be and as it will be when heaven comes down to earth and our earth life climbs heavenward as it grows in spirituality. The bonds between heaven and earth, which had been severed by humanity's apostasies, will have been renewed.

St. John's picture of a new earth is therefore not concerned with the physical earth, nor with the historical city of Jerusalem, but with the world of man's own making—his flawed human institutions and relationships and the misdirected ideals on which these are built. We look for a new earth, but St. John gives us to understand that first we must have a new "heaven"—new ideals. The most important feature of Revelation's new earth is therefore not its physical appearance—and certainly we do not expect it to have the pearly gates and golden streets and other features seen in St. John's vision, though as we have noted there is much symbolic significance in that picture. No, the really fundamental characteristic of the New Jerusalem is the close relationship that prevails there between God and his earthly children. All of them—all whom divine love's self-sacrifice could win—will in that new earth give full allegiance to the Heavenly Father and will be restored to their divine likeness and to their exalted position in his household as "heirs of God and joint-heirs with Christ our elder brother" (Rom. 8:17). And so St. John's first descriptive statement about the new Jerusalem tells us that "the tabernacle of God is with men, and he will dwell with them, and they shall be his people." And later he adds that they "shall serve him: and they shall see his face." In his First Epistle St. John enlarges on this, explaining that when the Savior comes we shall be able "to see him as he is" *because* "we shall be like him" (1 John 3:2)—another way of expressing the heightened spirituality, the closeness between God and man, that will prevail in the New Jerusalem. We will have cleansed our "heaven," our ideals, casting out the evil purposes and self-seeking and all the other wrongs that now pollute our earth life, and putting in their place the spirit and principles of the Lord Jesus.

In such an earth, in the new "city of peace" ruled by the King of Righteousness and Prince of Peace, all evil will have been eliminated for ever. There will be law and order, but it will be the law of love, written not on tablets of stone but on the tables of the heart and therefore self-enforcing, the perfect law of liberty. The glorified Son of man, acting as a great catalyst, will have transmuted all the base elements of earth life into gold, the loving kindness of heaven. Clearly the holy city, the New Jerusalem, is the embodiment of God's final purpose for humanity. it will be a world made new by the Word of God—a wholesome, glad, and glorious world that will rise from the ashes of the old, when the earth has been purified as by fire and restored to the fellowship of heaven.

It will be recalled that according to the interpretation of the Revelation presented here the second, third, and fourth acts of the apocalyptic worship drama all tell the same story. Each one tells of the great crisis of the ages, the final great day of Jehovah and the resulting changes in earth life, but with differing sym-

161

bolisms and with progressively greater detail. Only in the last act do we find the full picture of the new earth that will result, but in the third act there is a similar emphasis on close ties between earth and heaven, the seen and the unseen. There we find the vision of the Lamb of God on Mount Zion, the poetic symbol of the earthly Jerusalem—a picture therefore representing the Glorified Redeemer's return to earth. He is in the midst of a great throng of the saints of the Church militant, those still active in the life of earth. At the same time the unseen saints of the Church triumphant are heard as they sing a new song before God's throne in heaven. And at the close of that act, after the blowing of the seventh trumpet, we hear loud voices from heaven saying: "The kingdoms of this world have become the kingdom of our God, and of his Christ, and he shall reign for ever and ever" (11:15). In these words we see the fulfillment of the first petition of the Lord's prayer. God's kingdom will have come on earth, and his earthly children will do his will, even as it is done in heaven. That is another way of describing the ideal pattern of earth life promised in the consummation. That is the ideal toward which we must work.

THE PROMISE OF DIVINE HELP: THE LORD'S SECOND ADVENT

That ideal new earth cannot be brought into being, however, until the Lord has come again in his second advent. That coming, first promised in the Protevangel and foretold in many Old Testament prophecies, is the theme of St. John's Revelation, where it is pictured more fully and more vividly than anywhere else. He who came first as the lowly Nazarene bringing, at so great cost to himself, the life of God into the dying life of humanity, will come again, according to his promise. And in the Apocalypse we see him coming down from heaven riding on a white horse and accompanied by the resurrected hosts of the Church triumphant. He is armed with the sword of the mouth and a rod of iron with which he will "smite" and "rule" the nations, and he bears the name "King of kings and Lord of lords." He will rule in righteousness and bring all the world back into glad allegiance to God the Father.

St. John shows the returning Savior also as the Mighty One of the great day of Jehovah, and during the transitional period of the millennium he will bring about a thorough renovation of the whole of earth life, making it ready for the coming of the holy city, the New Jerusalem. The operations by which he will accomplish his task are represented by the various titles given him. He will be the Judge inexorable who by his truth will thoroughly sift the life of earth, eliminating all that is evil; and to those forces of unrighteousness that must be removed he will be the Mighty Avenger. To his own followers, however, the saints of the Church militant who will be watching and ready to receive him, he will come as the Mighty-to-Save, manifested as a spiritual presence, a great outpouring of spiritual power far beyond that received at Pentecost.

It is this great increase in spiritual power, sometimes known as the "rapture" of the saints, that is described in Revelation and by St. Paul (1 Thess. 4:17) as seeming to carry them up to heaven. Obviously it cannot be construed as actually taking these saints of the Church militant up out of the visible Church on earth, leaving that body a lifeless corpse just when it is vitally needed in the work of preparing for the Lord's second advent and of meeting him when he comes. In Revelation, for example, the "two witnesses" are described (11:12) as having this experience just as loud voices in heaven announce the second coming of the Savior, who is then seen as the Lamb on Mount Zion in the midst of the 144,000 of the Church militant, among whom the "raptured" saints must surely be included. This "rapture," then, must be interpreted as an increased spirituality that strengthens the link between earth and heaven, between the seen and the unseen, making those who experience it become more and more effective instruments for the accomplishment of the divine purpose.

In the unapproachable glory of his deity the returning Savior will be invisible to the merely earthly eye, even to his Church at the beginning of the millennium. To the world at large, therefore, his second-advent presence will be manifested only by this spiritual quickening of the Church, the body of which Christ is both the vitalizing Spirit and the living Head. And it will be the hands of the Church that will wield the rod of iron and the sword of the mouth by which the Lord's cleansing and renewal of earth life will be carried out. But as his divine power is poured out more and more mightily into the life of earth, the spiritual rapport between heaven and earth will become closer and closer, bringing an ever fuller and clearer manifestation of the presence of the Lord and his spiritual hosts. At last the veil between the natural and the supernatural will be rent in twain, and in the final consummation of the New Jerusalem, as noted above, we shall see him as he is, for we shall be like him. Then as King of kings and Lord of lords he will rule in righteousness in the world-wide commonwealth of spiritual Israel.

The Challenge To The Church

Achievement of the ideal—the supreme mutation in earth life pictured as the New Jerusalem—depends, then, on the Lord's second coming. But in turn that great event requires a necessary state of readiness in the Church militant and in the world at large. Here, then, we come to the challenge St. John's Revelation presents, to the Church as an institution and to the individual Christians who make it up. What must we do to prepare the way for the second advent—the Lord's coming as King of kings—and for the establishment of his world-wide kingdom of righteousness, his new earth? It is to the Church, the spiritual Israel of the New Covenant, that this task is given, just as it was given to the Israel of the Old Covenant to prepare the way for the Savior's coming as the Lamb of God.

The Church is called, then, to be the Lord's agent, the body in which he will be incarnate when he comes again. Through it he has worked on earth during all the Christian centuries, preparing for his second advent, and it is through it that he will continue to work during the transition period of the millennium, until he has accomplished his purpose of renewing the earth.

Renewal within the Church

Obviously, if we of the Church are to be effective agents toward that end of earth renewal, we must first renew our own institutions and our own members; and to Christians of today it is only too evident that the Church is in need of such cleansing and transformation. Within its various parts we can still find the same problems that are named in the Apocalyptic letters to the seven churches of Asia—backsliding, spiritual lukewarmness or even spiritual death, love of material riches, easy tolerance of apostasies. From our own experience we can add others, such as worldliness, narrow sectarianism, bigotry, pride, contentiousness, heresy, infidelity. The Church must be purged of such wrongs and re-inspired with the spirit of the Word of God. And what does the Savior himself recommend as the cure for such spiritual ailments? In the letters to the churches he calls for *repentance*. We must recognize our sins and our need for divine help and ask for it. And he adds that he is knocking on the doors of our hearts, ready and waiting to give us this help if only we will open the door and let him in.

The Church must constantly strive by such cleansing and spiritual renewal to raise its ideals above those of the world around it and to become a more and more effective exponent of the mind of the Master. Only thus can it become worthy and able to carry out the great task that confronts it. It is well that the Church should be splendidly organized and highly honored, that vast multitudes should be enrolled in its membership, and that all the machinery of its propaganda should be unstintedly financed. It is well also that the Church should call upon art and music to beautify its temples and enrich its worship. In themselves, however, these things are of little value, and they become dangers if they are allowed to usurp the foreground of interest. Even worse, they become positively subversive, like wooden horses filled with deadly enemies, when they are no longer sought as mere means to the true ends of religion and become instead the coveted ends themselves. From such perversions the Church must be thoroughly purged at any cost. It must choose between Christ and the world, and not be led astray by the superficialties of life.

We of the Church must be ever aware of and more fully appreciative of our high calling and of our need for the cleansing and renewal that will equip us for it. The spiritual rebirth we need will of course be God's doing, but we must work with him to make it possible. It is our repentance that will enable him to give us the divine help we need. Only we can open the doors of our hearts and let the Savior in, and we can come to know him more fully only through our own faithfulness in Bible study and prayer.

Renewal of the World at Large

St. John's Revelation makes it clear that the Savior's promise of divine help for those who repent refers not only to the needs of the Church and its individual members, but also to the need of humanity as a whole. We can be altogether confident that the

Mighty-to-Save is indeed ready and waiting to mobilize the armies of heaven and come to the help of his earthly children in his second-advent presence, but again repentance must come first. In the Apocalyptic drama this is the lesson of the seven thunders, which "uttered their voices" just as the archangel with the "little book open" broke into the orderly sequence of worship; for the thunders remind us that in the Old Testament divine intervention came to the aid of the Israelites of old only in answer to their repentance. In recognition of this the archangel came with an urgent call for repentance—urgent because the coming of the fearful third woe was imminent, and only the Savior could countervail it. And it was in response to the resulting repentance, pictured as the faithfulness of the two witnesses, that the Savior's second advent was indeed hastened. Instead, then, of a vision of the third woe's devastation of the earth we see a vision of the Lamb of God on Mount Zion in the midst of the Church militant, the third act's version of the second coming.

Repentance, therefore, is the urgent need for the cleansing and renewal not only of the Church but also of the world at large, and to make the world aware of that need must be a major part of the task of preparing for the Savior's coming. There must be a world-wide heralding of the glad tidings of the Gospel—a continuation of the work of the great commission, baptizing men and women and making Christians of them. The Church must exalt the Lord Jesus unfailingly and bear testimony to the power of his great salvation; and by persevering, fervent, and confident prayer it must open the doors and windows of human thought, feeling, and motive more and more effectually to the free entry of the spirit of truth and love and to the overruling governance of the Master. Only as he is thus enthroned in more and more individual hearts can he at last be enthroned in the whole life of humanity—in its social and religious ideals and therefore in its social and religious institutions, its industrial and commercial activities, and its civic and international relations. This, of course, is the objective of the Lord's second advent and his establishment of the new earth symbolized by the New Jerusalem.

At the same time that the Church is preaching the Gospel and thus developing new values and new ideals in the hearts of individuals and increasingly in human society, it must also work against all the earthly conditions that cause injustice, destroy virtue, mar happiness; that exploit people economically, restrict their personal and civil rights, and are hostile to religion and truth. There are cumbering institutions, corroding customs, and deceptive ideals that have prevailed for so long that they seem almost to have become an inevitable part of the nature of human life on earth, and the world must be purged of them. Against them the Church must lift up its voice. And always, by voice and vote, it must carry on a ceaseless and forceful campaign for the ethical consideration of every public issue, big or little, everywhere.

In the language of the Apocalyptic letters to the churches we may say that we are called to be *overcomers*. Each Christian must strive, with God's help, to overcome the sins that threaten his own commitment to the Lord; and the Church must overcome first its own sins and weaknesses and then the evils that threaten the whole of earth life. We are called to overcome in these ways even if it requires sacrifice, as it did for the two witnesses in the Apocalypse and as it did for the Savior himself.

What is called for then, if we are to make the world ready for the Lord's second coming, is a campaign in the realm of ideals, an intensive campaign for personal and collective righteousness and for the application of the truth of the Gospel to all the practicalities of life.

In essence, therefore, we must wage a battle of right against wrong. Many Christians resist the use of military symbolisms to describe what we must do, fearing it might seem to suggest support for physical warfare, which of course is one of the great evils of which the world must be purged. To others, however, such symbolisms seem helpful. They remind us that the forces against which we are struggling are spiritually life-threatening and are therefore truly enemies; and we can win these battles over ideals only if we are committed to our cause with the same fervor and discipline as that expected of soldiers in a shooting war. Indeed, the task that confronts us is one that can be accomplished only by our whole-souled devotion to our all-conquering Leader. And if we are to have any hope of hastening his coming we must carry on the fight more zealously than in the past, with a new vigor that will differ from all our previously desultory conflicts with ignorance and evil as modern physical warfare differs from the battles of Caesar or Napoleon.

167

How difficult the battle can be is represented symbolically by the visions of the Apocalypse. They portray a world beset by evils that attack not only visibly and outwardly in human society but also invisibly and inwardly within the hearts and minds of individuals. So threatening are these evils that they are described as demons, dragons, wild beasts, the old serpent. They prey upon the earth, perverting both Church and State, and it is against them that the Savior is pictured as coming on his white horse, leading an army from heaven and armed with two weapons. He will smite the nations with the sharp sword of the mouth, but it will be the sword of truth proceeding from the mouth of his Church, as it continues the work of preaching the Gospel, championing all good causes, and assailing all wrongs. He will rule the nations with a rod of iron, but the hand that is to hold the rod is the hand of his Church as it continues its work of striking out against the evils that will not yield to the Gospel call. It will therefore be the Church in action, cooperating with the Savior, that will finally bind the old serpent and cast him and all his cohorts into the abyss—that will finally do away with all the evils that infect earth life and open the way for the new earth symbolized by the New Jerusalem.

WHEN WILL THIS BE?

When will this final triumph be accomplished? It was long ago that the watchman hailed the morning star at the Savior's birth, when he came to take away the sin of the world, and yet the night of sin still lingers on. When will he fulfill his promise to come again in his full-orbed presence as the King of Glory, the Sun of Righteousness? When will he who came first as the Paschal Lamb, whose heel was bruised by the serpent, come again as the Lion of the Tribe of Judah to crush the serpent's head? Why has he tarried all these weary centuries?

Regarding the question "when," the only possible answer is the one Jesus himself gave to his disciples: "Watch ... for ye know not what hour your Lord will come" (Matt. 24:42). In his Revelation, however, St. John reminds us that since we know not the hour of his coming, it behooves us not only to watch but also to be ready, for it might be today. This is suggested in the verse quoted at the beginning of this chapter, and we find it again in the closing verses of the book (22:10-17). There the revelator is directed not to seal the words of the book and save them for some future time, for they are needed even now. The time is short until the moral status of every person will be fixed, for the Judge is at the door with his rewards and punishments. Let all people know right now how blessed it is to wash their robes (v. 14 AST) —to change their moral and spiritual condition for the better while they still have time, so that when the New Jerusalem comes down from heaven they may have the right to enter it, enjoy the tree of life, and "take the water of life freely."

Regarding the question "why the long delay," we can be more definite. It is not because the Lord is unwilling or unready to come, but because he must wait to be called, chosen. The kingdom of righteousness he will establish when he comes as King of kings will be a democratic one, in which he will reign not only by hereditary right as the Son of God and our Elder Brother but also by the free choice of his people. It will be in our hearts, not in some palace, that he will be enthroned, and he cannot enter any heart until its owner opens the door and invites him to come in. During all the Christian centuries the high privilege of his presence in our hearts has been offered freely to all, but when and where has it been really appreciated and fully accepted? Only on some great occasion, such as Pentecost, or in the glow of a great revival or in the fire of persecution, has the Savior found the doors of many hearts wide open in response to his unwearied knocking; and even then the welcome he has found has often been only that of a casual guest. Clearly the lukewarmness of the Laodiceans represents a problem common throughout Christendom.

It is our own slowness and perversities, then, that have caused these weary centuries of delay. We of the Church, the spiritual Israel of the new Covenant, have been called to prepare the way for the Savior's second coming, and we have not yet completed our task. We should change our questions therefore, and instead of asking when he is coming and why he has waited so long we should ask when we are going to make that coming possible, that coming that is so urgently needed, as is represented in the Apocalypse by the archangel's urgent call for repentance. Not until we are fully responsive to his every purpose can the Savior be enthroned as a spiritual presence in our hearts and lives. Only then can he rule over us as individuals and through us establish his world-wide kingdom of righteousness and peace.

Our prayer, then must be: Come, Lord Jesus! Come into our hearts, and through us come into our world.

NOTE

Many aspects of this challenge to today's Church are discussed also in the last chapter of the author's earlier work, *The Lost Prophecy* (Fleming H. Revell, New York, 1924).

THE APPENDICES

APPENDIX 1

The Primordial Apocalypse of the Stars

The Ancient World View
  The Galactic Universe
  The Zodiac
  Earth's Counterposed Mountains
  Earth's Two Axes

Interrelationships of These Cosmic Symbolisms
  The Zodiacal Gateways
  The First Advent
  The Second Advent
  God and Humanity

The Dramatis Personae of the Apocalypse

APPENDIX 1

The Primordial Apocalypse of the Stars

Primordial religion found in astronomy, the first of the sciences, a loyal handmaid, whose primal cosmography was able to furnish its theology with symbols that are perennially faithful and that constitute a complete apocalypse, the original of all apocalypses, written immutably upon the scroll of the heavens. There, where from time immemorial all of every age and region must see it, in a picture-writing that all of every language and culture may read, is the story of the redeeming work of the Savior of the world—the wounded but finally victorious Seed of the woman, the Lamb-Lion.

These great astral symbols can be recognized as the common source from which the ancient ethnic cultures developed their many varying cosmologies. Of these the most complete and consistent was that of the Euphratean region, from which the ancient Hebrews came. Supremely excellent though it was, however, this cosmology was sadly encumbered with many gods and with the countless demons of Babylonian magic. And yet in the redaction of it used by Moses as the theological prologue of the Torah we find no remnant of these excrescences, nor even any lingering suggestions of them. Israel's religion was purged of all the polytheistic and magic elements of its Chaldean heritage in the great reformation and mutation that accompanied the exodus.

In the Torah, then, we find a cosmology that provided a perfect frame of reference for its ancient parables, old even in the time of Abraham. This cosmology was used by St. John as the background of his Apocalypse. It is a pictorial drama enacted in the starry heavens, with the world view of the ancient cosmology providing the settings of the drama and the heavenly bodies forming the actors seen on this stage. And for the interpretation

175

of these settings and actors we can appeal to the symbolisms and myths that had gathered about them through the ages; to the temple structures and furnishings that were patterned after them; and to the symbolic uses that had already been made of them in earlier apocalyptic writings, especially those found in the books of Ezekiel, Daniel, and Zechariah.

The Ancient World View

To understand the setting of the apocalyptic drama we must inquire into the ancient concepts of the universe as a whole and of the earth's place in it.

The Galactic Universe

In the cosmography of St. John's Revelation, based on the Ptolemaic world view, the earth was of course thought to be at the center of the universe; and around that center, it was believed, revolved all the stars making up the galaxy.

Three important constructions within this universe must be noted because of the symbolisms they provide for St. John's Apocalypse. First there is the galactic circle itself, which we know as the Milky Way, the great band of closely packed stars that represents the edgewise view of our disk-shaped galaxy. In all early folklore this bright belt has been interpreted as a great celestial highway or river, and since it arches somewhat irregularly across both the northern and southern skies it leads both to the northern heaven of heavens and to the underworld of the south. This Milky Way cuts across two great circles marked off on the face of the heavens. One is the projection of the earth's own equator; and the other, at an angle to it, is the ecliptic, the annual path the Sun seems to follow around the celestial sphere. The relation between these two great circles accounts for the earth's seasonal variations, and wherever the four seasons are experienced they have been marked, in early cultures, by special festivals. In St. John's drama the symbolisms associated with them in ancient Israel play a significant role. (See Appendix 2.) By itself the ecliptic has additional symbolic significance, for it is marked off by the constellations of the zodiac (see below).

Lying close to the ecliptic, the path of the Sun, are also the orbits of the Moon and the planets. In ancient thought the term "planet" included all the bodies that follow the ecliptic, the Sun

176

and Moon as well as the true planets, of which only five were then known—Mercury, Venus, Mars, Jupiter, and Saturn. Because these bodies move, they were interpreted as bridging the void between earth and heaven, between time and eternity. Earth does not stand alone and isolated, far from the distant heaven whose fixed stars cannot move to help her. Instead, she is surrounded by the moving "planets." The ancient Hebrews considered these to be God's messengers, the seven archangels—mighty intelligences sent forth from heaven with messages and influences and ministries to help and direct the life of earth and to bring it into conformity with what it ought to be. In St. John's symbolism they are "the seven spirits of God" (Rev. 4:5). The number seven has here, of course, the usual mystic significance of completeness (see Appendix 4), and it was a felicitous ignorance that found just that number among the celestial attendants of the earth.

These "planets" contributed also to the old concept of the structure of the universe. It was assumed that they moved around the earth in seven concentric hollow spheres, and this was the basis for the concept of seven heavens and seven infernos. The galactic axis around which they moved was pictured as passing through the center of the earth, at right angles to the plane of the ecliptic, and extending up through the whirling spheres of the seven heavens to reach the north pole at the top of the universe, the heaven of heavens, where the throne of God was located. This, the only way from earth up to heaven, was the "way of the tree of life" of the Genesis story of Eden.

God's throne, to which the way of the tree of life leads, is far nearer this earth of ours than might be thought, for, as has been noted above, the galactic universe is flattened, making it watch-shaped rather than spherical. Thus the transcendent God is also imminent, "not far from every one of us" (Acts 17:27). In the ancient temple that concept of God in the midst of his people was symbolized by the Shekinah, the fiery cloud above the mercy seat.

All of St. John's visions are described as having been seen "in the spirit," and nearly all of them were seen from the vantage point of heaven (4:1), the northern part of the universe. Thus the whole celestial sphere was open to his view, save only what was hidden by the earth in the immediate region of its south pole. This cycloramic prospect from the top of the northern heavens enabled the revelator to see the whole array of the starry hosts known to the ancients, all of the 48 constellations (sometimes construed as 49 or 50) recognized at that time. Around these star pictures there had grown up many myths and legends, and the symbolisms associated with them had formed the basis of all earlier apocalyptic writing and were therefore available for St. John to use in his great apocalyptic drama.

The one unfailing consensus of the ancient apocalyptic uses of the lore of the stars is the assignment to them of moral and spiritual qualities on the basis of their celestial latitude. In general, the constellations in the northern sections of the heavens were interpreted as symbolizing righteousness, progress, and life more abundant. They represented the supernal influences heaven continually sends to the help of earth life. In contrast, the stellar figures of the southern skies symbolized sin, regression, death—the infernal influences by which hell beguiles and seeks to destroy earth life. At its southern end the galactic axis passes through the seven infernos to reach the south pole of the universe, the "abyss" or the inferno of infernos, where dwelt the great dragon and all his minions. These symbols of recrudescent chaos, devolution, and evil were thought to maintain a continuously evil-working and disaster-threatening hostility toward humanity. Only when earth life has been thoroughly purged of the perversities they personify will this horde of evil doers be driven out of the universe and cast into the utter destruction of the lake of fire and brimstone (20:7–15).

The Zodiac

Midway between these northern and southern regions are the twelve constellations of the zodiac, a zone that encircles the celestial sphere along the ecliptic and extends about eight degrees to the north and south of it. In their apparent revolution around the earth the "planets" seem to move through these constellations.

This zodiacal zone was thought to represent human existence as it now is, for it is a battleground of contending influences—those from the north that would restore the lost image of God, and those from the south that come from the venom-engendering spirit of the serpent. The constellations of the zodiac are therefore open to two opposite interpretations, depending on which influence is given dominance. In their pervert construction,

178

as they were shown in the old Babylonian cosmology, the zodiacal figures represent the agents of Satanic influence on earth life. On the other hand, in their ideal and ultimate construction they symbolize the Church and the State, the two divinely ordained social agencies at work in this battleground of earth life.

It is through these two institutions that God's great salvation is to transform and restore the life of earth, and their affairs were thought to be supervised by the "angels" of the seven "planets" as they moved through the constellations of the zodiac. Those twelve constellations were assigned as "houses" to the seven planets—one each to the Sun (Leo) and the Moon (Cancer) and two to each true planet, one being associated with the Sun and one with the Moon. Included in the solar group were Virgo, Libra, Scorpio, Sagittarius, and Capricornus, assigned respectively to Mercury, Venus, Mars, Jupiter, and Saturn. The lunar group, assigned to the planets in the same order, included Gemini, Taurus, Aries, Pisces, and Aquarius.

From these solar and lunar "houses" the planetary "angels" supervised the affairs of Church and State respectively. Because the individual houses of the Sun and the Moon were associated with both the five solar houses of the planets and the five lunar houses, the zodiac as a whole was divided into two overlapping groups of seven houses each, symbolizing that the activities of Church and State are both separate and intermingled. In the Apocalypse these two groups of seven constellations are symbolized as two seven-branched candlesticks.

From time immemorial and all over the world the zodiac has been recognized as the central feature of the ancient cosmography. Its astronomical uses have been such that it has well been called "the most precious, if not the oldest, scientific heirloom of the human race."[1] Even more precious, however, has it been in its religious uses, so that its constellations have been very appropriately represented by precious stones. From of old these constellations had been accepted as the most significant features of what was regarded as the divinely devised celestial chart of the universe, and the oracles of divine revelation were made known through them. Among the ancient Hebrews this was accomplished by the use of the Urim and Thummim with the jeweled breastplate of the high priest. On it the twelve zodiacal constellations, assigned as heraldic devices to the twelve tribes of Israel, were represented by their identifying jewels.

The Hebrew name associated with that jeweled breastplate belongs, therefore, also to the figure that gave it its significance, the zodiac pictured by its jewels; and that name, *chosen*, is indeed the best possible characterization of the zodiac as it was conceived by the ancients and as it is employed in religious symbolism; for that name finds an exact equivalent in the Greek word *cosmos*, "ordered beauty," an arrangement with an end in view. The zodiac is truly a "cosmos," for it brings into the picture the concepts of ordered time, ordered elements, and ordered life.

Ordered time was the zodiac's primary contribution to the conception of the universe as a realm of law and order, for it is first of all the dial of a great chronometer on which the Sun and Moon and all the planets register the orderly forward march of the months and seasons and years and cycles. It is these time units, culminating in the grand eras marked by the precession of the equinoxes, that the apocalyptists employed to measure their "times" and "ages." And here it is to be observed that indeed, as revelation and science and philosophy agree, it is in ordered time that we must find the beginning of cosmic creation. Revelation tells us that the first and fundamental cosmic reality brought forth by the brooding Spirit of God and announced by the creative Word was "light" (Gen. 1:1–3); and from Pythagoras to the modern physicists, our thinkers and investigators have found the ultimate of their analyses in number, rhythmic vibration, ordered time.

From the zodiac we receive also the concept of *ordered elements*. The second step in creation may be conceived as the ordering of its rhythm into meter, its energy into the elements of matter; and the material cosmos may be conceived as sufficiently advanced for the service expected of it when these elements are ordered in accordance with the requirements of that service. A full picture of that consummation can be found, of course, only in the cosmography as a whole; but, as we have observed, the zodiac includes all other features of the cosmography in its implications, and it is specifically charged with the analysis of the cosmic substance into constituent elements and with the representation of their orderly intermingling and distribution. Here, of course, we can expect, for the suggestion of the elements, only a symbolism employing the means at hand, the conceptions of remotest antiquity. And in those old concepts matter

180

was broken down into earth, water, air, and fire. In ancient cosmology the orderly intermingling and distribution of these four "elements" in the cosmos were represented by the zodiacal trigons. Each element was identified with three different zodiacal constellations, and imaginary lines connecting these three inscribed an equilateral triangle or trigon within the circle of the ecliptic. These trigon associations, with the leading constellation of each group named first, are: (1) Earth—Taurus, Virgo, Capricornus; (2) Water—Scorpio, Pisces, Cancer; (3) Air—Aquarius, Gemini, Libra; (4) Fire—Leo, Sagittarius, Aries.

The four points of the compass are conveniently associated with the zodiac through the bright stars, or lucidae, of the leading constellations of the four trigons. These so-called "royal" stars, denoting respectively the east, west, north, and south, are: Aldebaran, in Taurus; Antares, in Scorpio; Fomalhaut, in Aquarius; and Regulus, in Leo.

Having set before us a physical cosmos sufficiently advanced, the zodiac comes now to its real task, one indicated by the fact, to which its modern name alludes, that all save one of its constellations picture living creatures. It tells, therefore, of the grander work for which the material cosmos of the elements was formed—the creation of a living cosmos, *ordered life*. The development of conscious forms of life is conceived as having begun with a germ planted in the primal deep and to have developed, on the one hand, the outer or bodily and material forms of which the elements are symbols, and, on the other hand, the forms of conscious life of which the consummation is found in man.

This new order of creation involves a new principle. Here the creature must cooperate with the Creator in the development, the unfolding, the evolution, of the nature with which he is endowed. In the apocalypse of Genesis this truth is stated exactly, for we are told that when God created man he "breathed into his nostrils the breath of life; and man became a living soul" (Gen. 2:7).

Furthermore, in this new order of creation, as a consequence of the possibility involved in the self-determination exemplified in evolution, we find also its fearful opposite, devolution; and both evolution and devolution are set forth in the living creatures of the zodiac as they are expounded by the cosmic myths that have come down to us and as they are construed also in those recensions of the apocalypses of the stars, the apocalypses of the written word. In the ancient Babylonian creation tablets these living creatures make their first appearance as the monsters of the zodiac of Tiamat, the old dragon of chaos, and must be conquered and conformed to the cosmos; and it is only too abundantly evident that the dragon of chaos is ever seeking, and all too often successfully, to bring earth life back to the state pictured by those monsters. For example, the ninth chapter of the Revelation pictures the living creatures of the zodiac in their demoniacal aspect and shows the forces of human life under the perverting dominance of the powers of darkness. And in the twelfth chapter the prototype of the great harlot of the Apocalypse is represented by Tiamat's fearful harpy Lakhamu, usurping the place of Virgo, the Church of Christ.

It follows, accordingly, that the zodiac's pronouncements concerning life must deal above all with its re-ordering, with its salvation from the ruin entailed by devolution; and so we find, as the supreme treasure of this precious heritage from antiquity, an apocalyptic exposition of the Protevangel, that ancient foreshadowing of the two advents of the Savior. This is revealed by the changing relationships of the zodiacal constellations and their "signs." Because the figures of these twelve constellations are very unequal in their measurements, they served at first as merely approximate signposts marking the sequence of the months and seasons. When the progress of astronomy made it desirable to note the time element of astral phenomena more accurately, the ecliptic was divided into twelve equal arcs of 30 degrees each, to correspond with the 360 days of the accepted solar year. These arcs were constructed so as to correspond as nearly as possible with the zodiacal constellations and are called the "signs" of the constellations with which they were first associated. When they were first established, the Sun was just entering the constellation Aries, thus also the sign Aries, on the date of the vernal equinox, which marked the beginning of the Hebrew sacred year. Aries, thus associated with the first month of that year, was therefore the "head" of the signs, while Pisces, associated with the last month, was the "heel." Because of precession, however, the vernal equinox shifts westward along the ecliptic, making a complete circuit in about 26,000 years. The Sun of the vernal equinox is therefore now seen in the next constellation, Pisces, although in terms of signs it is still said to be in Aries. The "head" sign has thus encroached upon the "heel" constellation, as in the first prediction of the Protevangel. In doing so, however, it has lost its head position, for the constellation Pisces has taken its place as the marker of the first month of the sacred year.

Thus, while the zodiac was in the first place simply a representation of God's beautiful creation, it was finally employed also to represent God's even more wonderful re-creation, the salvation of the human world gone wrong.

Earth's Counterposed Mountains

As has been noted, the universe was pictured as a series of concentric spheres within which the seven "planets" moved. It followed naturally that its earthly center or core was also conceived as essentially spherical. This concept was supported by the commonly accepted celestial projections of the equator and its meridians.

To the thoughtful among the ancient inhabitants, however, the material earth itself was not the central point of interest. They were more concerned with its relation to the spiritual and moral verities symbolized, on the one hand, by the heavens above them, and on the other by the hells beneath. And so the essentially spherical earth, viewed as a conditioning dwelling place with reference to these two realms, was represented as two counterposed mountains—the *chthôn* and *antichthôn* of the Greeks. Traditionally these were conventionalized into foursquare pyramids, and their peak was conceived as passing altogether through the first crystalline sphere, that of the Moon, and on into the second, that of the Sun. Thus from the great equatorial ocean one world mountain climbed up into the heavens of the north, extending even into the second of the seven heavens, endowing earth life with the capacity to attain access even to the purely spiritual realm of the heaven of heavens, far beyond the limitations of this world of mortality. In similar fashion the other world mountain emerged into the hells of the south, leading to the nadir of human existence, in the abyss of abysses, the lowest pit of inferno.

It is true that we often find the ancients referring to the underworld, the realm of death and the abode of evil, in terms that would suggest merely a great cavern down deep in the solid earth, instead of the vast antipodal region of the celestial universe demanded by this cosmography. The origins of these cavern

183

features sometimes ascribed to the underworld are not far to seek. First, it was inevitable that the grave, the sepulcher, should add its characteristic features to the conception of the great realm with which it was so closely associated. In addition, for people who placed their shrines to the heavenly deities on the tops of pyramids representing the northern world mountain, rising up to the heavens, the only construction that would serve adequately as the shrine of a deity of their underworld pantheon was one that would suggest the apex of an inverted pyramid representing the southern world mountain. Accordingly we find that the temples of the Babylonian god Nergal, who was worshiped as the conqueror and ruler of Aralu, the vast realm of the underworld, were tomb-like excavations.[2] So likewise we find, in that ancient cosmographic monument the great pyramid of Egypt, a cavern, the "subterranean chamber" that is precisely the place required for this symbolism.

It was of course the heaven-attaining northern world mountain that was represented by the pyramidal staged temple towers of the peoples who developed and employed this cosmography. This pattern is also seen in the mountain city of Jerusalem, whose heights were crowned with the successively more exclusive terraced courts and the veiled sanctuaries of the temple.

Earth's Two Axes

Passing through the peaks of these two conventionalized world mountains is the axis for the apparent diurnal revolution around the earth of the planets and their crystalline spheres and the "heavens" associated with them. Standing steadfastly perpendicular to the plane of the ecliptic, this axis was identified in ancient thought as the fixed center of the universe. It was constant in direction, and being the axis around which the universe revolved it represented the only line of no motion. It was therefore the only way from the northern peak of the earth mountain up through the whirling spheres of the planets and on up the steep ascent to the heaven of heavens at the galactic north pole, where was the throne of God.

The earth's own daily rotation, however, takes place around another axis, perpendicular not to the plane of the ecliptic but to the plane of its own equator. A notable and most significant characteristic of the planet earth is the declination of this equatorial axis from the ecliptic axis by an angle of 23-1/2 degrees, and the direction in which it points changes slowly as it precesses, like a spinning top. In a great cycle of 26,000 years it makes a complete swing around the ecliptic axis. Thus, pointing in many different directions and never up through the planetary spheres, it cannot offer a way up to the heaven of heavens. It is therefore a snare and a delusion.

These characteristic differences between the two axes, representing the ecliptic and the equatorial orientations, correspond exactly with the two trees they represent in the Genesis story of the Garden of Eden. The ecliptic axis is the "tree of life," the supreme symbol of the infinite and the eternal and of life's only worthy goal. It can never cease to lead onward and upward, bridging the void between earth and heaven, between time and eternity. On the other hand, the equatorial axis represents the "tree of the knowledge of good and evil." In comparison with its rival it does indeed seem to be "a delight to the eyes" and "to be desired to make one wise" (Gen. 3:6), for it is well marked by successive pole stars and is therefore exceedingly useful to the traveler in his earthly journeys, while the north pole of the ecliptic is altogether inconspicuous and of no apparent significance or assistance to the traveler. Furthermore, as the tempter suggested to mother Eve and later to the builders of the tower of Babel, the terrestrial pole is a gate through which earth life can by its own exertion, without any supernatural assistance, climb up from earth to heaven and become "as gods." It leads only, however, into the second heaven, the realm of the Sun, which is indeed the source of life but only of terrestrial physical life. It cannot lead on up to the highest heavens but is a cul-de-sac, out of which there can be only a retracing of steps. If we content ourselves with the fruit of this tree we therefore remain earthbound, and continuing along our earthly journey we go beyond the furthest northerly point and return southward again. History shows us that again and again earth's vaunting cultures have followed such a downward path and have reverted to barbarism.

These are the symbolisms we find in the parable of Adam's "fall." In that story Paradise, represented by the Garden of Eden, was pictured at the top of the northern earth mountain, and Adam had won admission to it because he had reached the supreme earthly goal of a Godlike personality. That mountain top is not, however, life's utmost goal. It is the vestibule of heaven,

185

from which we can go onward and upward by the way of the tree of life, to achieve the grand mutation of our evolutionary development and win the moral worth that will make us truly children of God. Instead of following that upward way, Adam ate of the fruit of the tree of the knowledge of good and evil and turned and went back down the mountain, following the example of the serpent, the supreme symbol of regression and devolution—the vertebrate that has returned to the worm. It is this turning back, this decision not to press on toward the final goal, that we know symbolically as the "fall."

In the Genesis story, after Adam failed to take the path up into heaven it was barred by the guardian cherubim placed there by the Lord, each having "a flaming sword which turned every way, to keep the way of the tree of life" (Gen. 3:24). Of course God did not place these guardians at the gate of heaven because he was unwilling to permit humanity's further progress upward. The presence of the way invites attainment. But the story indicates the truth that it is indeed a steep ascent and that entrance to this way to the heavens can be gained only by those who are worthy. The guardian cherubim have power to open the gates as well as to close them and are commissioned to administer ready entrance to such as have the password and token. The password must of course be the confession of faith that Jesus is the Christ, the Son of God, and our Savior, while the token must be the cross of Christ.

Facing toward that supreme and only worthy goal, however, we ask how we can take even the first step in its direction, for in our few brief days on this little earth mountain we find ourselves on the brink of a measureless and plumbless abyss that represents a seemingly insoluble mystery. But God had a plan, ordained "before the foundation of the world," by which he himself was to intervene to save humanity from the venom of the serpent. The outline of this plan is set forth in the Protevangel (Gen. 3:15) in the apocalypse that begins the written word of God; and the Old Testament scriptures, from the temple sacrifices and the great festivals renovated and reinstituted by Moses to the Messianic visions of the prophets (Luke 24:27), foretell the initial sacrifice and final triumph of the wounded Seed of the woman who was to crush the serpent's head. In the Gospels we see the actual historic fulfillment of the foreshadowings of the first advent, the sublime condescension of the incarnation. It

186

was down the steep way of the tree of life that the Word of God came from the sapphire throne of heaven and in self-sacrifice and humiliation took flesh and dwelt among us as the Suffering Servant. The vivid apocalyptic drama of the book of Revelation portrays all that appertains to the second advent—the events leading up to it and its consummation. In the last vision of that book, with which the written word of God concludes, we see the New Jerusalem, Paradise more than regained, and the whole earth redeemed from the curse of sin, with humanity's world restored to the orientation that centers in the tree of life.

In the symbolism of these two axes, revealing the two "ways," with all the essential truth concerning them, the ancient cosmography and cosmology developed their most mystical and distinctive features, those that are most fundamental and most serviceable to apocalyptic. As might be expected, the temples of the Euphratean tradition, whose pyramidal form pictures the northern earth mountain, have two free-standing columns that represent the two axes and therefore the two trees of Eden. The temple in Jerusalem followed this pattern, and its columns are discussed in Appendix 3.

The concept of the heaven-piercing world mountain, conventionalized into a four-square pyramid up from which climbs the way of the tree of life, forms the background of three of the most notable visions of St. John's Revelation. These are: (1) the introductory vision of the throne of God and the heavenly hosts, fundamental to the imagery of chapters four through eleven and set forth specifically in chapters four and five; (2) the vision of the Lamb and the Church of the first-born on Mount Zion, recorded in 14:1–5; and (3) the concluding vision of the New Jerusalem (21:1–22:5), the new world "coming down from God out of heaven."

INTERRELATIONSHIPS OF THESE COSMIC SYMBOLISMS

As was indicated at the close of the section on the zodiac, that great celestial construct provides us with an exposition of the Protevangel. Since this requires the commandeering of all the resources of the ancient cosmography, including the earth mountain and its two axes, we must explore the interrelationships involved.

187

The Zodiacal Gateways

In the ancient cosmology, as has been noted, the constellations of the northern skies pictured righteousness and life, while those of the southern regions represented evil and death. The zodiacal zone, midway between the regions of life and death, and therefore a battleground between these contending influences, was thought to represent the present state of human existence.

Movement between these two realms was possible by means of the Milky Way, interpreted as a one-way celestial highway or river. That great starry baldric passes through both the northern and southern skies, crossing the zodiac at the constellations Gemini and Sagittarius. In ancient Semitic thought its northern part served as another symbol of the "way of the tree of life," the path that offers humanity access to the heavens. Coming up from Aralu or Hades, the abode of the dead, at Gemini, the Milky Way rises in a great arch up to the supernal region of the heaven of heavens and immortality. From there it descends back to the infernal regions by way of Sagittarius, which to the ancient Babylonians was ruled by Nergal, the mighty conqueror and master of the realm of the dead. Gemini and Sagittarius were considered therefore to be the inner gates at which the Milky Way crosses the circle of the ecliptic, and through which there can be movement into and out of the northern realm of life.

Similar significance attaches to the adjacent constellations, Cancer and Capricorn, which in ancient times were the stopping places of the Sun for the June and December solstices respectively. Their seasonal symbolisms (see Appendix 2) clearly identify them as partners respectively of Gemini and Sagittarius, offering movement in the same directions and serving therefore as outer doors.

On either side of these double gateways are guardian cherubim. Leo the Lion, with his gleaming sickle, and Taurus the Bull serve as the outer guardians of the Gemini-Cancer entrance portal into the realm of life, while Aquarius (known to the Babylonians as Ramann the Thunderer) and the fearful Scorpio guard the Sagittarius-Capricorn exit portal. These four guardian constellations, the so-called fixed signs of the zodiac, have often been interpreted not only as the cherubim of the Genesis story, guarding the way of the tree of life as represented by the Milky Way, but also as the cherubim of Ezekiel's theophany (Ezek. 1:10

188

ff.) and as the four living creatures of St. John's vision of the throne of God in heaven. St. John indeed identifies them by name: the first was "like a lion," the second "like a calf," the third "had a face as a man," and the fourth was "like a flying eagle" (4:7). The one apparent exception to perfect identity of these creatures with the zodiacal constellations is the metamorphosis of Scorpio into an eagle. Scorpio symbolizes the demoniacal character of the living creatures of the zodiac, as they were represented by the ancient Babylonians. In the Babylonian myth, however, those chaotic hosts of Tiamat were finally conquered and transformed into loyal servitors of order. Just so with the living creatures that appear in St. John's vision of the throne of God. All of them have been redeemed, as they themselves declare (5:9), but the transformation is most striking and absolute in the case of Scorpio. There was doubtless a hint of just such a mystical metamorphosis of the scorpion into the eagle in the notion of the old alchemists that iron could be transmuted into gold only when the Sun was in Scorpio. St. John appears to use both of these zodiacal symbols, for the scorpion woe of his ninth chapter is announced, in the last verse of chapter 8, by a lone eagle flying in the midst of heaven.

For the moment, however, we must return to the role these constellations play in the symbolism of the Genesis story. We have seen eight of the zodiacal "creatures" serving in various ways as wardens for the gates of the way of the tree of life as symbolized by the Milky Way, and the story speaks specifically of their barring the way. We must recognize, however, as noted earlier, that their function is not only to close the gates to those who are unworthy but also to open them to those who have the necessary password and token. Interpreting the Milky Way as the way of the tree of life, our symbolic first parents can be pictured as having climbed the ascending arc of the shining way, up from the realm of death to the summit of earth life. Because of their failure there, further movement along the upward way was closed to them, and they passed down the descending arc that leads to Capricorn's exit gate, back to the realm of death. Instead of going permanently into that infernal region, however, they were permitted to move back into the middle zone between life and death, the zone of the zodiac. From there we humans may climb again the way of the rising arc toward life and immortality if we will accept the promises symbolized by the

189

four remaining constellations of the zodiac. Aries and Pisces tell of the Savior's first advent and its offer of the password and token that will open for us the way of the tree of life. And in the symbolisms of Libra and Virgo we see foreshadowings of the second advent and the final triumph of the King of kings.

The First Advent

The first two of these constellations, Aries of the fiery trigon and Pisces of the watery trigon, stand before Aquarius, the outer guardian of the gate of the December solstice, the winter solstice of the Bible lands and therefore identified as the gate of death. They are symbolic of the first advent of him who is the Way, the Truth, and the Life, and they tell of his death and resurrection.

Because of his death for our salvation Jesus is known as "the Lamb of God that taketh away the sins of the world," the Lamb with whom we too must be "crucified unto the world"; and the zodiacal symbol of that sacrificial Lamb is the little constellation Aries, the Ram, a name that appears to be a hold-over from the zodiac of Tiamat. To the Hebrews, however, it was known as Toleh, the Little Lamb. In ancient times it was the constellation associated with the vernal equinox (see Appendix 2), and as the zodiacal symbol of the temple's brazen altar of sacrifice it represented the Church.

Clearly associated with it symbolically is its neighbor, the great constellation Pisces, the Fishes. In accordance with the ancient Semitic star lore, which assigned a zodiacal sign or constellation to every tribe or nationality, the constellation of the fishes was the accepted zodiacal cognizance of the children of Israel, and as the token of that peculiar people of God it was the symbol also of their Messianic hope. It represented the great deep from which we came and to which we must return—but not to die, for through the sacrifice of the Lamb we go endued with his life, to be washed from our sins and to begin our upward progress over again in newness and abundance of life. This is typified in the initiatory rite whereby we are "baptized unto his death" that we may be born again in his life. The Holy Spirit is again "brooding upon the deep," as at the time of the first creation, that we might become new creatures in Christ Jesus. Pisces has therefore been associated with the "seven spirits of God" (Rev. 1:4 for example)—that is, with the fullest manifestation of the work of the Holy Spirit, the work of renewal of life. To the ancient Semites this fish constellation was known as Nun, and the verb *nûn* means "to reproduce, to multiply." Because of the self-multiplying character of fish life the two fishes of Pisces are indeed natural symbols of the self-propagating and multiplying spirit of life in Christ Jesus that makes us free from the law of sin and death. They represent the worth of God's free gift to us, while the Lamb represents its cost to him. The self-devotion in which he shares his life with us must indeed be for him a sacrifice of which death, even the death on the cross, can be only a suggestive token.

A natural outgrowth of the long-accepted association of Pisces with the children of Israel, the people of the Old Covenant, was the use of the fish sign as the original token of the spiritual Israel of the New Covenant, the church of Christ. This was represented either by a picture of a fish, or fishes; or by the Greek word for "fish"—*ichthus*; or by superposition of the first two letters of that word—*iota* (I) and *chi* (X)—to form a six-armed monogram. The special significance of this symbol came chiefly, however, not from its historic association but because the word *ichthus* is made up of the five initial letters (capitalized here) of the Greek phrase: *Iesous CHristos THeou Uios Soter*—"Jesus Christ, the Son of God, our Savior." This is the one essential doctrine of the Christian confession of faith, and if it is not a mere formula of the lips but a testimony of the newness of life symbolized by Pisces it is the password that will open for us the way of the tree of life. The token that must accompany it is, of course, the cross of Christ, the Lamb of God—not the deceptive fetish of the overt cross but the inner spirit of sacrifice of which the cross is a symbol.

Pisces and Aries thus symbolize the first advent of the Savior and provide the password and token that enshrine the central truths of the Christian religion. Moreover, they are represented in the worship of the church of today—Pisces by the sacrament of baptism, to which Christ himself submitted in token of his voluntary humiliation and obedience even unto death, and Aries by the memorial sacrament of the Lord's Supper, which he initiated. These are the church's only "sacraments," the only ceremonial symbols that were authorized by Christ. They were foreshadowed, however, in the two essentials of the ancient Hebrew temple worship. In the temple's central object, the altar on which the sacrifice was offered, we see Aries represented, while

191

Pisces was represented by the "great sea" and its accessory lavers, in which both the priest and his offering had to be washed.

The Second Advent
The two remaining constellations, Libra and Virgo, are stationed by Leo, the sentinel gate of the June or summer solstice, which is the gate of life, and the keeper of whose threshold is Cancer or the Scarabeus, the emblem of immortality. Here St. John found the symbols of his wonderful Apocalypse of the second advent.

To the ancient Hebrews Libra, the sign of the autumnal equinox, was pictured as the "balances," suggestive of the weighing of evidence and just judgments (cf. Dan. 5:27). It was thought to be the zodiacal representation of the temple's holy place. This entrance room of the inner sanctuary was the audience chamber of Israel's divine King, whose throne was behind the veil, in the Holy of Holies, represented by Virgo. In the holy place, through the agency of the priest equipped with the "breastplate of judgment," Israel's Davidic kings and their predecessors (see Num. 27:21 for example) "enquired" of their divine suzerain by Urim and Thummim. They were sure of cooperative responses because their enquiries were prefaced by offerings of incense on the golden altar that stood in this chamber. Because that incense memorialized the sacrifices on the brazen altar, their pleas were based on the salvation, the reconciliation, made possible by the sacrificial intervention of their sure foreshadowings.

Accordingly, in St. John's Apocalypse Libra and Virgo represent the two great rival but sometimes coalescing institutions of the State and the Church. But in his visions the place of the true Church of Christ is sometimes usurped by Lakhamu, the fearful harpy of Tiamat's train, who is the prototype of the great harlot of the Apocalypse. Likewise the State, represented by Libra, is shown as having been seized and held, now by that false Church, the counterpart of Virgo, and now by a marauding empire, as represented by Scorpio. This reflects an ancient uncertainty as to the constitution of that part of the ecliptic, for it was at times attached to one or the other of the adjacent constellations. Its association with the offices of government, the administration of the law, and the meting out of justice was

192

developed early by the Babylonians, however, for they assigned the associated month Tisri to Shamesh, the divine judge.

In Shamesh we have an unperverted symbol of the "Sun of Righteousness," who is to come as "a consuming fire" and yet "with healing in his beams." He is *Shiloh,* the one whose right it is to reign and to execute judgment upon the earth. This is the promise of the Feast of Tabernacles, which comes in the month of Tisri (see Appendix 2) and which looks forward to a new era that will be ushered in and established by the strong hand of the Son of the virgin, who to that end will smite the nations with a rod of iron. He is symbolized by Leo, the great Lion "of the tribe of Judah," who guards the gate of Cancer. (In Jewish astrology Leo was the sign of the tribe of Judah.) In the Apocalypse this Lion is strikingly identified with the little "Lamb standing, as though it had been slain" (5:5–6 AST) and is indeed that Lamb revealed as the mighty conqueror of sin and death and the grave.

The truth of this interpretation is symbolized by the fact that the autumnal equinox, which in very ancient times gave character to the stars of Libra, has long passed, because of the precession of the equinoxes, into the stars of Virgo. At the time of the first advent it was marked by that constellation's beautiful lucida, the pure white Spica. Now, though it is still among the stars that are construed with Virgo, it is moving toward the arc that belongs to Leo.

Here then are prophetic symbolisms of the second advent of the Savior. This Lamb-Lion is to rule the world as the divine head of the Church, his multiplied incarnation, symbolized by Virgo. It seems strange at first to find this symbol of the Church so far away from the symbols of the altar and the baptismal font, and at the opposite portal of the way of the tree of life. There are similarities between the two, however. While Virgo denotes the true Church of all the ages, it is still a symbol of prophetic rather than of historic import. So it was with regard to Aries and Pisces during the many centuries when they were the celestial counterparts of the smoking altar and the molten sea. But as the types and shadows of the temple service gave place to amazing realities at the coming of the Suffering Savior and his gift of the Holy Spirit, so the latent and invisible verities in the life of the Church will leap into glorious revelation at the coming of the Conquering Christ, the Judge Inexorable. The Christian era has been a season of sowing and of germination, and it is only the harvest that can give meaning to all that has gone before, and to which the plowman looks for his vindication. Until the return of her mighty Son the "woman," the true Church, is as it were hidden in the wilderness (12:14), and her place is often usurped by Tiamat's caricature of her, the great harlot, Lakhamu (17:1 ff.).

The Church as an institution truly representative of her Lord is today, and always has been, a fond hope, an ideal far away and often very dimly reflected. At best, it is only an earnest of expectation. But in the great day of his coming she is in very truth to become the multiplied reincarnation of her Lord, the body of which he will be the regnant and life-giving head. And that Church will be a body one and indivisible, for the saints of all the ages past, an invisible but puissant body, will rise up from the realm of the dead, through the eastern portal of the shining way, to join the hosts of the Church militant, and together they will be caught up into heavenly places in the spirit (1 Thes. 4:16–17). In the final contest with the powers of darkness, not completed until after a "thousand years" of the stern rule of the rod of iron, these hosts of the Church militant and the Church triumphant will wage uncompromising war against wrong in the flesh; and they will vindicate the right of redeemed humanity to march triumphantly through the portal represented by the Scarabeus, through the door thrown wide by the Lion of the tribe of Judah, and to climb once more the way of the tree of life to the Paradise of God, when earth shall at last become the vestibule of heaven.

The beginning of the end will be the last great day of Jehovah, when the Lion with his fearful sickle shall smite and bind the great dragon and destroy Lakhamu, the great harlot. Virgo, the pure and holy bride of the Lamb, will then be restored to full and undisputed possession of her house. The consummation will come with the transmutation of the fearful and deadly Scorpio, the house of Mars and the source of war, into the soaring eagle (4:7 etc.), the divine aspiration that was the original gift with which man was endowed when God breathed into his nostrils the breath of life. Then the balances of government, so long in dispute, will be gladly accorded, by universal acclamation, to him to whom they belong—to the true head of the Church, the King of kings and Lord of lords. Then he will sit upon the great white throne of judgment, and sin and death and hell will be judged and cast into the lake of fire, which is the second death; and he will reign over all as the Prince of Peace in a world made new, a new heaven and a new earth wherein dwelleth righteousness.

God and Humanity

Thus in the patterns and movements of the heavens we have a revelation of the fundamental truths of the relations between God and man that is in complete accord with the revelation contained in the written word of God. It is a comprehensive picture of the framework of the universe on which, as on an appropriate background, is painted an equally comprehensive picture of human destiny. And in it is manifest the power and wisdom and love of God as the Creator, Preserver, and Redeemer of mankind.

THE DRAMATIS PERSONAE OF THE APOCALYPSE

As we have seen, the action of the Apocalypse takes place in the starry heavens, and the actors on this stage are represented by stars or star figures.

Among all the ancient peoples it was assumed as a matter of course that all the starry hosts were servants of the unseen power or powers responsible for the universe. Among the "nations" they were conceived, therefore, as deities, or rather as symbolizing deities, each with his special function in the ordering of nature and the affairs of earth life. The Hebrews, on the other hand, thought of them as symbolizing angels of many hierarchies. All of them save Lucifer, the rebel morning star, and his fallen angels, were in the service of Jehovah of Hosts, the God of nature and the God of Israel; and each star was charged with a regular duty in nature and was subject to call for special service in behalf of God's people.

It would be unpardonable, however, to think so poorly of our ancestors as to suppose that they imputed a relationship of actual identity, either physical or spiritual, between a deity or an angel and his star or star figure. At most the relationship was conceived to be "mystical"; and in general it must have been held to be merely pictorial, conventional, symbolic, and hieroglyphic; and most of the star pictures were subject to several constructions, depending on the context in which they were set forth.

195

St. John, in his Apocalypse, therefore uses "star" and "angel" as synonymous terms; and here, as in all the sacred scriptures, the word "angel" implies a veritable spiritual being. Certainly some of the apocalyptic star-angels symbolize divine messengers intervening in the actual affairs of earth life. It must be recognized, however, that the star-angels of this drama stand in relation to those veritable angels as do the figures of a marionette performance to the persons they represent.

In this apocalyptic drama the actors, represented by stars or star-figures, are of three sorts:

1) First there are the archangels, represented by the seven "planets." These seven "watchers and holy ones" were conceived by the later Hebrews as the "holy overseers" of the hierarchy of heaven and of earth life. They surround the throne of God in the heaven of heavens and represent the regnant first-born of the realm of free intelligences with whom the Creator and Conserver of the universe shares his life and his work, his nature and his prerogatives.

Four of these archangels—Michael, Raphael, Gabriel, and Uriel—were universally regarded as especially the "angels of the face of the Lord," who stand in his immediate presence—before the throne, behind it, and to its left and right. They are therefore known as the cardinal archangels, and their cardinal relationships are reflected in the positions traditionally assigned to them as leaders of the heavenly hosts that guarded Israel's encampments in the wilderness; and since those encampments were an earthly representation of the zodiac, whose twelve constellations were the insignia of the twelve tribes of Israel, the cardinal archangels can be related to the cardinal points of the zodiac. This tradition, as it comes down to us through the Rabins, thus assigns Michael to the zodiacal east, Raphael to the west, Gabriel to the north, and Uriel to the south.

In the actual encampment, an earthly copy of the heavens, the terrestrial cardinal points were a mirror image of the heavenly, presenting a right and left reversal of the celestial original; and the axis in which the reversal took place would be at right angels to the line of vision. Since the "front" with the Hebrews was the east, the east and west positions remained identical with the original, like the top and bottom of a human figure seen in a mirror, while north and south, being at the left and right of the view, were reversed. On the ground, therefore, Gabriel was at the south of the encampment and Uriel was at the north.

Through these cardinal relationships these four archangels are associated, as has been noted, with the cardinal constellations of the zodiac and the trigons they lead; and the influence of the cardinal archangels within these elemental trigons is represented by the assignment to them of the brightest stars of the cardinal constellations—the so-called "royal" stars that mark the cardinal points of the zodiac. Thus Michael represents the earth trigon, led by Taurus; Raphael the water trigon, led by Scorpio; Gabriel the air trigon, led by Aquarius; and Uriel the fire trigon, led by Leo. The associated cardinal stars are respectively Aldebaran, Antares, Fomalhaut, and Regulus.

Since in the ancient cosmography it is the zodiac that relates heaven's activities to the needs of the life of the earth, it is these four cardinal archangels, with their relationship to the zodiac, who are assigned specific individual roles in the Apocalypse. They are sometimes represented by the cardinal stars associated with them, but constellations are assigned to them also—Boötes to Gabriel, Perseus to Uriel, Ophiucus to Michael, and Auriga to Raphael. In ancient cosmological stories these great heroic figures of the northern skies were pictured as messengers from the heaven of heavens; and the apocalyptist uses them in the same way, and also sometimes as the vehicles of the theophanic presence of the Lord.

The four cardinal archangels, therefore, sometimes appear individually and can be identified. No individual identification is possible, however, when all seven serve together as a group.

2) Second, there are stars and star figures which, by the ancient astral lore, had been endowed with characters and attributes that qualified them to serve as the heroes and villains of the apocalyptic drama. These have been identified as they appear in the action. Here it is sufficient to note their general nature. Some of them play the roles of bishops, priests, herald angels, and choruses. Others represent the great adversary and his angels—the dragon and various beasts and demons.

3) Third, there is the Divine Presence. It is an unseen presence on the throne of heaven (4:2) and on the great white throne, holding the scales of justice (20:11). The Savior, however, is represented visibly: as the great theophany of the opening vision (1:13); as the Lamb-Lion breaking the seals of the book sealed with seven seals (5:5–6); as the Lamb standing on Mount Zion

with the hundred and forty-four thousand of the Church militant (14:1); as the Heavenly Harvester (14:14); and as the Word of God, the King of kings and Lord of lords, riding forth on his white horse and followed by the armies of heaven (19:11 ff.).

The stars and star figures pictured in this Revelation appear in sequence as St. John, exiled on Patmos, might have seen them moving across the sky from east to west during the course of a night in the fall of the year. Last of all, rising in the east just before the dawn of a new day, appeared the great square of Pegasus, the astral symbol of the four-square city, the New Jerusalem.

* * *

It is evident, then, that the apocalypses with which the written word of God begins and closes are recensions of the primordial apocalypse of the stars, so ancient that its first form is attributed by tradition to the antediluvian patriarch Enoch. In it we find not only pictures of the paradise humanity has lost and is to regain, but also parables employing cosmic conceptions and astral figures as symbols to set forth, by the help of the myths and folklore associated with them, the essential processes of the great salvation outlined in the Protevangel. It is an age-long campaign of the Creator's intervention, working in and with the creature potentially endowed with his own nature. In this campaign, therefore, we must cooperate, and to it we have been summoned by a whole series of divine revelations. At great cost to himself the Creator, our Heavenly Father, has undertaken to make our restoration possible and certain—to show us how to parry the flaming swords of the guardian cherubim and find and climb the "way of the tree of life," the way that leads ever onward and upward toward the heaven of heavens.

NOTES

1. William Fairfield Warren, *The Earliest Cosmologies* (Eaton and Mains, New York, 1909), p. 119.
2. James Turley van Burkalow, *The Lost Prophecy* (Fleming H. Revell Co., New York, 1924), pp. 39 ff. and 52 ff.

APPENDIX 2

The Parables of the Seasons and
The Allegory of Israel's National Epos

Development of the Hebrew Versions of the Seasonal
Observances

St. John's Use of the Seasonal Festivals

The Hebrew Festivals of the Equinoxes
    The Vernal Equinox and the Passover
    The Autumnal Equinox and Its Festivals
    The Prophetic Symbolism of the Equinoctial Festivals

The Hebrew Festival of the Summer Solstice

The Omitted Winter Solstice and Its Symbolisms
    The Zodiacal Symbolism
    The Roman Saturnalia and Its Symbolisms
    Moses' Omission of the Festival
    Its Promises for Us

APPENDIX 2

The Parables of the Seasons and
The Allegory of Israel's National Epos

Like all primitive peoples, the ancient Hebrews found a deep spiritual significance in the changing face of nature as the Sun moved through the stars in its inevitable course that marked the months and seasons of the year. With all the other grateful and worshipful children of earth they observed especially the all-important seasons of seedtime and harvest, celebrating them with great festivals of joyful worship. These appear to be the oldest, most universal, and most inclusive of all the religious practices of the human race. Their observances involve prayer and praise and sacrifice, and their symbolisms offer all-sufficient hope and reveal the power, wisdom, and beneficence of God, the Creator and Preserver of the universe. At these great conclaves the people came together to give thanks for the bounties the season had brought, and to make sure of providential help in whatever vicissitudes the seasonal changes might bring.

DEVELOPMENT OF THE HEBREW VERSIONS OF THE SEASONAL OBSERVANCES

In the beginning these festivals and myths were doubtless concerned simply with thanks to God for the glad hope of seedtime and its blessed fulfillment in the harvest, and with prayers for his help against the fierce storms of winter and the burning heat of summer. When they first appear above the horizon of history, however, the inevitable discovery of their relation to the equinoxes and solstices had already been made and appropriately dealt with, and their myths had been gloriously enriched by the inclusion in them of the felicitously consonant parables provided by the movements of the "other" planets around the zodiac. (See Appendix 1.)

Unfortunately, however, in all the sadly degenerated ethnic

201

variations of the primordial religions the nature parables associated with the seasons came to be clouded and disfigured by polytheism and magic. Because of these perversions the Hebrew reformation, of which Abraham was the morning star and Moses the rising Sun, made a number of revisions. As a protest against the world-wide orgiastic features of the solstitial festivals, these were dispensed with, the winter one being omitted altogether and the summer one being replaced by the Day of Pentecost, which comes forty-one days earlier than the solstice. Furthermore, in the celebrations of Pentecost and of the equinoctial festivals the original nature festivals were largely eliminated. Substituting for them are the significant and indeed very pertinent features of Israel's national epos construed as a grand allegory of salvation. The festivals thus became instructive and inspiring rallying points, regulative of the social as well as the religious life of the Messianic people.

For the Hebrews, therefore, the seasonal festivals had acquired a prophetic significance because of their memorial association with the most distinctive movement in the history of that Messianic people—their pilgrimage from the bondage of Egypt to the settled liberty of the Land of Promise. That pilgrimage foreshadowed the Messianic parable of the final deliverance of the whole of earth life from its bondage to Satan and the establishment of the democratic kingdom of the Messiah. Thus it served to reveal the Creator as above all a Savior, a Re-Creator.

St. John's Use of the Seasonal Festivals

In this memorial and prophetic significance of the Hebrew festivals St. John found just the needed pattern for his apocalyptic drama, which foreshadows in more detail the events that are to result in that glad consummation. Here we see portrayed the wilderness journey of spiritual Israel down the Christian centuries, from the advent of Jesus, the prophet like unto Moses (Deut. 18:15; Acts 3:22–23), to his *parousia*, his second advent as the finally all-victorious Joshua of the New Covenant, who is to win for us the rest that remains for the people of God (Heb. 4:8 ff.).

Accordingly, St. John patterned his drama after the four great festivals of the ancient Hebrew calendar, each of his four acts representing one of them. All four were included in the first seven months of the sacred year, and this peculiarly worshipful period was sometimes known as the "week of months." In order of their occurrence the four are (1) the Passover, at the March or vernal equinox (the seasonal labels used here refer, of course, to the northern hemisphere); (2) the Day of Pentecost, coming a little earlier than the summer solstice, whose festival it replaced; and, marking the autumnal equinox, (3) Rosh Hashanah, or the Feast of Trumpets, celebrating the civil New Year, and (4) the Feast of Tabernacles and the great harvest festival of the final ingatherings of the fall.

In between Rosh Hashanah and Tabernacles comes the great Day of Atonement, represented in all four acts of St. John's drama. And following the fall equinox comes the winter solstice, the symbolisms of which St. John uses, even though it was omitted from Moses' calendar of festivals. The significance of the Day of Atonement and its role in the Apocalyptic drama will be considered in Appendix 3, but details and the zodiacal symbolisms of the other observances, including the winter solstice, are presented in the following sections of this Appendix.

THE HEBREW FESTIVALS OF THE EQUINOXES

The equinoxes are the times twice a year, in the spring and in the fall, when day and night are equal. On the spring equinox, when the Sun moves into the sign of Aries, "the ram" (called by the Hebrews Toleh, "the little lamb"), light, which has been gaining strength since the winter solstice, begins to prevail over darkness. In the fall, on the other hand, when the Sun moves into the sign of Libra, "the scales of justice," darkness, which has been recovering strength since the summer solstice, begins to prevail again over light.

The zodiacal constellations that carry these two crucial points in the contest between light and darkness are most appropriate to represent the institutions—Church and State—that have been divinely ordained to deal with the problem thus pictured: the one to proclaim the truth and further the increment of light, the other to war against the persistently recrudescent powers of darkness. We see these two aspects of the zodiacal symbolism reflected in the two-fold reckoning of the Jewish year. In ancient theocratic times only the sacred year was followed, beginning at

203

the new moon of the vernal equinox and symbolizing the Church. The civil year, instituted at a later time when Church and State were separated, begins at the new moon of the autumnal equinox, which thus symbolized the State.

In Israel's calendar, therefore, there were two Old Year and New Year celebrations, one in the spring and one in the fall. In each case the major celebrations (Passover and Rosh Hashanah respectively) were postponed to the full moons in order to dissociate them from the perversions of the new-moon celebrations of the Gentiles. As a result the references to the termini of the years were blurred, and they were further obscured by the overshadowing interest of the great allegory of the Exodus, memorials of whose salient features were superimposed upon the seasonal and zodiacal burdens of these festivals. There are nevertheless discernable likenesses to the ethnic Old Year and New Year celebrations, such as the Saturnalia, Beltane, Hogmanay, Yuletide, and Walpurgis; and these similarities do not result, as some early church fathers have suggested, from their all having been Satan's deceitful counterfeits of the divinely instituted services of true religion. Instead, all of these ethnic festivals and "mysteries" are survivals, more or less perverted by human predilections, of God's primordial revelation. The purity of that revelation and the genuine unfolding of its germinal truths were maintained in the worship of the Messianic people by virtue of the constant divine supervision and discipline ordained in their theocratic covenant.

As we have seen in Appendix 1, the zodiacal signs associated with the spring and fall equinoxes symbolize respectively the first and second advents of the Savior. The following discussion of their associated festivals will show that these carry the same symbolisms.

The Vernal Equinox and the Passover

At the time of the vernal or spring equinox the Sun comes up from its winter absence in the south, returning with light and warmth to renew summer in the lands of the northern hemisphere, where winter and death had held sway. Accordingly, the month Nisan in which this equinox occurs was the first month of the sacred year.

That sacred year began, not with any special New Year celebrations, but with a fast day in commemoration of the divine visitation of judgment upon the whole house of Aaron—when two of his sons, Nadab and Abihu, were punished with death because they "offered strange fire before Jehovah" and the other two, Eleazer and Ithomar, were rebuked by Moses because of careless disobedience in the discharge of their duties (Lev. 10). This was followed on the tenth of the month by a fast in memory of the death of Miriam, sister of Moses (Num. 20:1). On this date also the Joshua of the Old Covenant succeeded Moses, the law giver, as the commander of the hosts of Israel and led them across the Jordan River into the Promised Land of Canaan (Josh. 1:1 ff. and 4:19). The date therefore has prophetic significance, for it foreshadows the coming of the Joshua of the New Covenant, who is to lead spiritual Israel into the promised land of the kingdom of heaven. He came first, however, as the Lamb of God that taketh away the sin of the world, to deliver humanity from the bondage of sin and the curse of the broken law and the fear of death. And it was through the humble obedience of the namesake of the sister of Moses, her whose name we unwarrantably shorten when we call her the Virgin "Mary," that God provided the divine Paschal Lamb. Here again the prophetic significance of the date is evident, for on it every householder of Israel was expected to provide himself with a lamb for the celebration of the Passover four days later.

Passover, the great festival of the vernal equinox, begins on the fourteenth of Nisan, which was originally always on a Friday, and continues for seven days. It commemorates the deliverance of the children of Israel from the bondage of Egypt. More particularly, it recalls the strange fact that Jehovah accomplished that deliverance through the angel of death, who smote the oppressors but "passed over" and left untouched the homes of Israel—hence the name Passover. They were protected because upon their door posts and lintels they had sprinkled the blood of a lamb. Accordingly, the sacrifice of a lamb and the supper at which it was eaten, together with unleavened bread, on the evening of the fourteenth, constitute the characteristic features of the feast.

It is in harmony with this most significant symbol of the Hebrew ceremonial of the spring festival that in the immemorial picture-writing of the heavens the Sun at this time entered the sign of the constellation that symbolizes the temple's brazen altar of sacrifice, known to us as Aries, the Ram, but called

Toleh, the Little Lamb, by the Hebrews. (Because of the precession of the equinoxes the Sun is now in the constellation Pisces at the time of the vernal equinox, but it is still described as being in the "sign" of Aries. See Appendix 1.) The Passover festival is thus a prophetic foreshadowing of the sacrifice of the Lamb of God for the deliverance of humanity from the bondage of sin, whose wages is death. In fulfillment of those ancient foreshadowings, the great sacrifice of the love of God that makes possible humanity's deliverance from sin and death was consummated in the crucifixion of the Son of man on the fourteenth of Nisan, the day ordained for the sacrifice of the paschal lamb; and his glorious resurrection came three days later. As the blood of that sacrificial victim saved Israel of old from the visitation of death, so the blood of the Savior—his own divine life freely shared with us—will give life eternal to spiritual Israel; and as the flesh of the lamb eaten at that first paschal supper gave the Chosen People strength for the march out of Egypt to their new life as freemen, so the Savior's own spiritual presence provides the "bread of life" that will sustain all who believe on him.

Lest we forget that the essential purpose of this great sacrifice that fulfills the promise of Passover is removal of sin and not simply of death, which is only a consequence of sin, another distinctive feature of the Passover was the searching out and destroying of all the old leaven of the year just closed. Throughout, the seven days of the feast only unleavened bread is eaten; whence it is often called the Feast of Unleavened Bread. Thus the yeast for the year that follows must be an entirely new culture. Just so the old and degenerate leaven of the Scribes and Pharisees, the putrefaction that hides in the whited sepulchers of worldly wisdom and self-righteousness, is at last to be searched out and eradicated, a token of the final destruction of sin itself. Fulfillment of this feature of the old festival is represented by the Lord's Supper, and so we do well to eat it, not with the unleavened wafers of the Passover but with leavened bread, symbolic of the leaven of righteousness that came into the mind and heart and will of humanity with the birth of Him who was the Lamb of God. This new leaven of the Kingdom of Heaven is finally to leaven the whole lump of earth life (Gal. 5:9).

Like the other Mosaic festivals, the Passover had also a significant relationship to the seasons of seedtime and harvest. It comes at the time of spring sowing, when the seed is cast into the ground and dies, but with the sure hope that in due time it will spring up in a new and more abundant life. The only nature ceremony remaining in the festival at the time of Jesus was altogether expressive of that hope, for it was a celebration of the very first of the firstfruits. The barley sown the previous fall was now ready for harvest, and the first ripe grain of the season was presented before God as a "wave sheaf" offering on the sixteenth of Nisan, the third day of the feast, as an earnest of the harvests of grain and fruits that were to follow in the summer and fall. The wave sheaf was thus an assertion of the power of the spirit of life to triumph over death. Its promise has had its glorious fulfillment in the resurrection of our Lord as "the firstfruits of them that sleep," and the third day of the feast has been transformed into the joyous festival of Easter.

Thus Passover marks the birth of Israel as a nation and is the prophetic token of the central and essential feature, the very core, of their mission as a people—the Chosen People from whom the Messiah was to come.

At the beginning of the sacred year, therefore, we find both Old Year and New Year celebrations. The old year's failures were represented by its old leaven, which was thoroughly searched out and disposed of in preparation for the unleavened bread that, in the Passover feast, memorialized Israel's hasty flight from Egypt. Remembrance of the sins of the past was represented also by the initial fast day. The new year's hope was represented, not only by all the symbolisms of the Passover celebration but also, as in all new year celebrations, by bright illuminations, as of a newborn sun. In the Passover, primarily a household festival, the illuminations take the form of many lamps or candles in every home. Accordingly, in his Apocalypse St. John employs as his symbol of Passover the menorah, the seven-branched candelabrum or lampstand that lit the Holy Place of the house of God.

The Autumnal Equinox and Its Festivals

The seasonal festival of the autumnal equinox, the Feast of Full Ingatherings (with which Moses combined the Feast of Tabernacles), is celebrated at the equinoctial full moon, as is true of the spring festival of the Passover. It is preceded, however, by two related observances, the civil year's New Year's Day (Rosh Hashanah) and the great Day of Atonement.

The civil year of the ancient Hebrew calendar began, as has been noted, at the new moon of the autumnal equinox, on the first day of the month Tisri.

As in the case of the sacred year, the observances marking the beginning of the civil year included recognition of both the old year and the new. The old year's sins were acknowledged, repented of, and represented as expiated in penitential services during the first ten days of the year, concluding with the great fast of the Day of Atonement. And in the Feast of Tabernacles, marking the end of the wilderness wandering and looking forward to the prospect of crossing over the Jordan into the Land of Promise, the hope of the future was celebrated.

In contrast to the sacred year, the civil one is opened by a great New Year's Day celebration. Its solemn convocation, which includes special sacrifices, along with music, scripture readings, and prayers, is so strikingly characterized by the sounding of trumpets that it is sometimes called the Feast of Trumpets. At the same time this great New Year's Day or Rosh Hashanah is called also the Day of Judgment, an interpretation in keeping with the fact that at the autumnal equinox the Sun enters the zodiacal sign of Libra, the "balance scales" of justice, the celestial symbol of the Judge of all the earth. In Christian thought, therefore, the trumpets that marked that day of old have come to symbolize the final summons that is to assemble all, both the living and the dead, to appear before the great white throne. It is these trumpets also that furnish the symbols with which St. John, in his Apocalypse, marks the exit of the old order and prepares the way for the new.

The Day of Judgment introduces the penitential period leading to the Day of Atonement on the tenth of Tisri. The two are brought together at the beginning of the year to remind Israel of the judgments that led to the solemn covenant God made with them at the beginning of their history, and of their high privilege and deep responsibility as his Chosen People, called out of the nations and chosen from among their brethren. It was with Abraham that God made that first covenant, promising that through his seed he would bless all the nations of the earth (Gen. 22:18), for through them he would provide a sacrificial lamb, as he did for Abraham on Mount Moriah. The ram caught in the thorns there, provided by God for sacrifice as a substitute for Isaac, is a token of the sacrificial Lamb of God, born of the seed of Abraham, that should take away the sin of the world.

God's sifting out of the Chosen People continued through the generations, as he chose Isaac over Ishmael and the sons of Keturah, and went on to pass by Esau and elect Jacob. Finally he accepted all of Jacob's children and multiplied them into the twelve tribes of Israel. The Day of Atonement carries a reminder of this selection process in the ancient ceremony in which choice was made by lot between two goats. One was "for Jehovah," symbolizing his Chosen People, exemplified especially by Isaac and Jacob; and the other, the scapegoat turned out to wander in the wilderness, as did Ishmael and Esau, was "for Azazel."

In remembrance of these ancient covenant dealings the special Torah readings for the first two days of Tisri are Genesis 21 and 22, which tell of the selection of Isaac over Ishmael and of the sacrifice on Mount Moriah.

The fifteenth of the month marks the beginning of the seven-day celebration that the Jews were wont to call simply "the Feast," in recognition of its significance as the final and crowning festival of the year. In its seasonal role this was the Feast of Full Ingatherings, the harvest home when the promise of the spring planting and the firstfruits of Pentecost had been altogether fulfilled. In ordinary parlance, however, it was spoken of as the Feast of Tabernacles or Booths, for it commemorated the time when the children of Israel, having escaped out of Egypt, tabernacled in the wilderness on their way to the settled residence and peace and plenty of Canaan, the "rest" of the Land of Promise, which they reached under the leadership of Joshua. At the same time it interpreted that ancient migration as a foreshadowing of the journey of spiritual Israel through the wilderness of this world toward the "better country" seen of old "from afar," the new world upon whose summit will stand the heavenly city of the New Jerusalem (Heb. 11:9–16 AST). In like manner the Feast of Full Ingatherings self-evidently foreshadows the harvest-home of the age.

In remembrance of that ancient pilgrim journey the people dwelt in tabernacles or booths, as their forefathers did in the wilderness; and on each of the seven days of the feast they carried out special ceremonials to memorialize God's special care of his people in their wanderings. All night long great golden candelabra in the temple court were lit in memory of the pillar of fire, the Shekinah, that lighted and guided the ancient Israelites in the wilderness. Around these lights pious and distinguished men, even the great rabbis of the day, danced before the people with lighted flambeaux in their hands, singing hymns and songs of praise, which the Levites accompanied with harps, psaltries, cymbals, and all sorts of musical instruments. This continued until daybreak, when water was withdrawn from the pool of Siloam, the "well of salvation" (Isa. 12:3), in memory of the plenteous streams of water that flowed from the rock smitten by Moses at Meribah. This "outpouring of the waters," as it was called, was regarded as the most significant feature of the great feast. From the psalms and hymns and glad acclamations that were characteristic of these ceremonials the feast, and especially its great last day, was often given still another name, the Great Hosannah.

The Feast was followed, not by an immediate return to ordinary life, but by an eighth day of ceremonial observance, the Simchath Torah. This day of holy convocation marked the completion of the prescribed course of readings by which the synagogue services covered the books of Moses during the course of the year. It was suggestive of the "Sabbath rest" that remains for the people of God, a rest that the Joshua of the Old Covenant could not give the Israel of his day but into which the spiritual Israel of the Church is to be led by the Joshua of the New Covenant, the divine Redeemer, the Mighty-to-Save. But the ingathering of the autumn harvest involves judgment also, the casting out of the tares and the chaff; and before the Joshua of the New Covenant can confirm unto us our Christian heritage in that rest, he must drive out the abominations of the Canaanites that curse the land and make peaceful possession of it impossible. The dark shadow of the last judgment is therefore upon the background of the Feast of Ingatherings.

Clearly, then, the autumnal festival period looks forward to the end, not of the world or of earth life, but of this age of the seeming triumph of evil, of which the ancient wilderness wanderings are a type. That end will come when He who was rejected by the house of Israel will indeed return according to his promise as the Lion of the tribe of Judah, the King of kings and Lord of lords. As the Joshua of the New Covenant, the long-promised Son of David, he will lead spiritual Israel, which has gathered the full harvest of the fruits of the spirit, into the Sabbath rest when earth shall become the vestibule of heaven.

The Prophetic Symbolism of the Equinoctial Festivals

These two great nature festivals of seedtime and harvest are part of our common human heritage. Because the Hebrews added to that inheritance memorials of their own high calling as the Messianic people, their equinoctial celebrations form a remarkably complete exposition of the hope of Israel and of the world. They picture the coming of the promised Redeemer, first as the seed of the life of heaven on earth and the Lamb of God that taketh away the sin of the world, and finally as the Lion of the tribe of Judah who will reap both the harvest and the vintage of the earth. These are his offices as the great High Priest and the royal Judge.

The great moral truth taught in the Passover is its supreme formulation of the law of love and sacrifice. Jesus himself set it forth in one of his public discourses during his last Passover: "He that loveth his life shall lose it; and he that hateth his life in this world shall keep it unto life eternal" (John 12:25). This law holds good in all the relationships and activities of life; and the Son of God himself obeyed it. Laying aside the glory which he had with the Father, he took upon himself our nature and became obedient unto death, even the death on the cross, for the joy that was set before him in the union with him of redeemed humanity. All who would share that union with him, our Elder Brother, must obey this law; for they who wear the crown with him must also bear the cross with him. This is indeed the essence of Christianity and the significance of the first advent.

Just as the Passover sets forth the law of love and sacrifice, so the autumn celebrations set forth its sanction, the law of righteousness, the law of truth and justice, which will not permit love's sacrifice to be in vain. This will be writ large in the Savior's second advent.

The supreme essential of a life that is truly rational and ethical is the hope of immortality, and this hope is inherent in the fundamental symbolisms of both of these great festival periods of the Hebrew calendar. It is the first corollary of the law of love, and the firstfruits of that hope were represented by the wave sheaf of the Passover, whose glorious prophecy was fulfilled on the first Easter morning. But the fact of sin and its persistence call for the law of righteousness and the separation of the tares from the wheat, a necessary accompaniment of resurrection and an inescapable prerequisite of the new era that is to follow.

THE HEBREW FESTIVAL OF THE SUMMER SOLSTICE

The solstices mark the times, at the beginning of summer and winter, when the Sun, in its apparent journey north and south of the equator, seems to "stand still" at its northernmost and southernmost positions respectively. On its apparent journey around the ecliptic the Sun is at these times in the signs of the zodiacal constellations Cancer and Capricorn. It is also in these same general areas of the skies that the Milky Way, arching across the northern and southern skies, crosses the zodiac, the belt that was interpreted as the region of mortality, midway between the realm of eternal life in the heavens of the north and that of death in the southern region of Hades or Aralu. (See Appendix 1.)

These two constellations were therefore construed as gates in the zodiac, the only places where it was possible to leave the region of mortality, and such movement has to be along the Milky Way. Through Capricorn's gate that way led down into the realm of death, and there could be no return through that gate, for movement along the shining Milky Way was thought to be permitted in only one direction. Where the path led back up through Cancer's gate, however, it was possible to move from death back to mortal life, and from there, along "the way of the tree of life," on up to heaven and eternal life. From there the path led back to Capricorn, and this was the way by which the Son of God moved from heaven into the life of mortal man. Cancer was therefore the gate of both resurrection and eternal life, and Capricorn the gate of death.

As we have seen in Appendix 1, these zodiacal gates involved more than these two constellations, however. Cancer and Capricorn were construed as the outer doors of the gates, while the adjacent constellations, Gemini and Sagittarius respectively, were the inner doors; and each gate was guarded by a zodiacal cherub on either side—Gemini-Cancer by Leo and Taurus, and Capricorn-Sagittarius by Scorpio and Aquarius.

212

The Summer Solstice and Pentecost

Cancer, the Crab, the traditional home of the summer solstice, was thus from ancient times accepted as representing both the door to heaven and life eternal and the door of resurrection from the dead.

In the zodiac of the Egyptians, accordingly, this constellation was construed as a scarab. This beetle, which is first a grub, then a cocoon, and finally a winged creature, was their symbol of resurrection. As such it was esteemed above all other symbols and was engraved lavishly on the precious stones used in Egypt as seals and personal ornaments; and always numerous representations of the scarab were included in the furnishings of their dead.

Likewise among the Babylonians and their neighbors throughout the Semitic world the myth associated with the summer solstice, that of Ishtar and Tammuz, was based on summer's resurrection of earth's vegetation, after it had been killed by winter. The fourth month, corresponding to Cancer, was accordingly called Tammuz, and the Babylonian festival of the summer solstice was celebrated on the seventeenth of this month.

Among the Hebrews the Babylonian name Tammuz was retained for this fourth month, as was the earthly seasonal aspect and primitive significance of their summer festival, known as the Feast of Firstfruits. Its celebration was advanced forty-one days, however, thus effectively dissociating it from the sadly debauched Babylonian and Canaanitish celebrations of the myth of Ishtar and Tammuz. At the same time, and this is clearly the fundamental reason for the change, it was brought into close association with, and indeed became essentially an adjunct of, the immediately preceding festival of the Passover, coming just fifty days later. Evidently both of these festivals, the one in the spring and the other in early summer, were in their seasonal aspects "feasts of the firstfruits." The earlier of these firstfruits was of course the wave sheaf of the barley harvest, which was offered on the third day of the Passover celebration; and it was from that day that the fifty days were counted to fix the time of observance of the Hebrew summer festival (Lev. 23:15–16). That latter came, therefore, to be called the Feast of Weeks or more frequently Pentecost, the feast of the fiftieth day. It marked the end of the grain harvest, the grains being the

213

firstfruits that were to be followed all through the summer and fall by successive harvests of other products of the land, and by the final ingathering celebrated at the great fall festival.

Thus these two prophetic festivals were joined together and really formed a composite unit, merging the celestial cross and wave sheaf of the vernal equinox with the two doors of the gate of the summer solstice. This blending of the two is evidenced by the following sequence of events: the crucifixion of the Savior on Friday, the first day of the Passover; his resurrection from the dead and the offering of the wave sheaf on the following Sunday (the first Easter), which was the seventh Sunday before Pentecost; his ascension into heaven on the Sunday immediately preceding Pentecost; and on that feast day itself, the first Whitsunday, in accordance with his promises (Luke 24:49; John 16:7), his gift of the Holy Spirit to his waiting and spiritually exalted disciples. It was that gift that brought the Christian Church into being, gave her life, and enabled her to grow and work. As Passover is the story of the Word of God incarnate in Christ Jesus, so Pentecost is the story of the multiplied reincarnation of the divine life of the Word of God in the Church, the mystical body of which he himself is the head. And as the grain harvest was an earnest of the final fall ingathering, so that Pentecostal outpouring of the Holy Spirit in the upper room in Jerusalem is also prophetic. It is an earnest of the mightier baptism, the richer gifts, the fuller enduement with the spirit of life, that will enable the Church at last to win the world in the antitypical festival of full ingathering at the end of the age.

It was altogether in keeping with this prophetic significance, therefore, that the manifestations at the birth of the church were so unmistakably suggestive of the striking and characteristic features of the Festival of Full Ingatherings—the jubilant Feast of Lights and the Outpouring of the Waters, with its glad hosannas. For of that Pentecostal earnest of the full harvest St. Luke tells us: "And when the day of Pentecost was fully come, they were all with one accord in one place. And suddenly there came a sound from heaven as of a rushing mighty wind, and it filled all the house where they were sitting. And there appeared unto them cloven tongues like as of fire, and it sat upon each of them" (Acts 2:1–3).

As we have seen, the gate of heaven through which the Savior ascended is associated with the symbolism of the summer solstice. And in Biblical apocalyptic symbolism Cancer, the outer door of the gate of heaven, lends itself especially to the representation of spiritual exaltation and divine inspiration. In keeping with this symbolism Pentecost celebrates not only the Feast of Firstfruits but also the giving of the law of Moses, and this was one of the considerations in the shifting of this summer festival to a date forty-one days before the solstice. The Exodus story (Exod. 19:1–2) tells us that on the first day of Sivan, the third month, the children of Israel encamped before Mount Sinai, and after six days of inquiry on the part of Moses, of instruction and the offering of a covenant on God's part, and the acceptance of that covenant on the part of the people, the covenant was ratified (Exod. 19:3–24:11). That is, the essence of the law was completed on the sixth day of Sivan, which is the Day of Pentecost, for counting inclusively it is the fiftieth day from the sixteenth of Nisan, the day of the wave sheaf of the Passover service. The giving of the law in full was not completed, however, until forty-one days later, on the seventeenth of Tammuz, or the day of the summer solstice, for it was then that Moses came down from the Mount, where he had stayed forty days and forty nights in response to God's call. When he came down it was to find his people hilariously and obscenely worshiping the golden calf. Here then we have another reason, and no doubt the one that was really operative in the minds of the people, for moving the summer festival away from that day. It was finally devoted to a fast in memory of the final capture of Jerusalem, the result of an even worse apostasy on the part of its people.

The gate of the summer solstice, the gate to the way up to heaven, therefore represents the first of the two methods of divine intervention for our salvation. This is the method of revelation of the word of truth through divine inspiration, which is conceived not as given by the Holy Spirit coming down out of heaven, but as given to those who have been received up into heaven—that is, those who have attained a state of heavenly exaltation. So Moses climbed to the top of Mount Sinai, symbolic of climbing up into heaven; so the Savior was transfigured and communed with Moses and Elijah on a mountain top; so St. Paul was "caught up to the third heaven" (2 Cor. 12:2); and so St. John saw in the heaven an open door and heard a voice say, "Come up hither," and at once he was "in the spirit" (Rev. 4:1,2).

THE WINTER SOLSTICE AND ITS SYMBOLISMS

Although Moses did not include celebration of the winter solstice in the calendar of seasonal festivals (his probable reasons are discussed below), the symbolisms of that solstice and its zodiacal relationships contribute significantly to the story of God's great plan for the salvation of his earthly children and were used by St. John in his Apocalypse (see Act 3).

The symbolisms of this solstice are two-fold. From the agricultural point of view, present in the other seasonal festivals, this is the time for sowing the winter wheat and barley. From the astronomical point of view it is, on the one hand, a time of vivid remembrance of the southward retreat of the Sun, with the shortening of its daily ministry and the lessening of its vigor, and on the other hand a time of confident expectation that with the New Year there will be a new birth of solar glory and power and beneficence.

The Zodiacal Symbolisms

In the zodiac the winter solstice marks the gate to the downward arc of the shining way of the galaxy, which leads down from heaven, the realm of eternal life, down into either the zodiacal realm of mortality or the underground realm of death. Being conceived as an oriental fortress structure, this gate, like that of the summer solstice, has outer and inner doors, Capricorn and Sagittarius, and the guardian cherubs Scorpio and Aquarius are stationed on either side.

Capricorn, the Goat-Fish constellation, is the outer door of the gate and the entrance to the underworld. The double nature of this figure suggests the two entirely different ultimate goals of the mortals who enter that gate from time to eternity. Spiritual death is the goal symbolized by the "goat" feature of the constellation; but the "fish" feature commutes that doom to mere physical death for a season, this being granted to those bearing St. John's "seal of the living God," which is set forth by the fish-word *ichthus*. (See Act 2 and Appendix 1.)

Sagittarius, the Bowman, is the inner door of the gate, the one through which the shining way of the galaxy opens into the realm of mortality. Indeed, the galaxy shines most gloriously in this constellation, as befits the fact that it serves as the exit gate by which high heaven's divine interventions are represented as

216

coming to the rescue of earth life. We find, accordingly, that Sagittarius is the figure St. John employs in his vision of the King of kings and Lord of lords, who is coming to "destroy them that would destroy the earth," to establish here the Heavenly Father's kingdom of righteousness and peace, and to prepare the earth to receive the Holy City that is to take the place of the lost Garden of Eden. In the ancient Sumerian idiograms Sagittarius is represented as NER.GAL, "the great hero"—a title applied to the supreme symbol of divine power, the Sun in his fiery might. Moreover, in further accordance with St. John's employment of Sagittarius, this "great hero" was called also SHISH.GAL, "our elder brother," and NE.URU.GAL, "the conqueror of the realm of death"; and it was foretold of him that he was likewise to be the conqueror of all of earth's destructive hellions in the final world war described in the "Dibbara legend."[1]

Aquarius, the Water Pourer, is the man-faced cherub who stands at Capricorn's door. In accordance with Euphratean ideas concerning the so-called "dead," his stream of water sustains the underworld life represented by the fish feature of Capricorn.

Scorpio represents the cherubic monitor who stands at the door of Sagittarius. Hebrew apocalyptic changed this "scorpion" into a "flying eagle" (Rev. 4:7; cf. Ezek. 1:10); and that this reconstruction is intended to suggest transmutation, an absolute reversal of character, is evidenced by the fact that in the Semitic original the reverse of "scorpion" is "the pinions outspread" (as of an eagle—cf. Isa. 40:31). (See further discussion in Appendix 1.)

The celestial gate of this solstice, with its doors and their guardian and monitoring cherubim, symbolizes the Protevangel's revelations concerning the Savior's two advents.

In his first advent, the Son of God is represented as coming down from heaven through the door of Sagittarius and as going out into earth life through the door of Capricorn and on past the cherubic monitor Aquarius. Under the auspices of the winter festival's celebration of the season's sowing of wheat and barley, he was to become the wounded "Seed of the woman" foreshadowed by the cross of the vernal equinox. He himself said, however, that "except a grain of wheat fall into the earth and die, it abideth by itself alone; but if it die, it beareth much fruit" (John 12:24 AST). Thus, the seed of the winter sowings became the wave sheaf of the Passover and the firstfruits of Pentecost, the festival of the summer solstice marked by Cancer, the gate of

217

heaven. So, in accordance with the foreshadowings of the ancient conception of Sagittarius, the Savior became, on our behalf, the "conqueror of the grave" (NE.URU.GAL.), and "our Elder Brother" (SHISH.GAL)—the Redeemer of the confession of faith suggested by the fish symbolisms of the goat-fish and the water-pourer, "Jesus, the Christ, the Son of God, our Savior." The Sun's seasonal course through the zodiac from the heaven-descending gate of Capricorn to the heaven-ascending gate of Cancer therefore represents the life and work of the Savior in his first advent, as it is told in the Gospels.

In his incarnation the Son of God had become also a Son of man, to the end that the children of men, whose sin had lost them their high calling, might become one with him and therefore be children of God. At the cost of his supreme self-sacrifice the "law of sin and death" was countervailed by the "law of the spirit of life" in Christ Jesus. Having accomplished this object of his first advent, he returned to heaven and was glorified with all the glory that he had with the Father "before the world was" (John 17:5), though he is still and forever Jesus of Nazareth.

In his second advent he is represented as coming down from heaven again through the doors of Sagittarius and Capricorn, turning now in the direction pointed out by the cherubic monitor known in Gentile star lore as the Scorpion but, as we have seen, transmuted in the Bible's apocalyptic into the likeness of a soaring eagle. In the apocalyptic prologue of the Torah this constellation is identified with Enoch, the patriarch who represents the transmuted humanity that is to be "translated" so as not to see death (Heb. 11:5). In the Savior's second coming he is to lead transmuted humanity back to and beyond the Paradise it had lost, on to the holy and heavenly city that is to crown earth's summit as the consummation of the ages. This city, the New Jerusalem, is the goal of the age-marking precession of the equinoxes, as is indicated by St. John in his account of the city's twelve jeweled foundations. He identifies these with the constellations of the zodiac, but he numbers them, not in the usual order of the movement of the Sun through the months of the year, but in the reverse direction, which is that of the precession. For example, in the several thousand years since these relationships were first recognized the vernal equinox has shifted from Aries to Pisces and the autumnal from Libra to Virgo. Thus the precessional way through the zodiac, from the heaven-descending gate of Capricorn to the heaven-ascending gate of Cancer, leads through Libra's balances of judgment and through Leo, the sign of the tribe of Judah. It was along this way that St. John saw the Savior coming down as the Judge Inexorable and as King of kings and Lord of lords, with all the hosts of heaven, to destroy them that would destroy the earth and to establish his all-inclusive kingdom of righteousness, goodwill, and peace. This is the Protevangel's conquering hero, the Lion of the tribe of Judah, who is to crush the head of the serpent tempter.

Saturnalia and Its Symbolisms

Notwithstanding its boisterous extravagances, the Roman festival of Saturnalia still carries all the symbolic features of the winter solstice. It originated in a celebration of the season's sowing of wheat and barley, in accordance with the primary significance of the name "Saturn," which is derived from the Latin verb "to sow." It later became an inclusive festival of the turn of the year, beginning on December 19 with dramatic celebrations appropriate to the year's end, looking back to the blessed ways of the golden age when good old Saturn ruled the land in righteousness and lovingkindness. Saturn and his age had vanished in the dim past, and the succeeding ages had been increasingly degenerate—ages of silver and brass and iron. But the promise of his return, bringing back "the age of gold," was represented in the celebration of the birthday of the Sun on December 25, the last day of the festival. Because of that hope for the future, the days of the festival were filled with mirth and jollity and the nights were gay and bright with the light of many lamps.

Moses' Omission of This Festival

In the allegory of Israel's national epos this hope for the future, with its foreshadowings of the Savior's second advent, was of course represented by the final and complete conquest of the Promised Land. The fourth and last of the great seasonal festivals would therefore seem to provide the natural and victorious conclusion of the Mosaic cycle of national convocations commemorating the history of the Messianic people and established for their instruction and inspiration. It also symbolizes the Savior's birth as the "Sun of Righteousness" risen "with healing in his wings" (Mal. 4:2), a part of the first-advent symbolism that is not represented in any of the other festivals.

219

Moses did not include it in his ritual, however, probably in part because the Promised Land was not entered until after his death and the completion of the Torah, and in part because of his determination to avoid association with the orgiastic perversions that had come to characterize the Roman Saturnalia. For a similar reason, it will be recalled, he had removed the summer Festival of Firstfruits from close association with the summer solstice.

Its Promises for Us

The omission of this ancient festival from the calendar of the people of the Mosaic covenant did not, however, annul its original promises. These were abundantly set forth by Israel's prophets and psalmists, and they are included in the calendar of the people of the New Covenant in the Feast of the Nativity. As we have seen, the really unitary and continuous nature of the divine intervention on our behalf is reflected in the inclusive foreshadowings of this final and therefore recapitulatory festival. Similarly, our Christmas celebrations make no effort whatever to distinguish between what we call the Savior's first and second advents. To be sure, it is more largely of the first that we sing, unfolding the promise of the angels' song of the "heaven-born Prince of Peace." But we sing also of the second, looking forward to that "age of gold" that has been "by prophet bards foretold," and acknowledging the human perversity, during "two thousand years of wrong" and war and strife, that have so long postponed it.

So also St. John was not content to leave the exceedingly significant festival of the winter solstice unused in his apocalyptic worship drama. There we find its foreshadowings giving assurance of the Savior's hastened parousia—his coming, in accordance with the second-advent symbolisms of the zodiac, as the King of kings and Lord of lords, to save the world from the utter desolation of the "third woe." (See Act 3.)

NOTES

1. Morris Jastrow, *The Religion of Babylonia and Assyria* (Ginn & Co., 1898), pp. 234, 528 ff., 582 ff.; and James Turley van Burkalow, *The Lost Prophecy* (Fleming H. Revell, New York, 1924), pp. 49–58.

APPENDIX 3

Rituals of Ancient Jewish and Early Christian Worship

The Temple Structure and Furnishings

The Jewish Rituals: (1) The Worship Service
    The Parashoth: Readings from the Law
    The Haphtaroth: Readings from the Prophets
    The Megilloth
    The Targumim or Translations of the Haphtaroth
    The Derashoth: Expositions of the Haphtaroth

The Jewish Rituals: (2) The Atonement Ceremonials
    The Great Day of Atonement
    The Anticipatory Day of Atonement

The Early Christian Worship Service
    The Spontaneous Oracles and Interruptions
    Scripture Readings
    Translations and Expositions of the Scriptures

St. John's Apocalyptic Worship Drama
    The Scripture Lessons
    The Day of Atonement in the Drama
    The Special Day of Atonement
    Spontaneous Oracles and Interruptions
    Prayers and Hymns
    Omissions

APPENDIX 3

Rituals of Ancient Jewish and Early Christian Worship

Worship is the theme from which St. John evolved the apocalyptic drama of his Revelation. In an established and intelligently purposeful ritual of worship each part, each "dotted line," has accepted implications and relationships. All of these had to be represented faithfully in the dramatization, for it is through them that St. John set forth his histrionic foreshadowings. At first glance the sort of determinism involved in such a ritual might appear to be a hurtful handicap, but in actuality the apocalyptist found in its calculable complex his chief asset, the *sine qua non* for the accomplishment of his purpose. For without the inescapable bonds of its ordered relationships there could be no Apocalypse, since without the sure clues they provide there could be no revelation.

The ritual that furnishes the pattern of the book is of course that of the early Christian Church, but this was modeled after the Jewish service of St. John's time. Both of these are reviewed here, and a summary of the Apocalypse shows how St. John adapted them in his worship drama. First, however, the symbolic structure and furnishings of the ancient temple must be reviewed, as they provide the background for this Apocalypse.

THE TEMPLE STRUCTURE AND FURNISHINGS

The temples of the ancient eastern world were conventionalized miniatures of the great temple of the universe. They were pyramidal staged towers representing a mountain climbing up from earth to heaven, like the earth mountain of the northern

223

hemisphere as it was pictured in the ancient cosmic symbolism. (See Appendix 1.) In its true conception such a temple represented the world, not as it is, but as it ought to be and as it is going to be, through the great salvation of the Savior. It is the heaven-piercing mountain of a new earth whose essential verity—its pattern, its ideal—must first have come down out of heaven. In St. John's Apocalypse it becomes the holy city, the New Jerusalem, coming down out of heaven from God, the symbol of an earth that will be a veritable Bethel, a house of God, and of whose new age the millennium is to be the prelude.

In accordance with this pattern the temple of God at Jerusalem was a four-staged tower, with the worship areas at the summit just as the Garden of Eden was pictured at the summit of the earth mountain. At the eastern end was an open courtyard containing the brazen altar of burnt offerings and its associated great "sea" or laver, required for ceremonial cleansings. Next to the west was a huge propylon or gate, before which stood two brazen pillars. That these represented the two trees of the Garden of Eden, which in turn represented earth's terrestrial and ecliptic axes as they were conceived in the ancient cosmology (see Appendix 1), is made clear by the names given to the two pillars. *Jakin*, on the right, stood for the tree of life, which symbolized the ecliptic axis. Its name is derived from the Hebrew verb *kûn*, "to be firm, fixed," and through the ages that axis has remained fixed. It is also, in that old view, the only way that will lead up through the whirling planetary spheres to the heaven of heavens. *Boaz*, on the left, represented the tree of the knowledge of good and evil, which symbolized the terrestrial axis. Because of precession it swings slowly around the ecliptic axis, pointing in many different directions and never offering a way up to the heaven of heavens. Its name can be construed as compounded of two elements: *bo* from the Hebrew verb "to go" and *az* from the word for "goat" and the verb *anaz*, "to turn aside, wander," as a goat does. Just so does the earth's axis of rotation "go turning aside"; and so too he who eats the fruit of the delusive knowledge of good and evil goes astray like a goat, as did Adam and Eve.

Here then was a symbolic suggestion of the Garden of Eden. But Eden, though it was situated at the summit of the earth mountain, is not the goal of humanity. It is indeed the goal of earth life, but from it we must begin a new march onward and upward to the possession of the universe. That final goal was symbolized by the sanctuary of the temple, which was entered through the gate and which consisted of two parts.

In the larger outer chamber or Holy Place was the golden altar of incense, the memorial altar with whose offering of incense all other offerings were to be seasoned as they were brought before God. Here too were the seven-branched golden candlestick and the golden tables of showbread, the "bread of the presence."

The way into the inner chamber or Holy of Holies was barred by a curtain called "the veil of the temple," a symbol of the barrier sin had interposed between humans and their Creator, for that small room, containing the ark of the covenant with its symbols of divine justice and mercy, pictured the heaven of heavens, where stands the throne of God. It revealed the divine reality of God's immediate presence with his people, while the great gate, the temple's most prominent feature, represented God's unapproachable majesty. So sacred was the Holy of Holies that it was entered only once a year, on the great Day of Atonement, and then only by the high priest, and there he carried out the first two ceremonials of that day of propitiation.

THE JEWISH RITUALS: (1) THE WORSHIP SERVICE

While the Jewish worship of St. John's day included prayers and hymns, its major features were prescribed readings from the ancient oracles that had been preserved through the centuries by nation-wide piety. These always included lessons from the law and the prophets, known respectively as the *parashoth* and the *haphtaroth*, and sometimes a *megillah* was added, one of the short sacred books. All of these were read in the original ancient Hebrew, which by then was a dead language. It had therefore become necessary for the readings to be followed by free translations and expositions or sermons (the *targumim* and the *derashoth*) in the vernacular of the place of worship.

The Parashoth: Readings from the Law

The fundamental feature of the Jewish service was the reading of the parashoth, the lessons from the Mosaic "law" found in the Pentateuch. Those five books had been carefully collected and arranged to set forth and define and illustrate Israel's covenants with God—the primal one of the Protevangel, those with the patriarchs, and the national covenant that made Israel God's chosen people. This Torah or "directive" is largely concerned with regulatory ordinances regarding temple sacrifices and observance of the seasonal festivals and the great fast of the Day of Atonement. Above all, however, it is concerned with setting forth in full detail the supreme allegory of Israel's wilderness pilgrimage from the bondage of Egypt to the *sabbatismos* of the Land of Promise.

From the olden times it had been required that the whole of the Pentateuch be read through in a fixed cycle of Sabbath lessons. Each Sabbath's assignment was divided into seven sections or chapters, which were read by seven different persons from the congregation, called up for this purpose in order of their ecclesiastical status—for example, a priest first, a Levite second, and so forth. Appropriate lessons from the law were provided also for religious services held on weekdays, but these, however important the day might be, were all shorter than the Sabbath lessons. There were six subdivisions in the lesson for the Day of Atonement, five for festivals, four for the new moon, three for Mondays and Thursdays. As on the Sabbath, the number of persons called up to read these special lessons always corresponded to the number of parts into which they were divided.

The Haphtaroth: Readings from the Prophets

Passages from the prophets had eventually been accepted as canonical and in full accord with the Torah, for it was recognized that these provided further unfolding of the germinal truth delivered to the saints of earlier times. Accordingly, it had become a regular part of the worship service to have the lesson of the parashoth reinforced by illustrative selections (the haphtaroth) read from the canonical prophets.

The Megilloth

The term "prophet" ascribed to the writers of the haphtaroth designates not a "fore-teller" but a "forth-teller"—a public speaker, a herald or preacher, a spokesman for God. He might also be a fore-teller, and often was; but a fore-teller, even a Daniel, who was not also a forth-teller was not a prophet in the canonical sense. Such works were known as "sacred writings" or hagiographa. A special category of such sacred writings was provided by the five short books known as the megilloth or "little rolls"—Ruth, Esther, Ecclesiastes, Song of Songs, and Lamentations. Although these are not prophetic in either the canonical or the predictive sense, on special festive occasions one of them was read in the worship service to supplement the haphtaroth.

The Targumim or Translations of the Haphtaroth

Although the lessons were traditionally divided into sections read by different persons, it was customary to have all the targums presented by one person, someone capable of providing a free vernacular translation of the ancient Hebrew.

The Derashoth: Expositions of the Haphtaroth

Originally each targum was followed by an exposition, known as the derashah, which served to resolve difficulties of obscure passages and to explain old customs that had been forgotten. By the beginning of our era, however, it had become common to have only one derashah following the last of the translations, and this was usually a discourse of some length, in every sense a sermon. It thus took the place of the spontaneous "oracles"—testimonies, exhortations, warnings—spoken by any among the worshippers who felt moved by the spirit of prophecy. Such prophecy, common in early times and revived during the exile, had later been suspended in Judaism;[1] and John the Baptist, the first prophetic voice since Haggai, Zechariah, and Malachi, had not awakened any echo in the accepted worship service.

THE JEWISH RITUALS: (2) THE ATONEMENT CEREMONIALS

In his worship drama St. John included also the ancient Jewish atonement ceremonials, both those of the great annual fast of the Day of Atonement and those of the special days of atonement that were introduced from time to time to meet special needs.

The Great Day of Atonement

In addition to the seasonal festivals described in Appendix 2, the week of months included also the Day of Atonement. This is not in reality a separate observance but the culmination of the ten days of penance that begin with the solemn convocation of

227

the Rosh Hashanah, which is called also "the Day of Judgment." A Day of Judgment naturally demands a Day of Atonement, and the two were brought together at the beginning of the civil year to remind the Israelites of the solemn covenant made at the beginning of their history. In it they had accepted deep responsibility for service as the priestly people through whom God should provide the lamb for the sacrifice—deep responsibility that was the answer to the high privilege to which God had called them out of the nations. And to that end all the notable features of the holy convocations that open the civil year have specific reference to the historic and prophetically significant events of those early days in the time of Abraham. The Day of Judgment recalls the fearful judgment visited upon Sodom and Gomorrah the same year that the covenant was made with Abraham. The Day of Atonement is foreshadowed in the story of the first sacrifice offered on Mount Moriah, the sacrifice of the ram caught in the thorns as a substitute for Isaac and as a token of the Lamb that God would provide through the seed of Abraham—the Lamb of God that should take away the sin of the world. So also that seemingly curious ceremony of the Day of Atonement in which choice was made by lot between two goats, of which one was to be "for Jehovah" and the other, the scapegoat, "for Azazel." Here there is a reminder of God's choice of Israel as his peculiar people, the people of the covenant, as exemplified particularly in the choice of their ancestor Isaac, while his brother Ishmael was left to become the wild rover of the desert, his hand against every man and every man's hand against him. Isaac was chosen for the service of Jehovah, as later Jacob was chosen over Esau. But Ishmael and Esau and all that they stand for, like the sins that are confessed upon the head of the scapegoat, are marked for entire removal from among the holy people.

The Day of Atonement therefore has to do with the call, choice, and purification of the people of the covenant. That these implications, if not originally obvious, are at least prophetically latent in the cycle of holy convocations at the beginning of the civil year, is confirmed by the fact that the special readings from the Torah assigned to the first two days of the year are the twenty-first and twenty-second chapters of Genesis, which tell of Isaac and Ishmael and the sacrifice on Mount Moriah.

The ceremonials of the Day of Atonement include sin offerings and sprinklings of blood symbolizing repentance, and the closing "devotion" of the scapegoat. How these are incorporated into St. John's worship drama, and more details concerning them, will be considered in the closing section of this Appendix.

The Anticipatory Day of Atonement

Near the end of Israel's desert wanderings, just as they were about to cross the Jordan, their great leader said: "From the day that thou didst depart out of the land of Egypt, until ye came unto this place, ye have been rebellious against the Lord" (Deut. 9:7). Because of this attitude Israel of old required not only the regular annual observance of the Day of Atonement all through their wilderness journey, but also special atonement observances at times of emergency and wrongdoing by the people as a whole (Lev. 4:13–21). The final one during their wilderness wandering occurred at Shittim.[2]

THE EARLY CHRISTIAN WORSHIP SERVICE

In all that was fixed and liturgical the worship of the early Christian church continued to follow the pattern it had inherited from Jewish worship. Nevertheless, it became completely and unmistakably Christian. As before, the services were interspersed with appropriate prayers and with "hymns and spiritual songs" (Col. 3:16; cf. Eph. 5:19), and there were readings from the law and the prophets. These readings were changed, however, in content and emphasis, to make them adequately inclusive of and worthily representative of all the new truths of Christianity—its new faith and hope and love and its new imperative. The character of their exposition changed also, to meet new needs. In addition the spontaneous oracles of ancient Israel, its *charismata*, were renewed and intensified.

The Spontaneous Oracles and Interruptions

The last mentioned change was evidenced especially by the new outpouring, lavish beyond precedent, of the gift of prophecy, which now centered, of course, on the story of Jesus and its meaning for humanity. The abundance and wonder of these prophetic utterances in the early Church are seen in the account of their first bestowal (Acts 2:1 ff.). There St. Peter's explanation reveals them as the Pentecostal firstfruits of spiritual enduement, which are to be given in full-harvest abundance for the accomplishment of the final task of world conquest. This is in accordance with the promise of the prophet Joel, who reports God as saying: "And it shall come to pass afterward"—that is, at the end of the age—"that I will pour out my Spirit upon all flesh; and your sons and your daughters shall prophesy, your old men shall dream dreams, your young men shall see visions" (Joel 2:28).

At any time and anywhere in the midst of the regular ritual, save only during the reading of the law of Christ, there was complete liberty for spontaneous utterances by any who had received spiritual gifts such as those of prophecy or unknown tongues. This is evidenced by the extreme license into which this sometimes degenerated, as seen in the itemized rebuke by St. Paul to the church at Corinth (1 Cor. 14:26–33).

Scripture Readings

Originally the parashoth of the liturgy consisted of the lessons for the day from the law of Moses. This was the accepted Torah or "directive" of the people of the Old Covenant—the fundamental law both of their religion and ethics and of their theocratic commonwealth. The people of the New Covenant were not long in discovering, however, that the law of Moses—partial, tribal, foreshadowing, and preparatory—had now given over its authority to the consummate law of the King of kings and Lord of lords, a law that is final, all-inclusive, and world-wide in its significance. From the first, therefore, the apostolic "epistles" were received by the churches as setting forth the mind of Christ and were always accepted as unquestionably authoritative. This was so even when they countervailed the ancient law (Acts 15:1–30; Gal. 2:1–10). Of course, then, these first elements of the New Testament, which has always been acknowledged as the Christian Torah, must have been accorded the old Torah's place of honor in the ritual of Christian worship and read as its parashah.[3]

The haphtaroth of the Jewish service were chosen from the canonical "prophets" to reinforce the lesson from the "law," in accordance with the objective of Jewish worship. This was the continuance, maintenance, and development of the religious, ethical, and civil life of the covenant people in accordance with the law, to the end that they should be ready for their Messianic mission at the coming of the promised Savior of the world. It

230

was of course necessary that they should be adequately informed concerning the Messianic hope and their own Messianic calling, and to this end all their sacred scriptures—the law, the prophets, and the sacred writings—were filled with Messianic prophecies, which they could not fail to hear. The Messianic hope, however, and their own Messianic calling were not stressed as the perpetual foreground themes of their public worship, but were rather an overshadowing influence and an abiding presence in the background. Theirs was not the Messianic propaganda directed toward the conquest of the world for the King of kings and Lord of lords. Theirs was still simply the self-development of recruits on the drill ground, of an army in the process of becoming.

On the other hand, the church was an army in being. It was made up at first of Jews who had received the training of the synagogue and developed under the discipline of the Mosaic law, and who were now persuaded, and anxious to persuade their fellows, that the long-promised Captain had come and was calling them to action. Their Torah, therefore, was his New Covenant; and interest in the Old Covenant and its sacred scriptures was no longer primarily in their wise prescriptions for right living. As good soldiers they must of course still obey these; but their interest was now chiefly in the Messianic prophecies of the scriptures as munitions for their Christian propaganda and as sources of light on the further and final outworking of the Christian hope.[4] For them, accordingly, the whole Old Testament—law, prophets, and writings—became, as it still is for us, a rich treasury from which to draw the haphtaroth lessons needed for the ritual.

As noted, the five little books used as megilloth to reinforce the haphtaroth on special occasions are utterly devoid of prophetic import of any kind. They could thus not long be retained in the Christian service. Instead, the Church turned to the devotional masterpieces of the centuries, collected and preserved in the five little books of the Psalms. In them there is a veritable treasury of Messianic foreshadowings, as the Savior himself pointed out (Luke 24:44). And so we must conclude that our present use of the Psalms in our worship services goes back to the very beginning of the Church. They must always have been employed, not merely in their original use with musical accompaniment for their devotional value, but also along with

231

other Old Testament readings, to provide background for better understanding of the lessons from the law of Christ set forth in the New Testament.

Translations and Expositions of the Scriptures

In the Greek-speaking "churches of Asia," when a lesson was read from the collection of scriptures accepted as belonging to the Christian Torah—most of these are now incorporated in our New Testament—there was of course no need for a translation. Where necessary, it would of course have been added. And for most of the early Christian churches translations would have been needed for scriptures written in ancient Hebrew.

The derashah or exposition originally followed the translation (if needed) of each portion of the parashoth and the haphtaroth. In the course of time, however, there came to be a single comprehensive derashah. At the beginning of our era this had become, in the Jewish service, a "sermon" of considerable length. It is evident, however, that when the early Church invaded strange lands and gathered Gentiles into her congregations, the Christian worship developed a need for the explanation of its readings from the ancient Hebrew scriptures—a need that originated from an ignorance immeasurably more profound and more extensive than that which had made the expositions necessary in the early Jewish worship. While there is no direct evidence concerning the custom of the early Church in this matter, it seems probable that multiple expositions were re-introduced; and the writings of the Church fathers give us glimpses of such usage, for they tell us that whenever several bishops were present at a service "sermons" were expected from all of them.

ST. JOHN'S APOCALYPTIC WORSHIP DRAMA

The pattern of St. John's worship drama is dominated by the scripture lessons, for these mark off its four acts. In each of these acts, however, the Day of Atonement is represented, and there is also a special Day of Atonement. Also there are prayers and hymns and, as in the early Christian worship, numerous spontaneous oracles.

The Scripture Lessons

Although the early Christian Church used the Jewish liturgical pattern it was possible, as has been noted, to introduce the Christian message by means of suitable scripture lessons and their translation and exposition. In the apocalyptic drama it was these parts of the worship, in their modified Christian form, that provided St. John with *tabulae rasae* on which to inscribe his histrionic revelation.

Following the ancient Jewish custom St. John begins his worship service with readings from the law (the parashoth); but following the custom of the early Christian Church he replaces the law of Moses with the law of Christ. For that purpose the early Church used apostolic epistles, and St. John uses the Savior's letters to the seven churches of Asia, which form Act 1 of his drama. Since these letters are presented in the vernacular of the churches that are to receive them, no targum or translation is necessary. And no exposition is given here, since it is presumed that each one will be read and expounded in the individual church to which it is addressed. This was the customary procedure with apostolic letters.

The haphtaroth of the Jewish service were chosen to support the parashoth, and this is the relation of the oracles of the seven-sealed book to the letters to the churches. The latter present foreshadowings regarding the development of the Church during the centuries leading up to the Savior's second advent, and the seal oracles supplement these with similar foreshadowings regarding civil developments. These oracles therefore serve as the haphtaroth of the apocalyptic worship drama (its Act 2), and their translations and expositions (Acts 3 and 4) are here interpreted as provided by the seven trumpets and the seven bowls of the wrath of God. This procedure—the presentation of all seven readings first, then all seven of the translations, and finally all seven expositions—differs from the ancient Hebrew custom of having each separate portion of the lesson followed immediately by its individual translation and exposition. St. John's method helps reveal the marked parallelisms between these three sets of oracles (see Appendix 5), and these parallelisms clearly support their interpretation as a seven-fold scripture followed by its translation followed by its exposition. Such use of multiple expositions was probably characteristic of the early Christian Church, as it gathered in more and more members who lacked a Hebrew background and therefore needed detailed explanation of the scriptures.

The Day of Atonement in the Drama

The great Day of Atonement was the one day in the year when the whole temple was in use, for its first two ceremonials furnished the only occasion on which even the high priest could enter the Holy of Holies. Only by portraying these ceremonials, therefore, could the drama consistently give us the glorious vision of its second act, in which we see the throne of God in the Holy of Holies of the celestial temple.

This is not, however, the reason for the inclusion of the Day of Atonement among the worship features of the drama. Its first three ceremonials represent repentance on the part of erring mortals and intercession on the part of their Redeemer, and the drama shows us that only such repentance can make possible the Savior's countervailance of the fearful third woe. The final ceremonial of the scapegoat symbolizes the fate of those who refuse to repent and who must therefore be destroyed so they cannot destroy the earth. One of these four distinctive ceremonials is represented symbolically in each act, in keeping with the message of the act. The first three involve the blood of a goat, presented as a sacrificial sin-offering, and the fourth involves a live goat. The four are:

1) A seven-fold sprinkling of the atoning blood of the sin-offering *upon* the mercy seat in the Holy of Holies, for the cleansing of the Holy Place, the symbol of the collective religious life of the people, the development of which is foreshadowed in the seven letters of the first act.

2) A seven-fold sprinkling of that blood *before* the mercy seat for the cleansing of the tent of meeting, the symbol of the collective civil life of the people, the development of which is foreshadowed in the oracles of the seven-sealed book of the second act.

3) A seven-fold sprinkling of that blood upon the golden altar of incense for the cleansing of the people individually for all the sins of which they have truly repented—repentance that is urgently called for in the third act, with its trumpet sounds of alarm and its threatened third woe.

4) The devotion of the scapegoat, upon whose head were laid all the iniquities, transgressions, and sins of Israel for which no atonement could avail. This was done at the door of the tabernacle, so that the scapegoat might carry these offenses off with him to his self-destruction in the wilderness. In this symbolism we see the only possible remedy for incorrigible evil, whether in the

individual or in society—whether it be an irredeemably offending "right hand" that would otherwise doom the entire man (Matt. 5:30), or the reprobate personality or nationality that sells itself to an ideology that would "destroy the earth" (Rev. 11:8). In the fourth act this is symbolized by the seven bowls of the wrath of God, and the final conquest of evil.

The instructions in Leviticus for the Day of Atonement also include ceremonials for the priesthood—the sprinkling of a bullock's blood as a sin-offering for Aaron and his sons—made in the same way and in the same places. With entire propriety this New Testament Apocalypse omits altogether the symbolism that might have been derived from these acts, for the Aaronic priesthood of the Mosaic law has been abolished. Christ Jesus himself is our mediator now, a High Priest who does not need "to offer up sacrifice, first for his own sins, and then for the people's: for this he did once, when he offered up himself" (Heb. 7:27).

It is equally appropriate that in these apocalyptic visions our Savior, now our High Priest, is represented both as the Glorified Savior seen in the theophany of the first act, whose rightful place is *upon* the throne, and as the little Lamb of Act 2, seen standing *before* the throne "as though it had been slain." He is not seen actually sprinkling the blood of a sacrifice such as foreshadowed the atonement of old, but this is represented suggestively by the temple background of the vision.

The Anticipatory Day of Atonement

In the Mosaic law provision is made (Lev. 4:13–21) for a prevenient atonement, to be used in emergencies. We find it most notably exemplified in the effective revivals brought about by repentance at the beginning and end of the judgments of Samuel (1 Sam. 7:3–11; 12:1–25), to which indeed the "seven thunders" of the Apocalypse allude (Rev. 10:3–4).

In the Apocalypse such an emergency is represented by the third woe, whose fearful horrors would have been unleashed by the sounding of the seventh trumpet and its translation of the unread text of the seventh seal oracle. Just before this could happen, and to prevent our learning by bitter experience the now most happily insoluble mystery of the third woe, the apocalyptist employs the prevenient or anticipatory atonement, unceremoniously introduced by the archangel Raphael into the course of the third act.

Spontaneous Oracles and Interruptions

In the apocalyptic drama of worship there are more than a score and a half of the spontaneous oracles and interruptions that had become so characteristic of early Christian worship. These include prophetic utterances or enactments by angels, archangels, and elders in the histrionic congregation; theophanic appearances of the Savior; songs and praises and voices from heaven; thunders; and even the significant silence at the close of Act 2.

Most of these interruptions are either merely interjectory or actually fit in with and form part of the context of the worship, corresponding with St. Paul's advice to the Corinthians that God wants peace in the worship service, not confusion (1 Cor. 14:33). In four cases, however, they are truly interruptions of the orderly procedure of the service, their unceremoniousness resulting, of course, from the urgent nature of their messages. The four are:

1) The angel who ascends from the sun rising with the seal of the living God (7:2), needed to protect the 144,000.

2) The silence in heaven for about half an hour (8:1), when the Savior refused to signify the oracle of the last seal of the seven-sealed book of prophecy—evidently because the hosts of heaven had read that oracle and had found it overwhelming in its fearfulness.

3) The angel who stood at the golden altar of incense to mingle incense with the prayers of the saints (8:3–5) just as the trumpet angels came forth to sound their horns, thus delaying the trumpet translations of the oracles of the seven-sealed book.

4) The startling appearance of the mighty archangel (10:1 ff.) whose hail was echoed by the seven thunders and who brought the "little book open," the megillah of the service, which initiated the parenthetic revelations of the tenth and eleventh chapters and their call for repentance.

Prayers and Hymns

As in the ancient synagogue and the early Christian Church, so in St. John's apocalyptic worship drama, prayers and hymns are part of the service. The songs of the Christian Church find their glorious representation in the matchless music of the heavenly choirs that echo through the pages of the Apocalypse, breaking into the regular order of worship from time to time as a special category of interruptions. The prayers of the saints go up continuously with the incense offered by the four and twenty elders (5:8); and in view of the ominous "silence in heaven" following the breaking of the unsignified seventh seal, the saints united in concerted supplication, censed by an angel at the altar with a golden censer (8:1–4).

Omissions

It is evident that St. John would have found it worse than useless to try to give a complete reproduction of the ritual associated with any of the worship features he employs. He was clearly justified in passing by such details as the wave sheaf of Passover, the loaves of Pentecost, the booths of Tabernacles, and the actual sacrifices of the Day of Atonement. His pictures are entirely unmistakable without them, and they would have cluttered up the stage and obscured the scenes without contributing a single item to the accomplishment of the drama's purpose. Just so is it with regard to some very important elements of the liturgy of the early Church. Nevertheless, every really essential element of worship that could not be employed in the action of the drama is given due recognition somewhere in the Revelation.

For example, the two original sacraments, baptism and the eucharist, are not specifically portrayed in any of the drama's scenes, and a comprehensive representation of the worship of the early Church would have to include them both, whether or not they were administered in every one of its assemblies. They do not, however, lend themselves to the purpose of the apocalyptist, and so he does not employ them, but he is very far from ignoring them.

Although the rite of baptism is not pictured, its outer form is brought to mind in the vision of the celestial temple, which provides the background of the second act's representation of the Feast of Pentecost, the birthday of the Church. There we see the "sea of glass," the heavenly original (Heb. 8:5) of the temple's laver and the Christian baptismal font. Its inner reality, the baptism with the Holy Spirit and fire, is indicated in the later and more specific vision of this same laver or font, where we find it a "sea of glass mingled with fire" (15:2). Its significance is made manifest by the victorious host of saints standing beside it and singing the song of Moses and the Lamb; for these are they to

237

whom white robes have been given (6:11), robes that are white because they have been "washed in the blood of the Lamb" (7:14).

There is no representation, either, of the holy eucharist, but three of its most familiar symbols are set before us—the "hidden manna" once (2:17; cf. John 6:49 ff.); the communion "supper" twice (3:20 and 19:9); and the "tree of life" four times (2:7, 22:2, 14, 19 AST). These symbols are always set forth in a context that contemplates a future subsequent to its own action. Evidently in the Church of St. John's day the sacrament of the Lord's Supper was not administered until after the dismissal of the public congregation, when it was doubtless merged with the agape or love feast, which was entirely separate from the public worship.

In like fashion, some formal confession of faith, such as the shema of the synagogue and the Apostles' Creed, would certainly have a place in the action of this drama if its purpose required a complete representation of the early Church's worship. It would have halted the forward march of the foreshadowings, however, and would have presented an insoluble problem to the reader who, accepting this Apocalypse at face value, tried to construe such a confession as in some way predictive. Thus nothing of this sort is put into the mouths of the histrionic worshippers in the drama. On the other hand, this Apocalypse could not afford to ignore such an important element of public worship; nor was there any difficulty in representing it in full measure without making it the burden of an action that could be misconstrued as predictive. The great doctrines of salvation, all the essentials of the creed of the Church, are implicit in the drama's other symbolisms—in the nature parables of the ancient festivals; in the prophetic allegory of the pilgrimage represented in the great memorial convocations of the week of months;[5] and in the symbolic rites of the Day of Atonement, which both picture the background and reveal the objective of every scene. Furthermore, the most vital and most immediately pertinent of these truths are echoed in the songs and choruses and lyric pronouncements with which the action of the drama is punctuated, while the Christian's fundamental confession of faith in "Jesus the Christ, the Son of God, our Savior," is set before us in the "seal of the living God."

NOTES

1. See 1 Mac. 4:46; 9:27; 14:41.
2. See Num. 25:1 ff.; 31:16; Deut. 4:3–4
3. See Col. 4:16; 1 Thes. 5:27; 2 Pet. 3:2,15,16.
4. Cf. Luke 24:26 ff.; John 5:39; Acts 17:11, etc.
5. Cf. John 6:32 ff.; 1 Cor. 10:1–11; Heb. 3:7–4:11.

APPENDIX 4

The Symbolisms of Numbers

Auspicious Numbers: The Two Fundamental Ones
 Three
 Four

Auspicious Number Combinations
 Twelve
 Seven

Numbers with Definitely Evil Import
 Six
 Eight

APPENDIX 4

The Symbolisms of Numbers

In ancient Hebrew thought special mystical significance was assigned to many numbers. This was true first with regard to those found notably employed in the work of the Creator as it was conceived in the ancient cosmology and represented in the zodiac and its appanages. To these it was natural to add numbers connoting outstanding events—ten, for example, referring to the giving of the law, and forty to the years of pilgrimage in the wilderness. Some of these mystic numbers were considered to be auspicious, while others were of evil import.

In the symbolisms of the Apocalypse the use of such mystic numbers is lavish and outstanding, and a recognition of their meanings, as they had been developed in earlier apocalyptic writings, contributes to our understanding of this book. This Appendix is chiefly concerned with the numbers thus used by St. John—seven and its augmented and diminished values (eight and six respectively), and twelve. However, since seven and twelve are derived respectively by the addition or multiplication of the two fundamental mystic numbers, three and four, these must be considered first.

AUSPICIOUS NUMBERS: THE TWO FUNDAMENTAL ONES

Auspicious qualities were ascribed to the numbers first identified as mystic—those that are represented outstandingly in God's perfect creation as it was pictured in the ancient cosmology. Of these, the two fundamental ones are *three* and *four*.

Three
Three derives its significance from ancient cosmology's three very different grand divisions of God's nevertheless unitary creation. These are "the heaven above," "the earth beneath," and "the water under the earth" (Exod. 20:4; Deut. 5:8; etc.). It is therefore the first and most fundamentally significant of the

mystic numbers employed in apocalyptic, and it is far more meaningful than appears at first glance.

The three great realms are divine reflections that tell of the administrative divisions of the cosmos as it was conceived by the ancients. They are also self revelations of the Creator who designed them; and in his sovereignty over each of these realms he was known to the ancient Hebrews by a different name: *Elyon*, the Most High or Lord of the Heavens; *Shaddai*, Lord of the Earth Mountain; and *Yamai*, Lord of the Deep (see Ps. 91:1–2). Abraham and his neighbors in Ur (Gen. 15:7) pronounced this latter name as *Yawa*, and without necessarily changing that pronunciation Moses, by divine command, spelled it *Yahweh*. By wordplay this change of spelling gives the name a new meaning—"He who will become [the promised Redeemer]"; and so it came to be the covenant name of Israel's divine King (Exod. 3:13 ff.; 6:3). These cosmic characterizations were authoritatively commended to the Hebrew patriarchs and were employed by them as divine names (Gen. 14:18–24; 15:7; 17:1; etc.), representing the three persons of the divine triunity. The later concept of the *trinity*, our supreme revelation concerning the Godhead, is thus rooted in the ancient cosmology's numerical symbolism of the deity.

Accordingly, *three* came to stand for the *Creator* because it was the number of the triad of characterizations in which primordial religion ascribed to him whatever reflections of his divine likeness could be seen in the ancient cosmology's three grand divisions of his creation.

Three represents also, therefore, the divine, the godlike, the spiritual, the religious. In the Old Testament this is reflected in the *three* times a year that the men of Israel were required to "appear before the Lord God" (Exod. 23:17; etc.); the *three* pronouncements of the Mosaic benediction (Num. 6:22–27); the *three-fold* declaration of the tersanctus (Isa. 6:3). To these St. John adds the *three-fold* time-equivalence of the divine covenant name—"the Lord which is, and which was, and which is to come" (Rev. 1:8).

Four

Four is the number of what the ancients called "elements"—earth, water, air, and fire. They saw these as the building blocks the Creator combined in various proportions to make real the three realms of his ideal universe. As some of the ancients suspected, however, we now know that instead of being themselves distinct material elements, these four merely represented the solid, liquid, gaseous, and ethereal states through which all the veritable "elements" of matter pass. Conceived in this way, they are indeed the building blocks of the visible universe. Moreover, the ancient listing of the four "states" of the "cosmic elements" was notably felicitous; for earth, water, air, and fire represent exactly the physical conditions required for the creation of a world that was to be the habitat of living creatures such as man.

Four thus came to stand for *substance* and *reality*. It represents the building materials the Creator employed to translate his plans into the actuality of the world in which we live. Thus when St. John saw the "holy city...coming from God out of Heaven" as the ideal of the new earth (Rev. 21:2) he described it as lying "foursquare" (21:16) to indicate that it was indeed to become a reality, one with the solid earth.

Auspicious Number Combinations

With *three* representing the Creator and *four* the materials he used, the stage is set for representations of the product of his creative activity and of the activity itself. We find these in the numbers resulting from the two combinations of three and four—their multiplication and their addition. These two combinations, *twelve* and *seven*, are oracular and summarize the two creation stories of Genesis.

Twelve

As the product of the multiplication of three and four, *twelve* represents the completion of the creation begun when light was called into being—the creation of the physical universe, nature's macrocosm. It stands for a four-square universe ruled by the triune God—our Father and Savior and Helper. This is the major theme of the first creation story, and the twelve constellations of the zodiac, its cosmographic symbol, actually indicate this multiplication. The "elements" are associated with the constellations in such a way as to suggest the orderly intermingling of the constituents of a cosmos. Beginning with Taurus, whose associated month was primordially the leader of the year, they are dis-

245

tributed, one to each of the constellations, in sequence—earth, water, air, fire. Thus each of the four is given out three times, to three different constellations; and for each element lines drawn within the zodiacal circle to connect its three constellations form a trigon, or equilateral triangle (see Appendix 1). The twelve constellations of the zodiac therefore represent the completion of nature's orderly or cosmic combination of the four elements. (It should also be noted that for some purposes the zodiacal circle is represented as a square, whose sides face the four cardinal points of the compass.)

As the number connoting the physical cosmos of nature and the properly ordered elements of our physical world, *twelve* came naturally to stand also for any other cosmos, and therefore for the properly ordered elements of our spiritual, moral, and social worlds. So, in the apocalypse of Genesis, the twelve constellations of the zodiac were employed to picture the twelve patriarchs. So in the Old Testament history the Messianic covenant people, called to become a spiritual cosmos, are represented as consisting of twelve tribes, each having as its insignia the gem of one of the twelve constellations of the zodiac. By the same token, the covenant people of the New Testament are described as a spiritual Israel of twelve tribes. These were at first represented by the twelve apostles; but when St. John saw them in his apocalyptic visions they were always mystically reckoned as twelve times twelve (or one hundred forty-four) thousand (Rev. 7:4; 14:1,3). And the Church of the consummation, which is to include the whole world, is represented in the Apocalypse by the City of God, the New Jerusalem, the zodiacally jeweled foundations of whose jasper walls are named for the twelve apostles (21:14).

Twelve is thus the number that stands for a cosmos, "a thing of ordered beauty, of perfection."

Seven

As the sum of three and four, *seven* suggests the Creator (three) taking in hand the elements (four) that were the preliminary entities of his creation and proceeding to effect its consummation. Thus, while *twelve*, the product of three and four, represents the product of the Creator's activity, the cosmos he created, *seven* represents his creative activity itself. This is symbolized by the "seven days" of creation in the Genesis story, and its completion on the last of those days is perennially commemorated in the Sabbath that hallows every seventh day.

Construed as the composite addition of three and four, or the Creator's contribution of somewhat of himself to something he has created, *seven* is a numerical rendering of the first oracle (Gen. 2:4–7) of the second creation story, which tells of God's last and consummate asynergistic act of creation. "And the Lord God formed man of the dust of the ground, and breathed into his nostrils the breath of life; and man became a living soul." (Cf. Gen. 1:30, which shows that this oracle applies equally to all genera and species of earth life.)

Construed as a discrete addition of three and four, or the Creator's association of his creatures with himself, *seven* tells of the synergistic divine activity that began with the creation of beings endowed with a living soul. This was an activity of creative evolution, whose final earthly mutation, which only man attained, is set forth in the second creation story's second oracle (Gen. 2:8 ff.). In this evolution the Creator and his creature cooperate to the end that the creature may attain the goal of his creation, his Creator's likeness; and in it, both as a help toward that attainment and as an earnest of his ultimate high calling, the creature is employed as the Creator's *agent*. In this sense *seven* signifies excellence and normal rightfulness, for it represents the *triune* God and the creatures of his *four-square* universe working together in perfect harmony.

In the ancient cosmography this ultimate celestial high calling, this goal of evolution, is found in the "seven planets" of olden times—Mercury, Venus, Mars, Jupiter, Saturn, and the Sun and Moon. All of these, moving round about and some of them to and fro among the constellations of the zodiac, were accepted as avatars of celestial intelligence used to supervise the operations of the material universe, the cosmos, and to shepherd the operations of earth life. These were thought of as mighty beings, and the polytheists of the decadent ethnic religions identified them with the major deities of their pantheons. Israel, however, knew them as Jehovah's angels, his messengers and agents.

It was clearly in view of this significance of the number that the apostles recommended the selection of "seven men," the seven deacons, to constitute the first administrative agency of the Christian Church. It was also clearly for this reason that St. John employed the seven-branched golden lampstand or candlestick of the temple's sanctuary, whose lamps indeed represented the seven planets (cf. Rev. 1:20 and 4:5), as his apocalyptic symbol of the Church as an institution, and set forth his foreshadowings of its development during the Christian centuries in seven letters. Further, his representations of the parallel developments of its companion institution, the State, were set forth in the oracles of a book "close-sealed with seven seals," which were translated by seven trumpeters and expounded by seven libation-pourers. The story of the activities and developments and interrelationships of these two institutions, the Church and the State, is the vertebral theme of St. John's foreshadowings. They are the two great social agencies through which God has chosen to shepherd humanity's march toward higher and higher attainments, both spiritual and temporal. When, in the exposition of the "little book open," the revelator's symbolism called for the representation of these two agencies by unitary figures, the "two witnesses," he introduced the number seven by synonymy, saying: "These...are the two [seven-branched] lampstands standing before the God of the earth" (Rev. 11:4; cf. Zech. 4:2). The seven thunders that translate that "little book" signify divine intervention at a crisis time.

Now we come to the explanation of an apparent inconsistency in St. John's use of these mystic numbers, his employment of both *seven* and *twelve*, two seemingly incongruous numbers, to characterize what appear at first glance to be two representations of the same spiritual entity. That is, the *twelve* tribes of spiritual Israel seem to be identical with the *seven* churches of the Apocalyptic letters. The truth is, however, that while the twelve tribes include the seven churches, the full equivalent of the former is found in the two seven-branched lampstands of the two witnesses (11:3–4). These represent God's people in their two great organized relationships and activities, those of the Church and those of the State. In the ancient cosmography these two sets of interlocked relationships and activities are represented by an equal but overlapping division of the twelve zodiacal constellations, making up a "solar" half and a "lunar" half. As was described in Appendix 1, the constellations were then assigned as "houses" to the seven planets—two each (a "solar" and a "lunar" house) to the five real but lesser seeming planets then known and one each to the Sun and Moon. Both of the latter, however, were included with the other five in enumerations and representations of both the solar and the lunar houses, making *seven* the number of each, as we see in the seven-branched lampstands. Only one such lampstand was provided for the Mosaic tabernacle, because its purpose in that connection was to represent, not the twelve zodiacal houses, but the seven "planets," the symbols of God's holy angels.

Seven is finally and supremely the *sabbatic* number, deriving this significance from God's use of the last of the seven "days" of creation, for we find it written: "And God blessed the seventh day, and sanctified it: because that in it he had rested from all his work which God created and made" (Gen. 2:3). Real rest, however, consists not in idleness but in turning to a new task, one that is more interesting even though it may be more difficult. Just so, as we have seen, the Creator turned from his asynergistic task of physical creation to the far more difficult but far more interesting one of spiritual creation. This is necessarily synergistic, and so he called upon the creatures involved to cooperate with him. To that end he made it mandatory for his Messianic people to set aside every seventh (*shebhii, shebhiith*) period of time for this same kind of spiritually active rest (*shabbath*) from merely temporal activities. The *Sabbath* of the seventh day was thus a memorial token of the Messianic covenant. The seventh week, month, and year bore similar significance. And after the completion of seven sabbatic years of re-creative evolution came the fiftieth year, the Year of Jubilee. This grand climatic year foretokened a new beginning, man's final spiritual mutation.

Fifty suggests also Pentecost, and all that it signifies in both ancient Hebrew thought and the development of the Christian Church.

NUMBERS WITH DEFINITELY EVIL IMPORT

The two numbers used by St. John with the most definite evil import are *six* and *eight*, which can be construed as perversions of *seven* (three plus four). As we have seen, seven symbolizes the divinely ordained cooperation between the Creator and his creatures. It represents the creature's right and proper service to his Creator and stands for God's faithful agents, whether angels or men. Accordingly, it is the number the Apocalypse uses to characterize the Church and the State, the two great social institutions, one spiritual and the other temporal, which God has ordained. When they are functioning properly they are the agencies through which we, God's now autonomous creatures, are to cooperate with each other and with him in overcoming the evils we have brought, and still bring, upon ourselves. By such cooperation we are to work out the salvation God has provided for us and attain the goal he sets before us.

When seven is construed in this way, the numbers *six* and *eight* can be taken to represent derelictions of duty. The one suggests a *diminished seven* that falls short (Rom. 3:23; Heb. 4:1) of what is rightfully expected; the other is an *augmented seven* that goes ahead presumptuously (2 John 9).

These suggestions, however, indicate only first steps toward the dire evils these numbers actually represent in the Apocalypse. These worse evils are not simply the result of failures in faithfulness indicated by the relation of these numbers to seven, the number of faithful agency. In addition, they stand for perversities in fundamental attitudes, indicated by the relations of these numbers to the constituent numbers that combine to form *seven*. As we have seen, these fundamental numbers are *three* and *four*, standing respectively for "God" and "the world."

Six

Six, the diminished seven, represents the evil that results from falling short of what is rightfully expected of us. The supreme evil for which it stands in the Apocalypse is revealed, however, when it is construed not only as "seven minus one" but also as "three plus three," thus doubling the number that represents divinity. In that sense, then, six represents a failure to keep the first of the Ten Commandments—"Thou shalt have no other gods before me." It is therefore the number used to identify the Antichrist of the Apocalypse and to "mark," with the number 666, the supreme apostasy that was to "worship" the wild beast of draconian world power (13:12,18, etc.). In the symbolism of the Apocalypse this can be construed as the sixth head of the scarlet beast, the sixth head of the beast from the sea, and the sixth head of the great red dragon.

Eight

Eight, an augmented seven, suggests the infidelity, the materialism, the worldliness, of one who "transgresseth" or goes beyond seven, and who "abideth not in the doctrine of Christ," and so "hath not God" (2 John 9). The godlessness of this apostasy is further defined and its insidious cause is revealed when its number is construed not only as "seven plus one" but also as "four plus four." We see then that the perfect number seven (*three* plus *four*) has been changed to eight by the deletion of three, which stands for the triune Creator, and its displacement by a second four, which stands for the Creator's building material and therefore suggests the material world. The divine has been dispossessed by the worldly.

Such godlessness is pictured in the Apocalypse as blatant atheism only in its latest developments (Chs. 9 and 16). It usually manifests itself in less obvious but often no less hurtful forms of pretense and hypocrisy. In these ways this apostasy's obsessing and finally all-possessing worldliness is largely dissembled. Its insidious nature is well represented, however, by the cryptic way in which its number, the augmented seven, is always set forth.

This augmentation appears first in the seven letters to the churches, whose number represents the assumption of innocence, of faithfulness, with which their examination of the churches begins. For only one of these churches, however, does its letter confirm that tentative assumption; and even that church in the "city of brotherly love" is found to have but "little power" (3:8 AST). Concerning Christendom as a whole, the letters make it very clear that the numerical symbol required to carry their verdict is the augmented seven. We do not see it set forth, however, until we recognize in Jezebel and her dupes a distinct type of church in the Christendom of the time of the end—a "church" on a par with the others but so apostate that it is excommunicate. Instead, therefore, of being addressed directly in a letter of its own, it is called to repentance through the "angel" of the fourth church, that of Thyatira (2:20–23). Thus understood, the letters are found to have passed the prophetic judgment of the augmented seven on a Christendom of *eight* churches.

It is true that a construction such as we find here could be merely casual; and so we would not be warranted in construing it in this way if it stood alone, with no supporting indication of design. However, paralleling the seven churches augmented to eight we find eight forms of the State represented in the book close-sealed with seven seals, with the increase occurring in the fourth seal. (See Act 2.) These augmented sevens, construed as a doubling of four, the number representing the world, tell us of worldly churches and purely secular states that have ceased to be the divine agents their ostensible number *seven* (three plus four) signifies that they ought to be.

We find that St. John uses a four-four division of the sevens in another way also, and for another purpose, this time as a means of fulfilling his basic purpose, to foretell the things that were about to begin to come to pass. It is evident that the interest of the book's foreshadowings centers, not in the beginning of these things, but in the consummation to which they were all to lead. Accordingly, we should expect to find in the symbolism that represents the action of the drama some device that would enable it to focus its emphasis upon the end of the age its foreshadowings cover. In the interpretation presented in this work, this is accomplished by having the first four in the series of seven present the significant features of the entire time between the first and second advents, dividing it into four periods, while the last four give us a four-fold survey of the end of the age. Thus the sevens are all divided into two equal halves of four each, each middle unit being counted with both halves. This can be represented by the carpenter's square (see the Prologue), in which the corner unit may be counted with either the upright or the horizontal arm; or by the seven-branched candlestick, the central stem of which may be counted with either of the two groups of three branches that flank it. In this usage the four-four pattern is not symbolic but structural and without evil import.

APPENDIX 5

The Apocalyptic Sevens and the Book's Recapitulations

The Divisions of the Letters to the Churches
    The Four-Three Division
    The Three-Four Division
    The Four-Four Division

The Divisions of the Seals, Trumpets, and Bowls of Wrath
    The Four States or Empires
    The Three Woes
    Four-Three to Three-Four to Four-Four

APPENDIX 5

The Apocalyptic Sevens and the Book's
Recapitulations

In the Prologue the concept of the pattern of the carpenter's square was introduced, a pattern by which the sevens of St. John's apocalyptic worship drama can be broken up into four-three and three-four divisions. These in turn may be commuted to a four-four division, with the middle item included in each part. The first group of four is here interpreted as telling a chronological story of four successive religious or civic developments in the interadvent years, down to the end of the age when the Savior will return as King of kings. The second group elaborates on conditions in the final or fourth period. In the four acts of the drama that pattern has been followed in the interpretation of the oracles of the letters, seals, trumpets, and bowls of wrath. This Appendix will present the evidence in the oracles themselves that supports such a four-four division, and will summarize the parallelisms between the sevens of the seal, trumpet, and bowl oracles.

THE DIVISIONS OF THE LETTERS TO THE CHURCHES

The letters to the seven churches have been variously interpreted, as simply a seven-fold survey of typical forms and degrees of religious life, or a seven-fold history of the Church of the present age. Following the pattern of the carpenter's square, however, they may be interpreted as falling into the two groups described above, with the Church of Thyatira, the middle one of the seven, being both the last of those that set forth the histori-

255

cal survey of Church development and the first of those that picture final conditions. To the casual reader such a division of the letters is not obvious, as it is in the oracles of the seals, trumpets, and bowls of wrath, but the evidence for it is scarcely hidden, and no one who looks for it can fail to find it. A four-three division is indicated in the introductions to the letters and a three-four division in their conclusions, with these groupings being commuted to a four-four division when Thyatira, the middle church, is counted in each half.

The Four-Three Division

In most of the manuscripts that represent the original Greek, the first four letters, which are here interpreted to be addressed to the generic or composite Church life of successive historic periods, are introduced thus, taking the Ephesian letter as an example: "To the angel of *a* church of Ephesus write..." In its primary application "Ephesus" refers simply to the Asian city of that name in St. John's time, and since there was only one church there, the message would seem to be to *the* church of Ephesus, and this is what we find in our English translations. But when "Ephesus" is applied apocalyptically and is construed as representing the whole Church of the first period of this conspectus of Church history, it is as if the message read thus: "To the angel of any church (whether Asian, African, or European) of the Ephesian period write..."

On the other hand, in the introductions of the three last letters, which are here interpreted as addressed to the several specific churches of the time of the end, the wording in the original Greek is "*the* church" of Sardis and Philadelphia and Laodicea. In its apocalyptic significance this must then be construed as: "To the angel of *the* Sardian (or Philadelphian or Laodicean) church of the time of the end, write."

The Three-Four Division

In all the letters, the last two sections are the promise to the overcomer and the summons to be ready for any further behests—that is, to keep listening for the mystic voice of the Holy Spirit, whose continuous presence as his Advocate the Savior promised in his last conversation with his disciples (John 14:16 ff.).

In the first three letters, those to the churches whose periods do not reach down to the end of the age and the great day of the Lord's return, the summons to listen to the Spirit comes first, and the following promise to the overcomer points to spiritual blessings and eternal life: "To him that overcometh will I give to eat of the tree of life, which is in the midst of the paradise of God." "He that overcometh shall not be hurt of the second death." "To him that overcometh will I give to eat of the hidden manna, and will give him a white stone, and in the stone a new name written, which no man knoweth saving he that receiveth it." (Rev. 2:7,11,17.)

The last four letters survey the Christendom of the time of the end, the Christendom that is to receive the Savior on his return and provide the base for the campaign of world conquest he is then to begin. These letters are closed by the summons, and the promise that precedes the summons always tells of a high calling on earth in connection with the Lord's return, when the saints are to be kings and priests unto God. The overcomers of the Thyatiran letter are to have "power over the nations" and "rule them with a rod of iron," and they are to enact the role of the "morning star"—the herald of the Sun of Righteousness in the gray dawn of the coming day. To the overcomers of the dead church of Sardis the Savior says: "They shall walk with me in white"—which suggests that they are to be martyrs and so are to be among those who live and reign with him for a thousand years (20:4). The overcomer of the church of Philadelphia is to be "a pillar in the temple" of God, thus serving, like the tree of life (see Appendix 2), as a gateway from earth to heaven. Overcomers of Laodicea are to share with the Savior the throne he shares with the Father. Thus, except in the case of Sardis, these promised blessings are appropriate only to soldiers of Christ who will be watching for his return and who are to share in the work of establishing his kingdom on earth.

Coming after such promises, the summons to listen for the voice of the Holy Spirit—"He that hath an ear, let him hear what the Spirit saith unto the churches"—is in effect an exhortation to watch and be ready to exercise the high callings promised when the Savior returns. To that same end the Savior voices specific exhortations and warnings to each one of these last four churches. They read as follows:

To Thyatira: "That which ye have already, hold fast till I come" (2:25).

257

To Sardis: "If therefore thou shalt not watch, I will come on thee as a thief, and thou shalt not know what hour I will come upon thee" (3:3; cf. 16:15 and 1 Thes. 5:2–5).

To Philadelphia: "Because thou hast kept the word of my patience, I also will keep thee from the hour of temptation, which shall come upon all the world, to try them that dwell upon the earth. Behold, I come quickly: hold that fast which thou hast, that no man take thy crown" (3:10–11; cf. 7:2 ff.; 8:13; 16:13–16).

To Laodicea: "I counsel thee to buy of me gold tried in the fire, that thou mayest be rich; and white raiment, that thou mayest be clothed, and that the shame of thy nakedness do not appear; and anoint thine eyes with eyesalve, that thou mayest see" (3:18).

It is as if, on the very eve of his long promised return, the Savior sought to prepare the saints of these churches for the "hour of trial" (3:10 AST) that his return would introduce. Here, then, is further support for the assumption that these last four letters are for churches of the time of the end.

The Four-Four Division

The letter to the church in Thyatira, being the middle one, has a double role. In its opening salutation it is like the first three letters, and thus like them it represents the church life of one period of the interadvent years, its period being the last one. On the other hand, the Thyatiran letter is like the remaining three in the nature of its promise to those who overcome, and in leaving to the very end its summons to listen to the Spirit. As has been suggested here, this last group of four can be interpreted as representing the varieties of Church life that will exist in the last time period.

In another sense also this letter has a double role, for while it is addressed to the angel of the church in Thyatira, it is clear that its messages are intended also for the so-called church of the scarlet woman Jezebel, a reference to the notorious Gentile queen who led ancient Israel into the spiritual harlotry of Baal worship. So pervert is this church of Jezebel that it cannot be counted among the true churches of Christ, and he cannot communicate with it directly. False though it is, however, it will be one of the conditions the Savior will meet when he returns, and so it cannot be omitted from the survey of that time of the end.

In the pattern of the carpenter's square, therefore, the Thyatiran letter is at the corner of the square and may be counted with both the vertical arm and the horizontal, making a four-four division of the seven letters.

THE DIVISIONS OF THE SEALS, TRUMPETS, AND BOWLS OF WRATH

In this interpretation of the Apocalypse the oracles of the seals, trumpets, and bowls of wrath, each seven in number, serve respectively, in the Apocalyptic worship drama, as the reading of the prophetic lessons in Hebrew, their translation into the vernacular, and the sermons based on them. They therefore set forth the same foreshadowings, each from a different point of view, and it is helpful to examine them together, for these three sets of oracles supplement each other. In them we find pictures of evil conditions that become progressively worse and worse, until finally, with the coming of the King of kings, the forces of evil are punished and overthrown, and the New Jerusalem is established.

These oracles will be presented in detail in terms of the obvious four-three division, interpreted here as four periods of government and three woes. Less obvious three-four and four-four divisions will also be noted.

The Four States or Empires

The four-three division stands out most surprisingly in the seal oracles, where the first four seals reveal the four horsemen of the Apocalypse, riding respectively on white, red, black, and pale horses. Paralleling these are the first four oracles of the trumpets and of the bowls of wrath, which in each case tell respectively of harm to the earth, the sea, the rivers and fountains of waters, and the Sun. The similarity of the trumpet and bowl oracles is obvious, and that the symbolism of the seal oracles is actually the same becomes clear when it is recognized that all three can be interpreted as reflecting an astral symbolism, the zodiacal trigons.

As noted in Appendix 1, each constellation of the zodiac had assigned to it one of the four cosmic "elements" recognized by the ancients—earth, water, air, and fire. Earth was assigned to

259

Taurus, Virgo, and Capricornus; water to Scorpio, Pisces, and Cancer; air to Aquarius, Gemini, and Libra; and fire to Leo, Sagittarius, and Aries. Any one "element" thus recurs regularly around the zodiacal circle, and an invisible line connecting all three of its occurrences forms an equilateral triangle or trigon within the zodiacal circle. Further, the first constellation named in each group is considered the leader of the Trigon, and it and its bright star or lucida mark off the compass directions. Thus Taurus, Scorpio, Aquarius, and Leo (representing respectively the earth, water, air, and fire trigons) indicate the east, west, north, and south of the zodiac.

For the first four trumpet and bowl oracles the trigon associations of the first, second, and fourth are obvious, for they tell of harm to the earth, the sea, and the Sun, which represents fire. The third oracles, which tell of harm to the "rivers and fountains of waters," may be related to the air trigon, because these waters of the land areas are supplied by rain that falls from the clouds. The leading constellation of the air trigon, the source of these waters, is known in our picture of the zodiac as Aquarius, the Water-Pourer; but among the ancient Babylonians this constellation was called Ramman, the Thunderer or the god of rain.

How all this relates the four horsemen of the Apocalypse to the zodiacal trigons is made clear by the vision of four colored horses seen by Zechariah, one of St. John's important sources of Old Testament apocalyptic symbols. In this vision (Zech. 6:1–8) the horses colored red, black, white, and grizzled are related respectively to "the four spirits of the heavens," and the black and grizzled are related to the north and the south—that is, to the air and fire trigons. No directions are named for the red and white horses, but the latter is not hard to guess. Ancient thought would inevitably have associated the white horse with Taurus, the Bull, leader of the earth trigon, for the color white was widely attributed to this figure (e.g., in Egypt the "white bull" of Osiris; in Greece the "white bull" that carried off Europa; in China the "white tiger"), and in direction that would indicate the east. The remaining direction, west, and the water trigon, must therefore be assigned to the red horse.

Returning, then, to the four horsemen of the Apocalypse, who rode on white, red, black, and pale horses, the trigon associations are clearly earth, water, air, and fire, just as in the first four trumpet and bowl oracles.

260

The relationships of the first four oracles of the seals, the trumpets, and the bowls of wrath may thus be summarized as follows:

1) The **first seal** reveals the rider on the white horse, which indicates the east, marked by Taurus of the earth trigon.

The **first trumpet** announces a visitation upon the earth, the trees, and the grass.

The **first bowl of wrath** is poured out upon the earth.

2) The **second seal** reveals the rider on the red horse, which indicates the west, marked by Scorpio of the water trigon.

The **second trumpet** announces a visitation upon the sea and its living creatures and ships.

The **second bowl of wrath** is poured out upon the sea.

3) The **third seal** reveals the rider on the black horse, which indicates the north, marked by Aquarius of the air trigon.

The **third trumpet** announces a visitation upon the rivers and fountains of waters, explained above as indicating the air trigon.

The **third bowl of wrath** is poured out upon the rivers and fountains of waters.

4) The **fourth seal** reveals the rider on the pale horse, which indicates the south, marked by Leo of the fire trigon.

The **fourth trumpet** announces a visitation upon the Sun, Moon, and stars.

The **fourth bowl of wrath** is poured out upon the Sun.

Let us note further the messages these three sets of oracles bring of ever more destructive warfare, with all its attendant social ills.

The rider on the white horse, to whom a crown is given, pictures victorious warfare that is comparatively inoffensive, for he is armed only with a bow. The first trumpet casts "hail and fire mingled with blood...upon the earth." And the first bowl reveals that, not withstanding the comparative ineffectiveness of the white horseman, he represents a time of downward trend, for already there were "men which had the mark of the beast" and "which worshiped his image."

The rider on the red horse brings a picture of continuous and all-devastating warfare, for he is armed with a great sword and has power "to take peace from the earth." The second trumpet tells of the death of one third of the creatures of the sea; but the second bowl paints a still more devastating picture, for it made

261

the sea become like "the blood of a dead man," and "every living soul died in the sea."

The rider on the black horse, carrying a pair of balances, tells a story of economic disturbances resulting from warfare. In the third trumpet oracle the rivers and fountains of waters are pictured as bitter, making many die; and the third bowl pictures these waters as blood, and acknowledges the righteousness of God in dealing with those who have "shed the blood of saints and prophets."

The rider on the pale horse is named Death, and he is followed by the hosts of Hell, who had "power...to kill with sword, and with hunger, and with death, and with the beasts of the earth"—all of war's direst evils. The fourth trumpet announces the coming of the three woes; and the fourth bowl brings power "to scorch men with fire," and men "blasphemed the name of God...and they repented not."

The Three Woes

The fifth, sixth, and seventh trumpet oracles, with their three woes, alert us to the kind of picture we shall find in the parallel seal and bowl oracles. Comparing all three series, as in the case of the first four oracles, we find here a story of dire troubles at the time of the end.

5) The **fifth seal** tells of the martyred saints in heaven and shows them being given white robes and being mobilized for the Savior's campaign against the demon hosts revealed by the fourth seal.

The **fifth trumpet** announces the invasion of locust-like demons coming up from the bottomless pit under the leadership of Abaddon-Apollyon and bringing in the **first woe**.

The **fifth bowl** brings darkness and pain upon the kingdom of the beast, and his people blaspheme God and will not repent.

6) The **sixth seal** assures the martyrs that their blood will be avenged and tells of upheavals of the great day of God's wrath.

The **sixth trumpet** announces the **second woe**—three armies of breast-plated horsemen. These and the locust demons of the fifth trumpet make up the hosts of Hell that follow Death, the rider on the pale horse, and they are a pervert parody of the Savior followed by the hosts of heaven.

The **sixth bowl** is poured out on the great river Euphrates to dry it up so as to prepare the way for the kings of the east—the

Savior and his heavenly hosts. They go forth to wage the battle of the "great day of God Almighty," fighting against the unclean spirits that come from the dragon, the beast, and the false prophet.

7) The **seventh seal** brings silence in heaven, indicating that its message, evidently the **third woe**, is so dreadful that it cannot be signified.

The **seventh trumpet** brings joy in heaven because the repentance following the reading of the little book open has made possible the Savior's hastened return to countervail the dreadful third woe. The Lamb is seen on Mount Zion with the 144,000 of the church militant; and the harvest of the earth is reaped, and the winepress of the wrath of God is trodden.

The **seventh bowl** is poured into the air, and a voice from heaven is heard saying, "It is done." And we see the visions of the fall of Babylon, the coming of the King of kings, the thousand-year imprisonment of the old serpent, the rebellion of Gog and Magog, the final casting of the devil into the lake of fire and brimstone, and finally the last judgment and the establishment of the New Jerusalem.

Four-Three to Three-Four to Four-Four

In terms of the pattern of the carpenter's square, the first four of the seal, trumpet, and bowl oracles can be thought of as the vertical arm, while the last three form the horizontal arm. The first four are here interpreted as providing a sketch of the civil history of the interadvent years, marked off into four successive periods of civil government. The last of these, representing the end of the age, is characterized by the three woes pictured in the last three oracles. However, if the fourth interadvent time period is grouped with its three woes, the obvious four-three division shifts to three-four. As in the case of the letters to the churches, either of these uneven divisions of the sevens can be commuted into four-four, with the fourth oracle, at the corner of the square, serving in both groups. It belongs both with the historical survey, of whose final period it tells, and with the three woes that characterize that period. And just as the fourth letter is really a double one, so is the fourth seal oracle, which shows Death, the rider on the pale horse, followed by Hell and his hosts.

INDEX

Abraham, 175, 202, 208f., 228

Adam and Eve, 32, 185f., 224

Advent, first, 6, 20, 55, 83, 87, 92, 95, 137f., 187, 190f., 211, 217ff.

second, 6ff., 8, 20, 22f., 29, 34f., 55, 57, 63, 73, 77, 81, 85, 87ff., 90, 92, 95ff., 99, 102, 104, 111, 115ff., 118, 121f., 123, 125, 138, 160, 162ff., 166f., 169, 187, 190, 192ff., 202, 211, 218ff.

Advocate, 23, 37, 90, 256

Altar, brazen, 44, 46, 49, 63, 190, 205, 224

golden, 44, 50, 55, 58, 63, 104f., 192, 225, 234, 236

Angels, 20, 45, 60, 64, 92, 112, 115ff., 119, 179, 236

Antichrist, 27, 31, 56f., 61, 74f., 94, 99, 105, 112, 116, 119ff., 122, 146, 151, 251

Apostasy, 25, 27f., 30, 33, 45, 82ff., 85, 90, 93, 99, 100, 112ff., 116, 146f., 149, 160, 251

Aquarius, 188, 190, 212, 217

Archangels, 8, 45, 47f., 60, 76, 85f., 88, 91f., 177, 196f.

Aries, 49, 182f., 190f., 193, 203, 205f.

Ark of the covenant, 52, 88, 90f., 110, 225

Armageddon, 63, 113, 117, 120, 122, 127, 151

Astral symbols, 13, 20f., 90, 148, 190, 197f.

Atonement, anticipatory day of, 8ff., 76, 85ff., 89, 103f., 229, 235ff.

Great Day of, 8, 10, 23, 35ff., 44, 50, 65, 85f., 103ff., 130f., 136, 138, 203, 208, 225, 227f., 234f.

Auriga, 47, 76

Axis, ecliptic, 177, 184ff., 187, 224

equatorial, 184ff., 187, 224

Babylon, 73f., 90, 95, 100, 110, 112ff., 114, 115ff., 129f., 135, 151, 263

Babylonian cosmology, 51, 179, 182, 184, 188f., 193, 213

Balaam, 28, 99, 139, 146f.

Baptismal font, 46, 64, 193, 237

Beast, the, 83, 100, 110, 112f., 114, 121

scarlet, 115f., 151

mark of, 94, 99, 100f., 109f., 112, 123, 127

seat of, 112

Beasts, two wild, 93ff., 115f., 150

Beloved city, 123ff., 135, 153

Blood of the atonement, 37, 65, 110, 112, 114, 136f., 229, 234

of the Lamb, 58, 61f., 65, 92, 118f., 125, 137, 206, 238

Boaz, 32, 224

Bondage, Eqyptian, 9, 37, 137f., 202, 205, 226

of sin, 138, 205

to Satan, 9, 202

Book of life, 126, 132f.

of works, 126

Boötes, 21, 47, 102, 197

Bottomless pit, 74, 83, 87, 114, 121, 129

Bowls of wrath, see wrath

Breastplate of the high priest, 21, 49f.,

105, 179f., 192
Bride of the Lamb, 89, 114, 118, 129ff., 136, 151f.
Bridegroom, the, 96, 113, 151
Burnt offerings, 44, 46, 49, 224

Canaan, 99, 138f., 205, 209
Cancer, 21, 66, 131, 179, 181, 188, 192f., 212ff., 217, 219
Candlesticks, 13, 20f., 27, 37f., 44f., 83, 179, 225; *see also* menorah
Carpenter's square, 13, 31, 56, 252, 255, 258, 263
Capricorn, 21, 50, 118, 131, 179, 188f., 212, 216ff.
Centaurus, 57, 94
Cherubim, guardian, 27, 32, 186, 188, 198, 217
Choir invisible, 97, 102, 109, 123, 150
Chosen People, 207ff.; *see also* Messianic People
Christ, 7, 9, 57ff., 79, 91f., 94, 100, 116, 119, 123f., 126, 151, 161ff., 182, 191ff., 230, 258
Church, 5, 7f., 11, 13f., 21, 23, 25f., 28, 31, 36, 56, 60ff., 65f., 77ff., 82ff., 84, 88ff., 92f., 96f., 98, 101, 115f., 118f., 123ff., 129, 131, 146f., 160ff., 165, 182, 190, 192ff., 214, 231ff.
militant, 60f., 97ff., 104, 118, 123ff., 148, 159, 162ff., 164, 166, 194, 198, 263
pervert, 82, 114, 116, 148f.
triumphant, 59, 97ff., 104, 109f., 121, 123ff., 127, 139, 150, 162, 194
Churches of Asia (seven), 8f., 13, 19ff., 22f., 25, 26ff., 37, 146, 164, 232f., 255ff.
Church and State, 5, 7f., 11, 13f., 21, 23, 25f, 28, 45, 53, 71ff., 74, 78, 82f., 85, 87, 91, 93, 98, 116, 124, 131, 135, 145ff., 179, 192, 203f., 249, 250
united, 150, 152f.
City of God, 152
Commission, great, 166
Communion, holy, *see* Lord's Supper

of saints, 96ff., 194
Confession of faith, 33, 49, 60, 97, 186, 191, 218, 238
Consummation, 6f., 12, 32, 38, 92, 114, 120, 122, 129, 135, 140, 152f., 162, 164, 180f., 187, 194, 202, 246
Cosmological symbolisms, 13, 21, 44ff., 55f., 102f., 109, 112, 120, 130f., 138, 175-179, 182, 188-193, 198, 247f.
Cosmos, 180f., 246f.
Countervailance, 55, 57, 63, 72, 77, 87, 104, 122, 137, 166, 234, 263
Covenant, new, 25, 36, 66, 78, 97, 140, 160, 164, 169, 191, 202, 205, 210, 220, 230f.
old, 25, 66, 159, 164, 191, 205, 208, 210, 220, 228, 230f.
Creation, 181, 183
Creator, 45, 54, 153, 181, 195f., 198, 201f., 225, 244f., 247, 249ff.
Cross, 45, 60f., 136, 186, 191, 211
Crucifixion, 92, 111, 137
Crystalline spheres, 177, 183f.

Daniel, 7, 20ff., 57, 94, 109, 176
Death, 58, 127, 262f.
Demons, 59f., 74f., 87, 149
Derashah, derashoth, 8ff., 109ff., 227, 232
Devil, 89, 121; *see also* Satan
Draco, 55f., 92, 121
Dragon, great red, 58, 89ff., 93, 113, 115f., 121, 149f., 194

Eagle, 53, 120, 189, 194, 217
Earth (world) mountain, 14, 27, 43, 129f., 133, 183f., 185, 187, 224
Easter, 37f., 207, 211, 214
Ecliptic, 45, 176f., 188, 192
Eden, *see* Garden of
Egypt, 9, 38, 73, 79f., 91, 99, 110, 112, 184, 202, 207
Eight, 251
Elder Brother, 54, 90, 96, 151, 161, 169, 211, 218
Elders, twenty–four, 48, 50f., 64f., 82, 88

265

Elements, cosmic, 12, 181, 245f., 259ff.
Encampment, Israel's, 131, 196f.
End of the age, 7, 12, 56, 67, 74, 102,
    114, 140, 210, 255f., 258
Ephesus, 26f., 31, 146, 256
Equinox, autumnal, 104f., 193, 203f.,
    207ff.,
    vernal, 60f., 182, 190, 203ff., 214
Eucharist, see Lord's Supper
Euphratean cosmology, 43, 126, 175,
    179, 187ff., 213
Euphrates River, 112, 139, 262
Exodus, 80, 204, 215
Ezekiel, 22, 53, 60, 176, 188

False prophet, 113f., 121, 125
Father, see God
Fire and Brimstone, see lake
Firstfruits, 35, 38, 96, 99, 113, 127,
    140, 207, 217
    Feast of, 66, 99, 213, 215, 220; see
    also Pentecost
Fish sign, 49, 60, 191, 216
Four, 245

Gabriel, 19, 21, 47, 102, 196f.
Galaxy, 176f.
Garden of Eden, 6, 14, 32, 53, 56, 130f.,
    177, 185f., 187, 217, 224
Gemini, 66, 188, 212
Genesis, 27, 92, 177, 181, 185f., 188f.,
    228, 245f., 247
Gentiles, 81, 94, 130, 135, 204, 232
God Almighty, 19, 48, 51, 64, 82, 112f.,
    117, 133
    children of, 186, 218
    Father, 23, 36f., 39, 48f., 54, 97,
    127, 139, 149, 161f., 178, 198,
    211, 218
    imminent, 44, 53, 91, 177, 225
    Most High, 50, 244
    spirit of, 180
    "seven spirits of", 55, 177, 190; see
    also planets
    transcendent, 52, 177, 225
Gog and Magog, 124f., 127f., 129, 133,
    152, 263
Good Friday, 38, 86, 214
Great Day of God, 26, 113, 115, 117,

119ff., 121, 129, 152, 194, 262

Haphtarah, haphtaroth, 8ff., 11, 43ff.,
    56ff., 71ff., 76, 226, 230
Harlot, 112f., 115ff., 121, 151, 182,
    192, 194
Harlotry, spiritual, 90, 98, 116, 139
Harvest, final, 72, 102f., 127, 140, 194
Heaven, 43ff., 58, 62, 65, 88, 97, 109
    of heavens, 27, 32, 44, 177, 183f.
Heavens, infernal, 13, 43, 91, 148, 178,
    188
    supernal, 43, 91, 148, 178, 188
Heavenly choirs, 8f., 64f., 97, 104, 109,
    118, 127
    Father, see God
    Harvester, 22, 198
    hosts, 57ff., 62, 65, 89, 104, 110f.,
    147, 262
Hell, 127
    hosts of, 58, 74, 262f.
Heracles, 55, 92, 95, 121
Herald angels, three, 99ff.
High priest (Jewish), 8, 23, 36, 44, 50,
    110, 136, 225
High Priest (Jesus), 23, 35, 37, 39, 85,
    124, 136, 151f., 211, 235
Holy city, 81, 129ff., 133ff., 140, 152f.,
    161, 163, 217, 224, 245
Holy of Holies, 8, 10, 20, 36f., 44, 50,
    52f., 58, 65, 82, 91, 105, 111,
    136, 192, 225, 234
Holy Place, 20, 44ff., 49f., 58, 82f., 105,
    192, 207, 225, 234
Holy Spirit, 28, 46, 48, 50, 55, 66, 84,
    90, 96, 101, 118, 124, 140, 150,
    190, 193, 214f., 237, 256f.
Horsemen, four, 56ff., 73, 119, 147,
    259ff.
Hydra, 91f., 94, 103, 112, 115
Hymns, 9, 78, 210, 229, 236f.

Ichthus, 60, 191, 216
Incense, see golden altar
Inferno of infernos, 173, 183
Ingathering, Feast of Full, see
    Tabernacles, Feast of
Intervention, divine, 5f., 37, 80, 86ff.,
    89, 92, 119, 192

Israel, new, 66, 78, 81, 85, 88f., 91, 104;
see also spiritual Israel
    old, 78, 81, 83, 85, 88f., 99, 109, 114,
    130, 135, 138f., 159, 166, 205,
    210, 229
    spiritual, 60f., 78, 81f., 95, 104, 110,
    131f., 140, 160, 164, 169, 202,
    209
    twelve tribes of, 97, 131, 180, 196,
    209, 246, 248
Israel's national epos, 9, 14, 37, 138f.,
    202ff.

Jacob, 29, 94, 209, 228
Jakin, 32, 224
Jehovah, 36, 49, 89, 120f., 138, 194f.,
    205
Jerusalem, 33, 81, 95, 120, 130, 134,
    140, 184
Jesus, 45, 166, 202, 218, 221
    Christ, 19, 27, 36f., 134, 145, 151,
    190
Jesus Christ, the Son of God, our
    Savior, see Confession of faith
Jezebel, 30, 98, 251, 258
Joshua, 83, 139, 205, 209
    of the new covenant, 97, 140, 202,
    205, 210
    of the old covenant, 205, 210
Judge, 23, 111, 169, 211
    divine, 25, 50, 117, 193
    inexorable, 128, 163, 193, 219
    of all the earth, 103, 115, 122, 126,
    138, 208
Judgment, Day of, 100, 102, 105, 122f.,
    126, 128, 133, 138, 152, 193,
    208, 228

King of kings and Lord of lords, 11,
    28f., 30f., 35, 57ff., 62, 73ff., 94,
    97, 103, 113, 115, 118ff., 120,
    123f., 125, 127, 129, 146f., 151f.,
    153, 160, 162, 164, 169, 194, 198,
    210, 217, 219f., 231, 259, 263
Kingdom of Christ, 58f., 75, 88, 124
    of heaven, 35, 206
    of righteousness, 121, 164, 217
    of the Lord, 79, 133, 159, 162

Lake of fire and brimstone, 114, 121,
    125f., 128, 133, 152, 178, 195,
    263
Lamb (of the Apocalypse), 6, 19, 47f.,
    54ff., 58, 60ff., 64f., 87, 93ff.,
    95ff., 99, 102f., 109, 118, 123,
    132ff., 137, 139f., 193, 197, 235
    of God, 6, 37f., 47, 54ff., 65, 86, 94,
    103, 115, 130, 133, 153, 162, 164,
    190f., 205f., 209, 211, 228
    paschal (Old Testament), 6, 39, 60f.,
    137, 206
    Paschal (New Testament), 121, 140,
    168, 205
    on Mount Zion, 95, 102, 118, 123f.,
    139, 150, 162, 166, 187, 197
Lamb–Lion, 48, 55f., 87, 118, 148, 150f.,
    175, 193, 197
Lamps of fire, 45
Laodicea, 33ff., 35, 48, 51, 146, 169,
    256ff.
Laver, 44, 46, 49, 64, 109, 127, 192, 224
Law, broken, 110f., 112f.
Leaven, 63, 125, 206f.
Leo, 21, 103, 188, 193, 212, 219
Letters, seven, 23ff., 26, 56, 71, 146f.,
    256ff., 263
Libra, 21, 49, 58, 105, 126, 138, 140,
    181, 190, 192f., 203, 208, 219
Lion of Judah, 6, 11, 54ff., 76, 87, 100,
    103, 121, 140, 153, 168, 193f.,
    210f., 219
Little book open, 8f., 10, 72, 75ff., 85f.,
    149, 166, 236; see also megillah
Living creatures, 20, 45, 48, 51ff., 64f.,
    181f., 189
Lord, 49, 58, 63, 82, 84, 88, 95, 113, 124
Lord's Day, 10, 19, 38
    Supper, 191, 206, 238f.

Marriage supper of the Lamb, 118,
    120
Martyrs, 31, 58f., 61, 82ff., 102, 109f.,
    118, 127, 151, 262
Megillah, 8, 10f., 76ff., 85f., 226f.
Melchizedek, 150
Menorah, 45, 83, 148, 207; see also
    candlesticks
Mercy seat, 20, 36f., 44f., 52f., 58, 65,

110, 112, 113f., 136f., 177, 234
Messiah, 9, 49, 89, 202, 207
Messianic calling, 81, 231
  hope, 60, 190, 231
  people, 46, 49, 60, 81, 140, 202, 204,
    211, 219, 246, 249
  prophecies, 48, 231
Michael, 47f., 91f., 196f.
Mighty Avenger, 22, 26, 72, 100f., 103,
  118, 121, 163
Mighty–to–Save, 22, 72, 101, 103, 118,
  121f., 135, 140, 163, 166, 210
Milky Way, 66, 76, 118, 131, 176, 188f.,
  212
Millennial kingdom, 57, 59, 63, 74,
  123ff., 151
Millennium, 84, 122–129, 134, 152f.,
  163f., 224
Moon, 21, 45, 104, 176f., 179f., 183
Moriah, Mount, 208f., 228
Morning star, 29, 120, 257
Mosaic law, 9, 23, 37f., 66, 77, 83, 215,
  225, 230f., 235
Moses, 46, 52, 66, 83, 85, 175, 186,
  202f., 205, 210, 215, 219

New earth, 129, 131, 160, 164, 166,
  224
New heaven and new earth, 5, 125,
  160, 195, 224
New Jerusalem, 6ff., 9, 12, 19, 26, 32,
  95f., 114f., 118, 122f., 125f., 129-
  136, 140, 151f., 153, 159, 161,
  163f., 166, 168f., 187, 198, 209,
  218, 224, 246, 259, 263
New Testament, 14, 23f., 26, 37, 159,
  230
New year, 71, 85f., 104f., 203ff., 207f.
Nicolaitans, 26, 28, 146f.

Old Testament, 14, 30, 46, 66, 78, 80,
  82, 86, 89, 121, 128, 130, 146,
  166, 186, 231
Ophiucus, 47, 91f., 121, 197
Overcomers, 27–35, 51, 123, 133, 167,
  256f.

Paradise, 55, 130, 135, 185, 187, 194,
  198, 218

Parashah, Parashoth, 8ff., 11, 19ff.,
  23, 56, 66, 225f., 230, 233
Parousia, 34f., 74, 77, 81, 95, 97ff., 99,
  128, 150, 202, 220
Passover, 6, 9, 37f., 61, 66, 86, 137f.,
  203ff., 213
Patmos, 8, 19, 94f., 198
Paul, Saint, 24, 33, 59, 80, 98, 124,
  126, 163, 215, 230
Pentecost, 9, 35, 66f., 84, 96, 99, 124,
  140, 163, 169, 202f., 209, 213ff.
Pergamum, 25, 28f., 146
Philadelphia, 31ff., 35, 133, 256ff.
Pillars, 32, 187, 224
Pisces, 49f., 60, 179, 181ff., 190ff.,
  193, 206
Plagues, 73ff., 111f., 117, 139
Planets, 21, 45, 131, 148, 176f., 249
Planetary houses, 179
Prayers, 9, 51, 63, 81, 88, 104, 162,
  166, 208, 229, 236f.
Precession, 132, 180, 182, 185, 218,
  224
Prince of Peace, 161, 195, 220
Promised Land, 6, 9, 12, 102, 138f.,
  202, 205, 208, 219f.
Protevangel, 6, 53, 55, 92, 95, 121, 138,
  162, 182f., 186f., 198, 217, 219,
  226
Providence, 48, 54, 78, 82, 84, 90, 92,
  114, 120, 133, 135, 139
Psalms, 77ff., 81f., 210, 231

Raphael–Labiel, 47, 76f., 80f., 85f., 87,
  196f., 236
Rapture of the saints, 84, 98, 124, 163
Red Sea, 46, 109, 139
Redeemer, 39, 83, 115, 119, 121, 123f.,
  162, 195, 210f., 218, 234
Repentance, 27, 30, 33, 79, 81, 85f.,
  100f., 104, 111f., 136f., 165ff.,
  229, 234ff., 263
Resurrection, first, 58, 97, 102, 123,
  127f.
  general, 36, 102
  of the Lord, 38, 66, 127, 138, 190,
  207, 214
  second, 102, 128f.
Retribution, divine, 86, 110f., 113, 125

Rod of iron, 7, 29, 35, 55, 90, 92, 118ff., 124, 162, 168, 193, 257
Rosh Hashanah, 9f., 104, 203, 208ff.

Sabbath rest, 133, 149, 210, 249
Sagittarius, 21, 50, 57, 94, 118, 188, 212, 216ff
Salvation, 6f., 13, 27, 34, 37, 48, 53, 55, 58, 61f., 86f., 89, 92, 95, 101ff., 114, 119, 122, 128, 133, 138, 153, 166, 179, 190, 192, 210, 216, 224, 238, 250
Samaria, woman of, 19, 48, 64, 134
Sardis, 26, 31, 146, 256f.
Satan, 9, 27f., 89, 91, 93, 121f., 125f., 129, 152, 202, 204; see also Devil
Savior, 22, 49, 57, 75, 87, 96, 101ff., 105, 118f., 122f., 137f., 153, 168f., 191, 193, 206, 214, 219ff., 231, 234, 236, 239, 251, 262f.
Scapegoat, 8, 10, 36, 86, 113f., 136f., 209, 228f., 234f.
Scorpio, 21, 53, 76, 111, 188f., 192, 194, 212, 217f., 259
Sea of glass, 46, 97, 109f., 139, 238
Seal of the living God, 29, 32, 58f., 60ff., 63, 95f., 104, 133, 148, 216, 236, 239
Seal oracles, 12, 56–63
Seasonal festivals, 202ff., 260ff.
Seed of the woman, 55, 90, 175, 186, 217
Serpens, 91f., 121
Serpent, 6, 90, 92f., 114, 121, 129, 168, 178, 219, 263
Seven, 12f., 20f., 23, 45, 71, 79ff., 87f., 110ff., 146, 247ff., 255ff., 263
Seven–sealed book, 8ff., 43ff., 47f., 54ff., 64, 71, 198
Shekinah, 20, 61, 91, 103, 135, 139f., 177, 210
Silence in heaven, 62f., 87, 236, 263
Sinai, Mount, 66, 110, 215
Six, 250f.
Smyrna, 29f.
Solstice, summer, 66, 131, 188, 202f., 212ff.,
    winter, 50, 87f., 131, 188, 190, 216ff.
Son of David, 55, 210

Son of God, 22, 30, 33, 35, 39, 48f., 55, 61, 86, 137ff., 169, 211f., 217f.
Son of man, 22f., 36, 39, 54, 102, 161, 206
    sign of, 7, 22, 102
Song, new, 54, 97, 99, 104, 162
    of Moses and the Lamb, 46, 109, 139, 238
    of victory, 118
Spontaneous oracles, 229, 236
Star angels, 20f., 196
    figures, 13f., 20, 197f.
    lore, 13, 176ff., 188ff., 195ff.
State, 5, 7, 11, 13, 21, 25, 28, 73, 79, 89, 110, 147f., 252
    pervert, 149
    and Church, see Church and State
Sun, 21, 45, 66, 90, 103f., 176, 179f., 183, 185, 188f., 203f., 205f., 208, 212, 218
    of Righteousness, 56, 87, 168, 193, 219, 257
Sword of the mouth, 28, 118f., 121, 124, 162f., 168
Swords, flaming, 27, 32, 186, 198
Synagogue ritual, 5, 8f., 22ff., 227f.
    Hebrew, 5, 23
    Christian, 11, 66, 75, 77, 99, 145

Tabernacles, Feast of, 9f., 38, 134, 137ff., 193, 203, 207ff.
Taurus, 76, 188, 197, 212, 245
Targum, targumim, 8, 10, 71ff., 227
Temple, celestial 20, 43, 46f., 53, 109, 113, 127, 234
    gates, 44, 46f., 53, 65, 224
    Jerusalem, 14, 44f., 53, 224f.
    Middle East, 14, 20, 32, 130, 187, 223f.
    structure, 223ff.
    veil of, 44, 105, 192, 225
Theophany, 20ff., 36, 39, 65, 76f., 95, 126, 197, 235
Three, 244
Throne, great white, 126f., 132, 195, 208
    He who sat upon it, 132, 194f., 197
Throne of God, 37, 39, 43f., 48, 50, 52, 64f., 90, 102, 105, 134, 162, 177,

269

184, 187, 189, 196, 225, 234
He who sat upon it, 48ff., 54. 64f., 197
Thunders, seven, 10, 79ff., 86, 166, 235f.
Thyatira, 29ff., 35, 55, 120, 146, 251, 255, 257
Torah, Christian, 24, 230, 232
Hebrew, 120, 175, 225f., 230
Transition, 122ff., 125
Tree of the knowledge of good and evil, 56, 185f.
of life, 27, 29, 32, 43, 56, 66, 130f., 132, 177, 185ff., 189, 191, 193f., 198, 224, 238
Tribulation, 22, 27, 62f., 102
Trigons of the zodiac, 57, 73, 75f., 181, 197, 246, 259f.
Triune God, 12
Trinity, 48ff., 96, 244
Trumpets, Feast of, 10, 85, 104, 203, 208; see also Rosh Hashanah
oracles of, 10, 71–75, 87
Twelve, 61, 245f.

Unleavened Bread, Feast of, see Passover
Uriel, 47, 103, 196f.
Urim and Thummim, 21, 44, 105, 179, 192

Victory, 58, 92, 115
Vintage symbolism, 113, 150
Virgo, 21, 91f., 104f., 134, 182, 190, 192ff.

Warfare, 7, 13, 28, 56, 59, 74f., 83f., 88, 89f., 91ff., 113, 115, 117, 119f., 122f., 125, 129, 148ff., 167, 179, 188
Wave sheaf, 66, 127, 207, 213f.
White horse (of the King), 94, 121, 162, 168, 198
robes, 31, 33, 36, 51, 57ff., 62, 64, 74f., 97, 102, 109, 113, 118f., 121, 124, 127, 152f., 238, 262
Wilderness, 9, 80, 89f., 115, 135, 138ff., 194, 196, 210
journey, 6, 9, 12, 14, 80, 85, 138ff.,

202, 209f.
Winepress of the wrath of God, 26, 30, 72, 100, 103, 113, 128, 137, 264
Witnesses, two, 10, 72, 77f., 81ff., 84f., 94, 114, 148, 163, 166
resurrection of, 79, 84
Woe, third, 62f., 73, 75, 77, 81, 85ff., 87, 89, 104, 122, 166, 220, 234, 263
Woes, first and second, 73ff., 85, 149
three, 72f., 77, 85, 262f.
Woman, the, 6, 89ff., 92, 115f., 194
Word of God, 91, 115, 118, 121, 123, 128, 161, 180, 186f., 195, 198, 214
Worship, 14, 19, 30, 51, 63ff., 82, 134, 223ff., 229ff
Wrath, bowls of, 8, 10, 12, 100ff., 119, 150, 259ff.
Great Day of, 30, 57, 59f., 121
of God, 10, 30, 72, 100, 103, 110f., 114
of the Lamb, 121
wine of, 113f.

Zechariah, 83, 134, 176, 260
Zion, Mount, 60f., 89, 95f., 102, 118, 123f., 130, 139, 150, 162, 166, 197, 263
Zodiac, 21, 27, 45, 47, 49, 52f., 66, 132, 148, 178ff., 189, 196f.
Zodiacal constellations, 43, 45, 52f., 83, 91, 131, 180, 189f., 218f., 246f.
gateways, 188